# INNOVATION IN NEW COMMUNITIES

M.I.T. Report No. 23

# INNOVATION IN NEW COMMUNITIES

Brown Miller
Neil J. Pinney
William S. Saslow

The MIT Press
Cambridge, Massachusetts, and London, England

# PUBLISHER'S FOREWORD

The aim of this format is to close the time gap between the preparation of a monographic work and its publication in book form.  A large number of significant though specialized manuscripts make the transition to formal publication either after a considerable delay or not at all.  The time and expense of detailed text editing and composition in print may act to prevent publication or so to delay it that currency of content is affected.

The text of this book has been photographed directly from the author's typescript.  It is edited to a satisfactory level of completeness and comprehensibility though not necessarily to the standard of consistency of minor editorial detail present in typeset books issued under our imprint.

The MIT Press

# PREFACE

Innovation in New Communities was a four month research project supported by Boise Cascade Housing Development, the Joint Center for Urban Studies of M.I.T. and Harvard University, and the M.I.T. Urban Systems Laboratory.

We are especially grateful to William L. Hooper, General Manager of Boise Cascade Housing Development, for initiating the project with us, providing its basic financial support, and contributing to its refinement and direction.

Professor Walter Rosenblitn, Acting Director of the Joint Center, and Professor Charles L. Miller, Director of the Urban Systems Laboratory, generously provided working space and administrative support.

At frequent stages throughout the project, many faculty members from M.I.T. and Harvard, too numerous to mention here, helped inform us of developments in their areas of expertise, reviewed our work and offered helpful suggestions for improvement of general and specific aspects of it. Professor Wilhelm V. Von Moltke, Director of Harvard's Urban Design Program, and Professor William L. Porter, Co-Director of M.I.T.'s Urban Design Program, were particularly helpful in these respects.

Finally, we are indebted to James Ebright for his assistance in programming the financial model and to Mrs. Patti Lerner for her stamina and accuracy in typing and proofreading this report.

Brown Miller
Neil J. Pinney
William S. Saslow

Cambridge, Massachusetts                    February 1971

# TABLE OF CONTENTS

# I. INTRODUCTION AND SUMMARY

The basic purpose of this investigation is to explore
opportunities for incorporating technological and programmatic innovations in new community projects. A secondary objective is to provide a source of facts and
analysis useful to design professionals, developers,
students and others involved or interested in new community development. A central premise which underlies this
effort is that new communities, as defined below, can be
planned and developed in a manner which accommodates changing
technologies and social requirements more efficiently than
existing communities. While this principle is often debated,
there can be little question that a major strength of new
communities must ultimately lie with the potential inherent
in any undertaking which can begin without displacing or
disrupting existing activities.

It is the realization of this potential which acts as the
focus for the issues discussed in this report. More precisely:

> What are the characteristics of new communities
> and of technological and programmatic innovations
> which determine the feasibility of applying ad-
> vanced technologies and/or social programs to
> large-scale development projects?

1

RESEARCH OF INNOVATIONS

The research method has been to (i) inventory and describe existing and potential innovations in urban primary networks that principally comprise and can be analyzed as public service systems;* (ii) identify social trends and problem areas that would influence and be influenced by technological innovations; (iii) predict the consequences of these impacts on settlement patterns in several main areas (transportation, communication, energy, waste): (iv) describe applicable legislation; and (v) develop an adaptable financial model for evaluating the feasibility of public service innovations at varying scales of development.

During the course of the investigation, it became apparent that one of the original objectives, to emphasize the evaluation of innovations, could be more fruitfully redirected toward descriptive and predictive goals. This was caused by a growing recognition that (i) data for evaluation (especially cost data) was unavailable or conveyed a low level of confidence; (ii) evaluation of the feasibility or impact of innovative technologies on a new community would

---

*Public service systems are defined here as those (i) which fulfill public service functions for a major portion of a community development project; (ii) whose characteristics can be expected to change at different scales of development; and (iii) in which operational or technological innovations are reasonably predictable. Several of the systems investigated may not necessarily lend themselves to delivery or management within a local public service framework but are selected where significant impacts on the community can be projected (many of the communications systems and large scale energy systems fall into this category).

be more useful within a location-specific context; and (iii) the other objectives, those of producing a useful tool for both the design and development communities, could be served more adequately by identifying a wide range of fundamental opportunities and issues rather than by evaluating only a few in depth. Therefore, the report should be considered more a summary study than a full treatise on the topics covered.

Innovations in housing have not been considered here since the proliferation of new housing systems as well as the potential for further innovation in all aspects of housing is now of such magnitude that it would merit a separate study. Nor are innovations in the design and planning process itself considered other than suggesting several methods for effectuating participatory design and planning.

## CHARACTERISTICS OF NEW COMMUNITIES

It is useful, at this point, to identify the characteristics of new communities which differentiate them from large-scale residential development projects. There is general disagreement over the definition of these characteristics; but, for the pruposes of this investigation, new communities are defined by the following attributes:

1. The inclusion in a project of commercial, recreational and institutional facilities required to serve the residential population and an industrial employment base for much of the population;
2. A development program undertaken as a comprehensive, coordinated effort safeguarded by appropriate land-use controls and enforceable performance regulations:
3. Provision of high-, medium-, and low-density housing not restricted to any particular socio-economic segments; and
4. Creation of a distinct administrative body (or bodies, public or private) to operate and maintain the communities public service systems.

3

In short, new communities are defined here as projects involving the creation of an urban environment rather than the development of limited-use projects in predetermined (or existing) urban patterns.  Almost by definition, new communities provide the opportunity to anticipate change and innovation and to accommodate that anticipation within the planning and development processes.

INNOVATION, CHANGE AND NEW
COMMUNITIES OVER TIME

During the months of this investigation and those following the force  of innovation and change over time became strikingly clear.  While timeliness is a principal characteristic of this study, the same timeliness makes the information and concepts presented subject to the pressures of current and future flux.  Thus, ideas and applications which may have appeared pioneering, speculative, or even highly unlikely a short time ago are now accepted and being applied -- some, even commonly so -- or have been superseded by more advanced ones.  The overall social, institutional and technological context has been undergoing pervasive changes which deeply affect the viability of specific processes or hardwares discussed in this study. New communities themselves, for example, are now recognized as a thoroughly legitimized, policy- and legislation-supported, media-publicized element in the mixed array of urban growth mechanisms, adaptable to the needs and aspirations of many regions.  A year ago -- let alone five years ago -- they were widely considered conceptually tenuous and economically hazardous.  The climate of innovation and change can be expected more easily to continue than to abate, further engendering innovation and the search for alternative, better ways of assembling the urban construct.  In this climate the requirement for anticipation, adaptability and vision overreach time-bound pressures of the present.  New cities and towns offer a logical and solid opportunity for meeting this requirement.

4

# A. SUMMARY OF THE REPORT

The investigation was structured around the description,
analysis and evaluation of innovative public service
systems within the context of anticipated social and
technological changes. To provide the basis for determining the relationship between innovations and scales
of community development, the study was divided into five
major areas of concern, each of which corresponds to a
part of this report and each of which is summarized below.

PART I: INTRODUCTION

The remainder of Part I sets the background against which
the potentials of innovations in new communities must be
measured. Section B of Part I elaborates on the opportunities inherent in new communities as vehicles for accommodating change and innovation and relates these opportunities to private developers as participants in the community development process. Three categories of opportunities are described: (i) those which encourage the initial
participation of private developers (particularly large
corporations) in new community projects by creating incentives (directly and indirectly) for private investment; (ii)
those which enhance the ability of developers to implement
significant innovations in new communities during the development period; and (iii) those which enable the developer to
gain experience from new community development applicable
to subsequent involvement in regional development programs
and redevelopment programs in existing cities.

Section C summarizes many of the social trends and projections which greatly affect the kinds of innovations currently
being developed and likely to be developed in the future.
These trends and projections have, of course, influenced the
selection of innovations discussed in this report and are

categorized as follows: (i) those which reflect the emergence of a post-industrial society in the U.S.; (ii) those which describe changing values and life-styles; (iii) those which illustrate changes in relationships between governments and their constituents and among levels of public and institutional control; (iv) those which define the expanding role of education within communities; and (v) those which describe reactions to technological impacts. The social trends discussed in Section C are closely related to the social and political factors identified in Part II of the report which is summarized below.

A summary listing of the innovations selected is presented in Section D with a preliminary evaluation of each innovation's potential impact on community form and settlement patterns.

Section E concludes Part I with a glossary of terms used throughout the report. These terms or phrases are defined so as to avoid ambiguity in the remainder of the report.

PART II:  TRENDS, GOALS AND SCENARIOS

Perhaps the most critical determinants of the feasibility of applying innovations to community development are the political and social environments which exist when an innovation becomes operationally and financially practical. Since most of the innovations studied here will be operational well within the next 10 to 20 years, it is important to determine, insofar as possible, what the political and social environments will be like during that period. Drawing on research of many widely divergent views of the political and social future (and present), Part II attempts to construct alternative future scenarios from observations of social and political forces which will have significant impacts on societal directions.

Of particular concern to the growth and development of new communities are the trends and public policies which will shape population distribution patterns on national and re-

6

gional levels. The references cited in Section A of Part II strongly imply that emerging public policies will be oriented toward dispersal of population away from the already heavily urbanized metropolitan areas. For the most part, these are policies which implicitly and explicitly will encourage the creation of new communities. Section A also discusses several issues arising from a comparison of residential density patterns (i.e., high vs. low densities) and activity locations (i.e., centralized vs. decentralized), issues which bear on the determination of community size and structure and which, in turn, relate directly to the physical and financial impacts of innovations at varying scales of new community development.

Section B of Part II identifies three of the basic goals toward which new communities might be directed: (i) ease of accessibility to activities and services by the residential population; (ii) participation by residents in decision-making processes throughout the growth of the community; and (iii) constructive interaction with the physical environment and ecological systems of which the community is an integral component. These goals were derived, in large part, as a natural extension of the social and political trends outlined in Section A.


A further extension of these trends into the scenario stage is described in Section C which identifies two distinct directions as the basic options for new community developments: (i) the community as a vehicle to enhance man's relationship to his natural environment and (ii) the urban community in which man foregoes close and continuous contact with nature for the excitement of human interaction in a highly active, densely populated setting.

## PART III: TECHNOLOGICAL AND PROGRAMMATIC INNOVATIONS

Part III of the report summarizes the range of technological and programmatic innovations studied during the course of the investigation and listed in Section C of the Introduction. Section A of Part III presents summaries of technological (or product) innovations in the following categories: (i) movement systems, (ii) energy systems, (iii) communications systems, (iv) waste management and (v) miscellaneous utility systems. Each of the innovations is discussed in terms of (i) stage of development, (ii) operational characteristics, (iii) scale characteristics and, where possible, (iv) cost information. In addition, references are listed which will enable the reader to find more detailed information for each innovation than could be included in this report.

Section B of Part III uses a modified case study approach to describe various programmatic (or process) innovations in three areas of particular interest: (i) health services, (ii) education and (iii) institutional control.

## PART IV: PUBLIC POLICY, FINANCIAL AND MARKET ANALYSES

The feasibility of incorporating innovations in community development is a function of several key factors which are external to the innovations themselves. Although various social, political and environmental issues which influence the potential for using innovations have been discussed throughout the report, Part IV concentrates on three issues of major importance: (i) emerging legislation and public policies, (ii) the ability of a new community to financially support innovations and (iii) the acceptance of innovations by the market which is to be served by them.

Section A summarizes the results of research conducted and interviews held with respect to the role of legislation and public policy in applying innovations to new community development. Pertinent federal legislation is described, and, to a lesser extent, state or local legislation is identified. Through discussion with officials in the legislative and executive branches and analysis of public media

8

reporting of the past two years, current federal attitudes toward new communities in general, and innovations in particular, were found to be highly favorable to the growth of public programs oriented toward encouraging private participation in new community development. The recent enactment, by several states, of legislation aimed at facilitating community development and regional planning is a particularly noteworthy trend in the definition and implementation of emerging public policies.

Section B of Part IV describes the preliminary construction and operation of a financial model designed to test the financial feasibility of public service innovations at varying scales of new community development. Although the model is currently operational only for illustrative purposes, it is capable of continual refinement as more data is found and as relationships between costs and community scale factors are more precisely defined. Ideally, the financial model would be the core of a highly developed analytical tool which incorporates public policy and market factors in an evaluation of a community's financial stability: the market factors would help define the limits of what a community's population might be willing to pay for a given mix of public services (e.g., tax rates and user charges), and the public policy factors would define the limits of public (state and federal) support for that same mix of services. Having established these critical limits, the financial model would (and currently does, illustratively) permit relationships to be established between community scale factors and public service costs and revenues.

A discussion of market factors which will affect the acceptance of innovations and new communities is contained in Section C. In particular, alternative mechanisms for informing potential users through the media are discussed in relation to private corporations which might participate in new community development as a vehicle for creating or broadening markets for their own products and services.

PART V:  ADVANCE DESIGN
OF NEW COMMUNITY PROTOTYPES

Many of the innovations investigated during the project,
particularly movement systems, have significant and deterministic impacts on the physical structure of a community.
Part V of the report describes the procedure used to evaluate these impacts at (i) the macro-form or community-wide
scale and (ii) the micro-form or service area (e.g., neighborhood) scale.  With respect to both scales,comparative
studies of existing cities and new communities were conducted to identify primary form characteristics which are
independent of topography and natural systems.  Prototypes at both scales were then constructed and used as the
basis for evaluating the effects of selected innovations on
dimensional characteristics, density patterns and activity
location and accessibility.

Section A of Part V identifies three primary macroforms,
one of which is characteristic of virtually all of the communities studied.  These macroforms basically reflect the
circulation system within a community.  By combining alternative population and activity distribution patterns with
the primary macroforms, comparative evaluations of various
community characteristics (accessibility, imageability,
etc.) can be made for each of the form taxonomies.

An analysis of physical form characteristic of smaller
areas within a community is the focus of Section C of Part V.
The "service area" concept is defined here and used to identify the scale characteristics (e.g., population levels) of
areas served by alternative mixes of activities and public
services.  It is not, therefore, a static concept.  Three
distinct types of service areas are identified:  (i) self-

contained, (ii) interrelated, (iii) community-wide oriented. The abilities of each type to accommodate various activities and services (and innovations) are compared on the basis of design criteria such as adaptability, interaction and service component characteristics.

## B.  THE FUNDAMENTAL OPPORTUNITIES IN NEW COMMUNITIES: TOWARDS A RATIONALE FOR CORPORATE PARTICIPATION

A rationale for corporate involvement in new communities must address itself to two questions:  What are the opportunities in new community development for participation by private corporations?  How are these opportunities affected by the potential for applying innovations to the community development process?  This section approaches these questions by describing three classes of opportunities:

  a.  Incentive opportunities for <u>attracting</u> corporations in the first place to new community development (<u>before</u> they are actually involved).
  b.  Opportunities for <u>applying</u> innovations in new communities (<u>during</u> corporate involvement).
  c.  Subsequent opportunities and dividends for <u>extending</u> innovative activities further in community <u>building</u> (<u>after</u> the first stages of corporate involvement).

The opportunities are discussed in this section in terms of rationale from the corporation's point of view.  Fundamental opportunities also exist from the government and user standpoints; whereas many of these overlap with the corporation opportunities, they are treated separately in Parts II and IV.

Given the impetus of emerging governmental policies and legislation and increasing financial feasibility (see Part IV), the opportunities [attracting (a), applying (b) and extending (c)] can be viewed as a continuously cycling and self-reinforcing series:

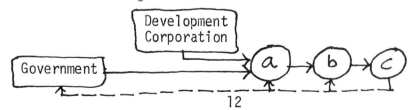

12

INCENTIVES TO ATTRACT CORPORATIONS
TO NEW COMMUNITY DEVELOPMENT (BEFORE)

1. <u>Construction of the future environment over the next
30 years</u>: The single greatest opportunity in new communities, from the developer's point of view, stems from the
often-cited fact that the next 30 years will witness the
construction in the U.S. of as many dwelling units (along
with attendant transportation, utilities and services networks, employment and recreation facilities and other human
settlement attributes) as have been built over the past 300
years (3,7). Simply from the standpoint of GNP, the portion
of national resources which will be applied to the construction of the future environment makes the undertaking one of
the largest sustained economic efforts yet started. It
stands to reason that the potential for development activity
and profit for the corporation will be substantial. Assuming one commonly accepted projection that only 7% of
the 300 million population in the year 2000 will reside in
new settlements (1) (equal to more than 10% of the existing
population and equal to 21% of the 100 million population
increase), it is clear that the new community component of
population accommodation and environment building will indeed be major. When viewed in the overall context of new
communities -- their regional impacts, applied innovations,
multiplier effects and self-propagating markets -- the opportunity for large-scale corporations to master comprehensively new community goals, development techniques and
systems integration appears unprecedented. The sheer bulk
of economic activity in the construction alone constitutes
a strong incentive, let alone the wide array of physical
components and economic activities associated with the
effort.

The National Committee on Urban Growth Policy recommendations illuminate the dimensions of the coming community and
city-building activity. The Committee recommends the building of 100 new towns of at least 100,000 population, and 10
new cities of at least 1 million population (2). Jerome
Pickard, an authority on metropolitan growth, projected a
potential need for the construction, between 1960 and 2000,
of 360 new communities of 25,000 each, or 180 new communities
of 50,000 each (3). The recommendations and the projections

13

are not binding; but they convey a reasonable measure of
the size of the new community "industry", for production
and marketing potentials and for the second-order fields
of frontier activity borne out of new communities. The
evidence of shifting national priorities and expanding
environmental emphasis amplifys the potential size and
significance of the new community thrust.


2.  Emerging governmental policy and legislation, federal
and state: The last ten years have seen the development
of urban, regional and economic development policies and
laws -- slow at first, but gathering momentum over the
last three years -- opening substantial opportunities for
new community development previously not there. As described
in Part IV, many of the serious impediments to large-scale
land development have been removed or considerably mollified
by the Housing and Urban Development Acts of 1968 and 1970.
The heavy and risky financial burdens of land acquisition
and front-end carrying costs have been reduced by provision
for loans and mortgage guarantees, and can be expected to be
reduced even further. A large number of federal supplemental grant programs have been focused on new communities;
and devices such as higher, accelerated depreciation rates
for new housing (as opposed to commercial development) have
increased the feasibility of new communities. The explicitly
stated federal goal of assisting ten new communities, containing social and technological innovations, by June,1971
reflects the direction of federal policy. If, as has been
forecast in numerous sources (5,6, also see Parts II and IV ),
growth policy should become a major focus for federal domestic activities in the 1970's, new communities and programs to boost their productive development will unquestion-
ably play a demonstrative and well-supported role. Such
programs would be congruent with emerging public policies
of population dispersal, regional economic development,
provision of housing and employment opportunities, technological and programmatic innovation and creative land use.

If, for example, the Executive Branch of the Federal Government chooses to employ carefully chosen federally owned land parcels for siting new communities (4), existing building codes and zoning restrictions retarding the application of desirable innovations could be lifted.  Additionally, provision of such land, by means of sale, transfer, or lease arrangements would remove a principal barrier to large-scale land development -- land acquisition and associated heavy front-end financing needs.  Similarly, major incentives to new community development can presently be provided through a host of means such as transportation, utilities and public facilities assistance, directing government activity and industrial location, and tax incentive measures.  The Report of the Advisory Commission on Intergovernmental Relations sums up the fundamental opportunity:

> As the problems resulting from the urbanization
> of the Nation's expanding population become
> more serious, the planning and construction of
> new communities may be viewed as an unparalleled
> opportunity to combine private enterprise and
> business objectives with the broader social,
> economic and political goals of American society (7).

Such goals are appearing increasingly in policy and legislation at the state level (see Appendix E).  In short, the array of government programs available -- in number and resources -- is vast and offers considerable incentives to those who will use them constructively.

3.  Coordinated application of social and technological innovations:  New communities offer ideal, and very likely the only, laboratories in which beneficial social and technological innovations can be applied and tested in a coordinated manner and which can subsequently be adapted for more general use.  New communities have long been thought of as logical places to develop markets for technological advances in housing oriented to performance standards  in-

stead of building codes. The same principle applies even more strongly to innovative transportation, utilities, energy, waste and communications systems as well as to forward-looking programs in health, education, community administration and social welfare.

A central assumption of this study is that the accelerating rate of social and technological change brings with it the imperative need to consider future alternatives and the role such innovations might play in a future of choice and design. The federal agencies have made it increasingly clear that they are pursuing a conscientious pattern of coordination between departments to encourage and develop priority innovative service and environmental systems (e.g., transportation, waste disposal and recycling, energy production and delivery). The sources for support are there for the new community developer to use. Not only do these opportunities for the developer overlap with public goals and policies; they offer the producers of new systems prime opportunities to test them and create their own markets, with all the profitability and multiplier effects built into the community development process. One example of this type of opportunity is the potential for generating innovative transportation systems in a new community linked with an innovative interurban high speed ground transportation line and a remote regional transfer airport (RRTA).

Because of the centralized control and management requirements inherent in community development, many mutually reinforcing innovations can be introduced simultaneously. Further, because of their model demonstration and transferability characteristics, they are eligible for solid governmental support. The simultaneity with which the innovations are considered maximizes assurance of high quality design and systems integration.

4.  Accelerated market aggregation and pace of development;
economies of scale; land appreciation; profitability:
Skilled entrepreneurial efforts can realize the major opportunity inherent in new community comprehensive development to control the rate and timing of return on investment.
Because of the comprehensiveness, relative capacity for
predictability and broad range of internal attractions of
large scale new communities (especially well adapted to
media presentation), they can achieve accelerated market
aggregation and pace of development, economies of scale,
land appreciation and ultimate profitability not possible
in smaller developments.*  The increments in land value
accruing in a comprehensive new community, as opposed to a
standard subdivision, stand to be much larger, thus providing great incentive for both the developer and the
community itself.  A portion of the increment in land values
accruing from the conversion of underdeveloped land to more
intensive use can be returned to the community for provision
of community facilities.  Since land appreciation is in most
cases the prime economic incentive for the developer to
build the community, it is clear that his control process
can allocate the proportion of this increment which goes
into community facilities and that which goes into corporation profit.  For the industrialized housing producer, a
particular opportunity exists in new community development
because the community represents potential for a rapid
growth rate and aggregated market -- the original incentive
for him to invest the heavy commitment required for indus-
trialization in the first place.

5.  Comprehensive planning, regional and economic base
integration:  The comprehensive planning process implicit
in new community development mandates establishment of an
integrated economic base and thorough regional resource

---

*Valencia, California, for example, plans a tenfold increase
 in present population of 4500 to 45,000 within just the next
 five years. (The Exchange, November 1970, p.19)  It may be a
 precursor to a more widely followed pattern of telescoped
 development periods.

and social accounting. Therefore, the developer possesses
the opportunity to marshal and focus public and private
resources in accordance with objectives favorable to both
public and entrepreneurial interests. In the case of new
community development in conjunction with an economic development program (e.g., a growth center in a depressed
region), unusual potential would exist for synchronously
concentrating economic forces in accordance with an overall
strategy which optimizes social, economic and environmental
benefits. Hence,the forces external, as well as internal,
to the new community borders would be mobilized to enlarge
the regional magnet attributes and economic base of the
area (e.g., industrial location patterns, employment opportunities, recreation facilities, regional shopping complexes, cultural attractions, neighboring land values, etc.).

The advantages of efficient land use development are inherent in the comprehensive planning process of new communities for at least three reasons. First, the usually
large land cost savings in a new community create competitive savings which can be passed on to the developer, community and individual housebuyer. Second, unified land
planning achieves the benefits of efficient and amenable
open space, transportation, utilities and services patterns.
The reduction of street lengths, sidewalks, utilities and
street furniture, made possible by skillful comprehensive
design, frees funds that can be devoted to other community
services. Third, even with expanded project size, tighter
control over the staging process becomes possible due to
the continuity of the same management and the greater
ability of the developer to adapt the community to user
response and unforeseen change over time. The greater
utilization of industrialized building capacity can sharply
reduce the development time frame necessary for past community development.

6. Marketability, profitability and the congruence of new
communities with emerging societal values: New communities
offer an unprecedented opportunity to respond to emerging
values and rising expectations in a way that existing urban
communities cannot. They represent a fresh chance not only
to meet known present needs, but also to anticipate and plan
imaginatively for future problems and opportunities by applying the best present- and future-oriented knowledge of
community needs, processes and design. This means not only
responsiveness to present and future market demands, but
also market creation, a leading capability of new communities.

With the emergence of forceful popular momentum supporting
environmental and ecological issues, new communities can
focus renewed attention and respect on nature, inhibit environmental despoilation, and implement technological and social
service systems compliant with the renewed attention. They can
accommodate the increasing ground swell of the back-to-
nature decentralization forces, articulated most forcefully
in the recent past by Orville Freeman (8). This set of
values is not entirely new,* but ample indicators signal
that it is gathering renewed vigor. New communities offer
an important vehicle for demonstrating the capacity to
reintegrate urban, man-made systems with rural and natural
systems in a positive, even poetic manner that satisfies
basic spiritual cravings for which the suburbs (and central
cities) have proved inadequate.

A 1968 Gallup Poll showed that 56% of Americans, if given
the chance, would choose a rural life. Only 18% would
choose a city, and 25% a suburb (9). In the light of an
incipient national population redistribution policy and the
growing recognition that urban and rural America cannot be
dealt with any longer as though they were separate

---

*As applied to communities, it has been around at least
 since the Utopian Communities, Ebenezer Howard's Garden
 City and Frank Lloyd Wright's "Broadacre City".

problems*, the popular disposition evident in the Gallup
findings may find considerable satisfaction in the urban-
rural reintegration and accessibility possible in new communities. Symptomatic of the reality of the popular trends
is the increasingly stated desire of industries to provide
their employees with a good environment and access to amenities, and the industries' consequent interest in locating
where they can attract employees by offering them the best
in schools, recreational access to the countryside,and other
features of the urban-rural balanced community (10). This
seems a reliable indicator of both potential marketability
and profitability.

APPLICATION OF OPPORTUNITIES
IN NEW COMMUNITIES (DURING)

Having described incentives to attract corporations to
new community development, the discussion moves to outlining
the opportunities for applying innovations in a new community
during the development process.

1. Provision of accessibility to comprehensive technological and social services: Innovative technological and social
services comprise the major portion of the subject matter
in this study and are not elaborated on further here. The
belief inherent throughout is that their application "from
the ground up" is one of the central opportunities of new
communities, frequently impractical in existing cities.

2. Achievement of social balance, and adaptability to different ways and elements of daily life: The opportunity in a
new community to provide for social balance and the mixing
of different economic, social and ethnic groups has not yet
been realized; but if it will be, it will yield exemplary

*The strongest indicator of this is the pending creation of the
 Federal Department of Community Development which subsumes HUD
 and Department of Agriculture   rural housing interests.

20

effects for other communities. Since the federal government and HUD are supporting only those new communities which embrace this principle, its achievement can be accelerated. This opportunity does not ignore the counter-trend toward a simultaneously increasing separation of various groups. But in terms of long-range goals and overall perspective, this latter tendancy is subordinate to the preeminant thrust toward increasing reconciliation and constructive interaction between different social groups. While it is true that for the immediate future, the appeal of such integrated balance may be limited to certain clusterings of age, income and education characteristics, it is probable that the movement toward this type of balance will diffuse and accelerate. The new community offers a singular opportunity to accelerate the process: to bring together different groups attracted by the existence of new values and open facilities which supersede older causes of social and economic separation and which promote in their place common interests and sources of enrichening interaction.

Within new communities there would be no resistance from pre-existing patterns of population distribution, nor any entrenched interests. Thus, the urban structure can be conceived so as to make "racial and economic integration a taken-for-granted reality -- a beneficial reality -- from the very beginning." (11) The developers who anticipate this social thrust and are among the first to realize it will successfully create their own market, which will probably grow larger in time.

In addition to accommodating low and moderate-income residents (in proportion to their relative population) the new community can spur the integration or reintegration of age groups, particularly the elderly. This possibility suggests the more general opportunity of reintegrating common activity and place elements of daily life frequently estranged from each other in existing communities (e.g., work and recreation; home and education; urban and rural; income, age and class groupings; citizens and political institutions; commerce and culture; etc.). This theme affects land planning and physical location criteria; it also speaks to the enlarged possibility of citizens playing multi-career roles in their community as a matter of course, rather than exception, including different activities phased over daily, weekly and age-level cycles (e.g., worker, teacher, social paraprofessional, artist, children, the elderly, etc.). The need and opportunity to accommodate emerging and alternate life-styles and values can be fulfilled in the new community.

The promise of greater community adaptability to changes over time is reinforced by the potential for integrating diverse resident group participation into the decision-making processes of local administration.

3. Design of an urban environment responsive to natural determinants, and of land use patterns beneficial to community-shared interests: Through comprehensive and rational design, the new community can achieve more beneficial settlement patterns than megalopolitan overgrowth, on the one hand, and costly scattered suburban sprawl on the other. The prospect of new communities being "more beautiful and sensually satisfying than most of our cities and suburbs" (1) is a persuasive incentive to the developer as well as to the users for providing models which have the effect of creating their own demand (let alone influencing heightened expectations and change in older cities).

From the start, an opportunity lies in the strong adoption of the use of natural systems and site characteristics in community design. This may not appear innovative or fundamental until one realizes that few towns and cities have been built which fully realize the potential of natural assets such as shore line, river or incline or even drainage patterns. At a time of renewed attention to the elimination of polluted waterways, opportunities exist for imaginative use of water networks in inner community situations -- canals, fountains, shorelines, etc. -- which could restore to urban living the benefits previously realized by medieval and Renaissance Moslem, Spanish and Italian architecture in a number of the most widely admired human settlements in history.  In present day America, many Florida communities (islands, canals, shoreline marina configurations), California seacoast towns -- even artificially created lake towns in the Arizona desert -- attempt to apply these principles. What makes the opportunity especially notable are trends of increasing outdoor recreation and restoration of clean rivers with  consequent recreational potentials.  European new towns have generally succeeded in employing superior landscape design, including the generous use of berms, terracing and plantings to enhance the reintegration of urban and natural systems.  Since these methods can often be applied to great benefit at low cost, there is little reason why the American new community could not achieve constructive results by the application of the same techniques.

Through improved street patterns, increased walking and cycling paths, shorter distances to destinations of daily or frequent visits, the capital savings from reduced total road length and, in some cases, school buses, can be utilized for other community services.  The comparison between Bridgeport, Connecticut (a representative American city of 100,000 population) and the new community of Columbia, Maryland, planned for 110,000, is illustrative.  Bridgeport's streets cover 23% of its land; in Columbia, only 8% of the land is used for streets.  Thus 15% more land can be used for other purposes -- parks, school grounds, etc. Such patterns can also reinforce the growing interest in community-shared -- as opposed to privately held -- natural attributes and service facilities.*  Enlightened conservationist land use mechanisms already widely practiced at

_____

*The Henry George argument for returning unearned increment in privately-held land value to the community is reawakening and may pertain directly to those new communities with land holdings impinging on major natural amenities.

23

the planned unit development (PUD) scale are much more
strongly appropriate at the new community scale.  Cluster
developments, natural conservation easements and other
open space zoning devices, as well as the ecological
guiding principles contained, for example, in McHarg's
Design with Nature (12), can be employed to preserve the
important natural features of the community.

In short, the new community offers the developer the opportunity to apply natural determinants to an urban environment.

4.  Application of innovative processes affecting the development phase and the community structure:  Innovative processes which represent strong opportunities for the corporate  developer of a new community are disaggregated here
into three classes: (i) those involving major actor groups
during the development phase, (ii) those which would indirectly affect the community physical form but which would
not cost more than present systems,and (iii) those which
would indirectly affect the community physical form but
which would cost more than present systems.

A prominent opportunity affecting the development phase is
the ability to form new combinations of strategic actors
in the development process, particularly industries and
financial  sources with a permanent stake in the new community (i.e., industries, business and public service system
companies).*  The new community can provide the vehicle by
which different profit-oriented entities cooperate to reinforce each other's market positions.  An example is the opportunity for a primary developer in a non-metropolitan area

---

*Examples of this type of alignment exist already in Jonathan
 (Stanford Research Institute, Olin Corporation, Northern Natural
 Gas Company, Jonathan Development Corporation, Burlington In-
 dustries, Inc.); Columbia (Connecticut General Life Insurance,
 Chase Manhattan Bank, The Rouse Company); Walt Disney's EPCOT
 (Experimental Prototype Community of Tomorrow), Florida, and
 several others.

to align himself with an airline or aircraft manufacturer,
thereby developing the urban/rural access capabilities
through innovative transportation. This possibility seems
promising when viewed in the context of the expanding role
air transportation is playing in the distribution of freight
and the easing of leisure access. Similar opportunities
would apply to producers of other transportation modes as
well as to providers of utility and communications services
and others.

Another opportunity during the development process is the
potential of conscious manipulation and use of media, discussed in Part IV. This seems to be an under-utilized
method of accelerating pace of development.

Process innovations potentially affecting community physical
form and probably not costing more than present systems can
be simply enumerated:

> ·early involvement of community participation in plan-
>  ning of educational and health services;
> ·manpower training and employment programs, especially
>  those which involve workers' permanent stakes in the
>  community;
> ·integration of industry, business and cultural in-
>  stitutions into the community-wide educational net-
>  work;
> ·disaggregation and dispersal of industries and em-
>  ployment facilities;
> ·provision for intentional communities or "living groups"
>  as sub-units of the community;
> ·establishment of a surrogate constituency for the
>  future new community citizens in the early stages of
>  the planning process; and
> ·dispersal of government centers and community control.

Process innovations potentially and indirectly affecting
community physical form but probably costing more than
present systems are:

25

·extended health services;
·orientation service (an expanded version of "Welcome Wagon");
·monitoring of the impact of the community on natural systems;* and
·monitoring of the impact of technological and social innovations on the resident population.*

SUBSEQUENT OPPORTUNITIES AND DIVIDENDS FOR EXTENDING ACTIVITIES FURTHER IN COMMUNITY BUILDING (AFTER)

A leading critic of new communities concedes, "...there is little doubt that new towns might have a powerful demonstration effect and assist greatly in the diffusion of design innovation." (1)  He also points to the need to require that new community findings be transferable to other areas and that they be monitored for their effects.  In an age crying for images of a more fulfilling urban environment, new communities -- at the minimum -- will perform needed experimental and demonstrative image-making roles.

<u>Transferability of new community achievements to other new communities and to existing cities</u>:  The demonstration and transferability characteristics of new community activities represent a great opportunity for subsequent innovative activity by the corporate developer.  James Rouse illustrates one example; from his initial new community effort at Columbia, Maryland, and smaller development projects in the Baltimore area, The American City Corporation, a subsidiary of The Rouse Company, has prepared a proposal for a new city of approximately 400,000 in South Richmond, Staten Island, and a regional proposal for Hartford, Connecticut which subsumes a galaxy of satellite communities, presumably with his company providing the planning and development.  It is understood that Rouse is extending a similar pattern of operations to the greater

---

*These monitoring mechanisms, while causing an additional cost to operate where there was none before, would doubtless contribute toward an overall cost saving when total social and ecological costs are accounted for.

Boston area. Clearly, the corporations with sufficient financial, productive and managerial power to develop one new community will benefit considerably by developing sufficient in-house skills to operate effectively on potentially forthcoming development problems after their first new community effort has proved the demonstrability and transferability of innovative systems.

REFERENCES

(1) William Alonso, "The Mirage of New Towns," The Public Interest, No. 19, Spring 1970.

(2) Donald Canty, ed., The New City, Report of the National Committee on Urban Growth Policy, published for Urban America, Inc., Praeger, New York, 1969.

(3) Jerome Pickard, Dimensions of Metropolitanism, Urban Land Institute, Washington, D.C., 1967.

(4) U.S. Public Land Law Review Commission, One Third of the Nation's Land, Government Printing Office, Washington, D.C., 1970.

(5) A. James Reichley, "George Romney is Running Hard at HUD," Fortune, December 1970.

(6) National Goals Research Staff, Toward Balanced Growth: Quantity with Quality, Government Printing Office, Washington, D.C., 1970.

(7) Advisory Commission on Intergovernmental Relations, Urban and Rural America: Policies for Future Growth, Government Printing Office, Washington, D.C., 1968, p.98.

(8) Ward W. Konkle, ed., Providing Quality Environment in Our Communities, Graduate School Press, U.S. Department of Agriculture, Washington, D.C., 1968.

(9) James L. Sundquist, "Where Shall They Live?", The Public Interest, No. 18, Winter 1970.

(10) "It's Mountain Standard Time: Boom Time in the Rockies,"
     _Fortune_, September 1970.

(11) Victor Gruen Associates, _New Cities USA, A Statement of_
     _Purpose and Program_, prepared for the Department of
     Housing and Urban Development, brochure, 1966, p.25.

(12) Ian McHarg, _Design with Nature_, Natural History Press,
     New York, 1969.

(13) The American City Corporation, _The Hartford Process_,
     reproduction, Columbia, 1970.

## C.  SUMMARY OF SOCIAL TRENDS

In acknowledging the main trends that have influenced
the identification of innovations in this report, the
simplest procedure is to enumerate them in the following
summary.  Many of these factors are discussed more fully
in other sections of the report.

A.  The emergence in the U.S. of a Post-Industrial Society
    (1) characterized by the following trends:

    1.  There will be an increase to seven in ten persons
        employed in service occupations by 1980 (as com-
        pared to the employment of six in ten persons in
        primary industries, characteristic of an industrial
        society) (2).

    2.  There will be a decrease to two in ten urban workers
        employed in manufacturing by 1975 (3).

    3.  The single largest employment group by 1980 will be
        professional and technical personnel (2).

    4.  The axial principle of society will shift from the
        emphasis on state or private control of investment
        to an emphasis on knowledge, its codification and
        dissemination; and on communications as the key
        technology (2).

    5.  More free time to spend for purposes of cultural enrich-
        ment, leisure, recreation and avocation will be available.

    6.  The emergence and decentralization of craft and
        personal service activities as avocations will

occur. These will be a source of stable, purposeful engagement and an ongoing sense of accomplishment for a substantial number of individuals (4).

7. Guaranteed income will cover a large share of those not in the work force (4).

8. A greater proportion of discretionary income will be spent on services and momentary, comsumable pleasures. This will strengthen the trend toward a service-, rather than a product-oriented economy and will reinforce the primacy of services in the community.

9. Increasing pressure on corporations and other profit-making entities will continue to mount, requiring them to assume socially constructive roles, e.g., training assistance to disadvantaged groups, protection of the natural environment, and consumerism (4).

B. Changing values and life-styles with a high probability of occuring in the 1975-to-1985 period:

1. Increasing upward social mobility from lower classes will be most evidenced by racial and ethnic minorities; some increase in downward mobility will be most evidenced by white middle class.

2. Traditional class stratification will diminish in importance; new class distinctions will arise with the centralization of knowledge and power in a technocratic-managerial elite (4).

3. Short-range "supersensate" cultural values will become more pronounced (5): work, advancement and achievement-oriented values will continue to erode

as a "counter-culture" grows in numbers. Some
drugs and marijuana, emblematic of this overall
trend, will become more accepted. Humanistic,
secular and perhaps self-indulgent criteria will
become central (6).

4. Long-range "ideational" cultural values will grow
   in strength, inner-directed, subjective, meta-
   physical, religious and mystical values becoming
   stronger. Some mixture of the ideational and
   supersensate values are observable in today's
   youth. Sorokin, in his monumental historical
   cultural study, predicted the shift to ideational
   cultural values in the last decades of this century
   (5).

5. New careers for women will open up (4).

6. Women and ethnic minorities will assume full
   equality in job and social opportunities (4).

7. The strength of the nuclear family as a child-
   raising unit will continue to decline (2).

8. With women devoting more time to non-household
   activities, there will be increased demand for
   prepared meals, delivery service for prepared
   meals, inexpensive family cafeterias for multi-
   dwellings, maintenance service companies for
   dwellings (7), day care centers, and community-
   run, 24-hour child-rearing centers.

9. Non-marital arrangements for raising children will
   be widely accepted (4).

10. A possible trend may emerge for more families to
    have two sets of age-clustered children (5).

11. Teenagers will to some degree leave parental
    households earlier to join communities focused

around the themes of work and education (4).

12. Alternate life styles will become more commonplace and accepted; e.g., non-kinship extended
families of couples, age groups, working groups,
class groups, creative groups, therapeutic groups
(8). Prototypes: communes, intentional communities, mutual adoption clubs (A. Huxley), Rossmore
Leisure World, Sun City, South Bay Swinging Singles
Clubs, half-way houses, Synanon, T-groups, etc.

13. There will be shorter working times for the employed, with the extra time being spent for avo-
cation and leisure activities -- a good portion
of which will be home-centered.

14. There will be higher levels of discretionary income
for most citizens, of which a larger part will be
spent on recreation and leisure activities.

15. New non-productive concepts of leisure will grow,
similar to deGrazia's definition, "The freedom
from the necessity of being occupied."

16. The elderly, through guaranteed incomes, greater
vitality and health, will be a generation of greater
visibility and cultural integration (5).

17. Second careers, travel and community service will
keep life meaningful for the elderly, thus reducing
the risk of their increasing alienation from society.

18. Simultaneously with successful integration, the
black separatist movement will grow. There will
be many almost totally white communities, many integrated ones, and many totally non-white (4).

19. Nationwide and worldwide travel will become more
commonplace and increasingly accessible to all but
the poorest. Reinforced by the "global village"

communications explosion, travel of citizens to other countries, as well as travel of other nationals to this country, will result in increasingly global values, growing ecumenism and internationalism.

20. Higher mobility in an environment of continuing rapid social change will result in sequential careers, marriages and social associations which will place greater value on the immediacy and intensity of the ephemeral relationships shadowing the "temporary society" as described by Bennis (9).

21. The growth of the "temporary society" trend will likely lead to the simultaneous emergence of a counter-trend, in which some groups consciously strive to repossess older values.

22. Between now and the year 2000, there will be a requirement for from four to twenty times the amount of recreational facilities that now exist (10).

C. Changing relationships within public and institutional control mechanisms:

1. More Councils of Government (COG's), metropolitan or region-wide, will be instituted. Some may be special purpose districts for the management of extra-civic concerns such as transportation, pollution industrial location, population migration, taxes, and central information processing units (11). Prototypes: Association of Bay Area Governments (ABAG), Port of New York Authority, etc. More often they will be county, multi-municipality or multi-county coordinated multi-purpose governmental structures.

2. There will be some polarization of elite groups, government, university and managerial meritocracies versus grass roots groups seeking elimination of social, personal, and environmental alienation by their

participation in decision processes.

3. The revolt against institutions that deny individual participation may, as today's youth emerges from student status, lead to new mechanisms of participation in government, education, place of employment, etc. (4).*

4. Instant referenda and public opinion monitoring will be increasingly important in shaping the direction of public policy (4).

5. Increasing speed in obtaining feedback on community opinion will allow greater speed for change in community values (4).

6. Local community control of services, schools, health and welfare will become stronger (4). Prototypes: Little City Halls, tenants' councils, neighborhood associations, home owners' associations, tenants' or owners' management corporations.


D. Expanding role of education:

1. The "communiversity" will emerge as a community institution to serve the total community including the unemployed and the aged (4).

2. Adolescent education may in some instances change to combine work with study (4).

3. Education will become much more decentralized, diversified and integrated into the workings of the community (4). Prototype: Philadelphia Parkway Plan,

_____

*John Gardner's Common Cause may represent a precursor of this trend.

34

in which a high school's "physical facilities" are comprised of the city's major cultural institutions lining the Benjamin Franklin Parkway.

4. With knowledge as the axial principle of society, education will grow in demand; and with accelerated social change, there will be need for continual education and education for modified or new careers. This will also be stimulated by individuals living longer and having a greater number of productive years.

E. Reactions to technological impacts:

1. The alienation brought about by technology will take a more tangible form if a substantial number of people find themselves separated from the labor force by being made nonessential (4).

2. There will be greater individualization of what are now the mass media (4).

3. Progress in social technology will specifically call for the establishment of monitoring and predictive devices for relating impacts of technological change (4).

REFERENCES

(1) Daniel Bell, "Notes on the Post-Industrial Society," The Public Interest, No. 6, Winter 1967.

(2) Daniel Bell in lecture at Harvard University, Fall, 1970.

(3) Barton-Aschman Assoc. Inc., Guidelines for New Systems of Urban Transportation, Vol. I: Urban Needs and Potentials, HUD, 1968.

(4)  Paul de Brigard and Olaf Helmer, <u>Some Potential Societal Developments: 1970-2000</u>, Institute for the Future, 1970.

(5)  Pitirim Sorokin, <u>Social and Cultural Dynamics</u>, 1962.

(6)  Herman Kahn and Anthony J. Wiener, "The Next Thirty Three Years: A Framework for Speculation," <u>Daedalus</u>, Summer 1967.

(7)  Gloria Steinem, "What It Would Be Like if Women Win," <u>Time</u>, Vol 96, August 31, 1970.

(8)  Carol Burke, Kellner-Oshrey Associates, Boston, Mass.

(9)  Warren Bennis, <u>The Temporary Society</u>.

(10) Marion Clawson, <u>A Place to Live, The Department of Agriculture Yearbook</u>, 1963.

(11) Karl Deutsch and Richard Meier, <u>Confederation and Decentralization of Urban Governments: How Self-Controls for the American Megalopolis Can Evolve</u>, unpublished paper, Harvard University, 1968.

## D.  List of Innovations

The tables on the following pages contain an extensive list
of technological and programmatic innovations, many of
which are discussed in Part III of the report.  On the basis
of the research from which this list was compiled, a preliminary evaluation of the potential impact of the innovations on community settlement patterns was prepared.  More
detailed and systematic studies of the design impact of
several of the innovations (particularly movement systems)
were undertaken at a later stage in the investigation (see
Part V).  It was useful, however, to estimate preliminary
impact potential as a step toward identifying those innovations whose consideration in a new community project is, at
least in part, a determinant of settlement patterns.

MAJOR DETERMINANT OF PATTERN
- (1) OVERALL PATTERN
- (2) SUBSET OF PATTERN

COULD HAVE INFLUENCE ON PATTERN
- (3) OVERALL PATTERN
- (4) SUBSET OF PATTERN
- (5) NONE

| | (1) | (2) | (3) | (4) | (5) |
|---|:---:|:---:|:---:|:---:|:---:|
| **A. MOVEMENT SYSTEMS** | | | | | |
| Dial-a-bus System | ● | | | | |
| Dashaveyor System | ● | | | | |
| Transtech System | ● | | | | |
| Alden Capsule Transit System | ● | | | | |
| Varo Monocab System | ● | | | | |
| Minirail System | ● | | | | |
| Sky Car Transivator System | ● | | | | |
| Vehicle Distribution System | ● | | | | |
| V/STOL airbus service (extending to destinations outside of N.C. boundaries) | | | ● | | |
| **B. ENERGY SYSTEMS** | | | | | |
| All-underground power transmission | | | | | ● |
| Total energy (gas) and total electric | | | | | ● |
| Fuel cells (in residential units) | | | ● | | |
| Nuclear energy | | | | | ● |
| Magnetohydrodynamic energy | | | | | ● |
| Tidal energy | | | | | ● |
| Geothermal energy | | | | | ● |
| Solar energy | | | | | ● |

|  | MAJOR DETERMINANT OF PATTERN | | COULD HAVE INFLUENCE ON PATTERN | | |
|  | (1) OVERALL PATTERN | (2) SUBSET OF PATTERN | (3) OVERALL PATTERN | (4) SUBSET OF PATTERN | (5) NONE |
|  | (1) | (2) | (3) | (4) | (5) |
| **C. COMMUNICATION SYSTEMS** | | | | | |
| Digital carrier systems data network |  |  | ● |  |  |
| Cable Television (CATV) |  |  | ● |  |  |
| Personal two-way wireless TV |  |  | ● |  |  |
| Computer utility |  |  | ● |  |  |
| Video Casettes |  |  |  |  | ● |
| Facsimile reproduction machines |  |  | ● |  |  |
| Projected outdoor holograph images |  |  | ● |  |  |
| Holographic 3-D video |  |  | ● |  |  |
| **D. WASTE MANAGEMENT - SEWAGE** | | | | | |
| Vacuum home sewerage system (Liljendahl) |  |  |  |  | ● |
| Grinder pump/pressure system |  |  |  |  | ● |
| Waste tamer |  | ● |  |  |  |
| Municipal sewage treatment (Unox System) |  |  |  |  | ● |
| **E. WASTE MANAGEMENT - COLLECTION** | | | | | |
| Automated vacuum collection (AVAC or Centralsug) |  |  |  | ● |  |
| Pneumo-slurry system |  |  |  | ● |  |

COULD HAVE INFLUENCE ON PATTERN

MAJOR DETERMINANT OF PATTERN

| | | | | |
|---|---|---|---|---|
| (1) OVERALL PATTERN | | | | |
| (2) SUBSET OF PATTERN | | | | |
| (3) OVERALL PATTERN | | | | |
| (4) SUBSET OF PATTERN | | | | |
| (5) NONE | | | | |

| | (1) | (2) | (3) | (4) | (5) |
|---|---|---|---|---|---|
| **E. WASTE MANAGEMENT - COLLECTION (continued)** | | | | | |
| Prepacked system | | | | | ● |
| Garchey system | | | | | ● |
| **F. WASTE MANAGEMENT - TREATMENT** | | | | | |
| Pyrolysis disposal system | | | | | ● |
| CPU-400 disposal system | | | | | ● |
| Composting disposal (biōstabilization) | | | | | ● |
| Anaerobic digestion | | | | | ● |
| Home solid and liquid waste treatment and water recycling | | | ● | | |
| Municipal solid waste recycling | | | | | ● |
| Fusion torch recovery | | | | | ● |
| **G. MISCELLANEOUS UTILITY SYSTEMS** | | | | | |
| Grouped utility corridors or "Utiladors" | | ● | | | |
| Tube Parcel Delivery System | | ● | | | |

| | MAJOR DETERMINANT OF PATTERN | | COULD HAVE INFLUENCE ON PATTERN | | |
| --- | --- | --- | --- | --- | --- |
| | (1) OVERALL PATTERN | (2) SUBSET OF PATTERN | (3) OVERALL PATTERN | (4) SUBSET OF PATTERN | (5) NONE |
| | (1) | (2) | (3) | (4) | (5) |

**H. HEALTH**

| | (1) | (2) | (3) | (4) | (5) |
| --- | --- | --- | --- | --- | --- |
| Dispersed* community clinics | | ● | | | |
| Adaptable hospital or clinic design (acute, extended, or nursing care bed & facility adaptability) | | | | | ● |
| Computer assisted diagnostic service | | | | | ● |
| Prepaid Medical Program | | | | | ● |
| Multiphasic health screening | | | | | ● |
| Alcoholic, drug, and mental disturbance hot line services | | | | | ● |
| Paraprofessional dispersed* psychiatric consultation services | | | | | ● |
| Centralized monitoring of remote outpatients | | | | | ● |
| Abortion clinics | | | | | ● |
| Human Potential Center for encounter or T group and sensory awareness seminars, etc. | | | | | ● |

**I. EDUCATION, CHILD CARE, AND HUMAN POTENTIAL**

| | (1) | (2) | (3) | (4) | (5) |
| --- | --- | --- | --- | --- | --- |
| Dispersed* day care centers | | ● | | | |
| Dispersed* 24-hour child rearing centers (creche's) | | ● | | | |
| Dispersed* primary schools with local community control | | ● | | | |
| Decentralized educational facility components for higher schools with close school-community ties | | ● | | | |

| | (1) | (2) | (3) | (4) | (5) |
|---|---|---|---|---|---|

COULD HAVE INFLUENCE ON PATTERN

    (5)  NONE
    (4)  SUBSET OF PATTERN
    (3)  OVERALL PATTERN

MAJOR DETERMINANT OF PATTERN

    (2)  SUBSET OF PATTERN
    (1)  OVERALL PATTERN

| | (1) | (2) | (3) | (4) | (5) |
|---|:---:|:---:|:---:|:---:|:---:|
| **I. EDUCATION, CHILD CARE, AND HUMAN POTENTIAL (cont'd)** | | | | | |
| Use of teaching machines & computer assisted instruction | | | ● | | |
| TV and computerized educational service accessible to homes & care centers | | | ● | | |
| Educational credit vouchers given to head of household of school age children to be spent on education of choice | | | | | ● |
| Educational programs for second careers for the retired | | | | | ● |
| Educational programs for mid-career "retooling" for professionals | | | | ● | |
| Educational programs for serious careers for women out of school | | | | | ● |
| **J. CITIZEN PARTICIPATION, GOVERNMENT, AND WELFARE** | | | | | |
| Sampling of potential user preferences for planning purposes | | ● | ● | ● | |
| User participation in the planning of community facilities | | ● | ● | ● | |
| * Star after "dispersed" facilities indicates those which are within a 10 to 15 minute walk or 1/2 mile radius of most remote dwelling unit. | | | | | |

42

| | MAJOR DETERMINANT OF PATTERN | | COULD HAVE INFLUENCE ON PATTERN | | |
| | (1) OVERALL PATTERN | (2) SUBSET OF PATTERN | (3) OVERALL PATTERN | (4) SUBSET OF PATTERN | (5) NONE |
|---|---|---|---|---|---|
| | (1) | (2) | (3) | (4) | (5) |

**J. CITIZEN PARTICIPATION, GOVERNMENT, AND WELFARE (cont'd)**

| | (1) | (2) | (3) | (4) | (5) |
|---|---|---|---|---|---|
| User participation in the design of their own dwellings | | | | ● | |
| Community forum for ratification of on-going planning decisions | ● | ● | ● | ● | |
| TV broadcast to the home on planning alternatives. Instant feedback, remote referendum and ratification | ● | ● | ● | ● | |
| Multi-service centers (employment, educational, vocational, marital and family counseling; legal, accounting and employment service; entertainment and recreation) | | | | ● | |
| Prepaid legal and accounting service | | | | | ● |
| Ombudsman service | | | | | ● |
| Orientation service for new arrivals | | | | | ● |
| Dispersed* government centers (little city halls or in multi-service centers) | | ● | | | |
| Monitoring societal impact of technological and social innovations | | | ● | ● | |
| Monitoring impact of community input-outputs on natural systems | | | ● | ● | |

* Star after "dispersed" facilities indicates those which are within a 10 to 15 minute walk or 1/2 mile radius of the most remote dwelling unit.

COULD HAVE INFLUENCE ON PATTERN

               (5)  NONE
         (4)  SUBSET OF PATTERN
     (3)  OVERALL PATTERN

MAJOR DETERMINANT OF PATTERN

   (2)  SUBSET OF PATTERN
 (1)  OVERALL PATTERN

| | (1) | (2) | (3) | (4) | (5) |
|---|---|---|---|---|---|
| **K. SOCIAL ORGANIZATION** | | | | | |
| Areal demarcation of neighborhood size subculture units for special interests, age, etc. | ● | | | | |
| Planning for inclusion of alternative life styles | | | | | |
|     Intentional community (or commune) areas in overall plan | | ● | | | |
|     Housing availability for living groups, (both kinship & non-kinship) | | | | ● | |
| **L. EMPLOYMENT** | | | | | |
| Dispersed* small industries (for business or employment opportunities) | | ● | | | |
| Dispersed* small commercial facilities (for business or employment opportunities) | | ● | | | |
| Employment training programs for underskilled | | | | | ● |
| Screening of industries for worker-alienating characteristics | | | | ● | |

* Star after "dispersed" facilities indicates those which are within a 10 to 15 minute walk or 1/2 mile radius of the most remote dwelling unit.

|  | | (1) | (2) | (3) | (4) | (5) |
|---|---|---|---|---|---|---|

COULD HAVE INFLUENCE ON PATTERN

    (5)   NONE
    (4)   SUBSET OF PATTERN
    (3)   OVERALL PATTERN

MAJOR DETERMINANT OF PATTERN

    (2)   SUBSET OF PATTERN
    (1)   OVERALL PATTERN

| | (1) | (2) | (3) | (4) | (5) |
|---|---|---|---|---|---|
| **M. PUBLIC SAFETY, FIRE PREVENTION, & LAW ENFORCEMENT** | | | | | |
| Grade separation of pedestrians and cars at major intersections | | ● | | | |
| Computer assisted police patrol and detection | | | | | ● |
| Sensitivity training for police officers | | | | | ● |
| Television surveillance of high-potential accident, crime, and fire areas | | | | | ● |
| **N. RECREATIONAL, CULTURAL, AND ART AND ARCHITECTURE** | | | | | |
| Computer/TV games | | | | | ● |
| Development of dispersed* craft enterprises | | ● | | | |
| Use of mobile and inflatable or otherwise highly adaptable structures for community buildings | | | | ● | |
| Covered central public functions with large dome or other structure | | | | ● | |
| Underground parking (for high density areas) | | | | ● | |
| Automated parking structures (for high density areas) | | | | ● | |

* Star after "dispersed" facilities indicates those which are within a 10 to 15 minute walk or 1/2 mile radius of the most remote dwelling unit.

COULD HAVE INFLUENCE ON PATTERN

MAJOR DETERMINANT OF PATTERN

| | | (1) OVERALL PATTERN | (2) SUBSET OF PATTERN | (3) OVERALL PATTERN | (4) SUBSET OF PATTERN | (5) NONE |
|---|---|---|---|---|---|---|
| | | (1) | (2) | (3) | (4) | (5) |
| **O. RELIGIOUS** | | | | | | |
| Dispersed* chapels or meditation places | | | ● | | | |
| Ecumenical churches | | | | | | ● |
| **P. HOME SERVICES** | | | | | | |
| Computer assisted television shopping | | | | ● | | |
| Robotic machines for household chores | | | | | | ● |
| Sonic cleaning devices and air-filtering systems | | | | | | ● |

* Star after "dispersed" facilities indicates those
  which are within a 10 to 15 minute walk or 1/2 mile
  radius of the most remote dwelling unit.

# E. GLOSSARY

In order to clarify such terms as density, centralization, decentralization and dispersal, used throughout this report, they are defined in the following way:

High density: settlements with over fifteen dwelling units (over 50 persons) per net residential acre.
Medium density: settlements with between seven and fifteen dwelling units (or 25 to 50 persons) per net acre.
Low density: settlements with between two and six dwelling units (or 7 to 24 persons) per net residential acre.
Very low density: settlements with one dwelling unit (less than 7 persons) per net residential acre or less.

Centralization: concentration of population, activities, services and political control in large centers.
Decentralization: diffusion of population, activities, services and political control into small autonomous centers.

Dispersal: the movement of population and the establishment of activities in areas either (i) outside of metropolitan districts or (ii) outside of the 12 major urbanized regions.

Service areas: geographical living areas, primarily residential, which are characterized by the range of integrated activities (schools, health clinics, commerce, cultural, recreational and institutional facilities) and service systems (transportation, utilities, street networks, etc.) necessary to support the populations contained within them.

Activity centers: integrated centers, large or small, of many activities for which people have reason to be connected. Centers would include job and shopping opportunities, health care, education and recreation opportunities.

# II. TRENDS, GOALS AND SCENARIOS

The purpose of this section is to identify and describe those factors which must be recognized in any analysis of new communities and large-scale development. Principally, these factors reflect emerging social and technological change, the objectives toward which new communities might be directed, and the evolving life styles toward which society may be moving. For community design, these factors are essential in understanding total urban systems and their dynamic behavior. For development, they are essential in understanding emerging investment and marketing opportunities.

SUMMARY

In the coming decade, a national growth strategy will probably be implemented to establish growth poles outside of the metropolitan areas and the major urbanized regions of the nation. These growth poles will attract people from the large cities and suburbs by offering a dramatically better quality of environment, higher levels of services, and superior design. They would be instituted as de novo "new communities" and as community growth centers in conjunction with existing small towns of under 50,000 population. New-towns-in-town, communities within the dense areas of existing metropolitan areas, will also be developed. Improved opportunities for recreation, shopping and employment will occur within new communities; and there will be vastly improved user-oriented delivery systems for education, health care and social services of greater variety than presently exist or would exist at that time in central city or suburban areas.

Access to opportunities and services within and outside of these communities will be improved by innovative systems of movement and communication. Concurrent with trends toward

greater centralization of decision making and greater alienation  -- trends that are currently being encountered by
people in existing cities -- there will be mechanisms for
decentralized and participatory decision making in some new
communities.  This will both ease and complicate the development process but will improve the general attractiveness
of the communities where those mechanisms exist.

By 1980, professional and technically-employed persons will
be the largest employment group in new communities, followed
by skilled laborers.  There will be more discretionary income and free time which will be used in pursuit of education, recreation and art, craft and skill avocations, much
of which will be home- or neighborhood-based due to improved
communication technologies and the decentralization of activity  centers.  There will be more demand for "living groups,"
people with similar interests living in small groups of
houses or apartments, clustered around a shared facility
such as a common group living-dining area, a multi-media
communication room or a purposeful facility such as a craft
or special skills enterprise.  Living groups would have the
options to undertake child day-care, shared cooking and
maintenance arrangements.

For high and medium density communities, individual dwellings and/or several living groups of various sizes would
form the basic building blocks or sub-culture units of larger,  more heterogeneous neighborhoods, which then would form
larger districts containing almost all of the activities
that would be desired by the residents within agreeable
walking distance.  A high degree of local political control
would be exercised at the district or service area level
(10,000 to 15,000 people).

For low and very low density communities, made more feasible
by the availability of dwelling-based energy production and
waste treatment, the socio-physical units would be less hier-
archically structured;but local political control would still
be exercised.  These communities will be highly nature-ori-
ented in that the siting and design of individual or multi-

49

family dwellings and other structures will be strongly influenced by the site conditions.            •

All components of the communities will be screened for pol-
luting characteristics and the community input/outputs will
be periodically monitored for effect on the environment.

## A. POPULATION DISTRIBUTION AND GROWTH TRENDS

The population "explosion" in the U.S. is rapidly being discounted. Since the post-war baby boom from 1945 to 1960, when fertility rates reached about 3.75 births per woman, there has been a sharp rate decline, due in part to more widespread use of birth-control measures. The latest Bureau of the Census fertility projection (series D) is 2.50, and the National Goals Research Staff projects it as low as 2.11 by 1980, which is close to the replacement rate or zero population growth (1).

The growing concentration of the U.S. population in large urban masses has resulted in a perceived, and in some ways real, lowering of the quality of life in urban and rural areas (2); and "population dispersal" is a concept that may well influence federal policy in the White House and the Congress during the years to come.

COMMUNITY DEVELOPMENT AND NATIONAL GOALS

Major environmental and service problems have occured together with population growth in the twelve major urbanized regions in the United States, as evidenced, for example, by power shortages and by physical and psychic pathologies due to air, water and noise pollution and excessive population densities in the concentrated parts of these regions. Congestion, resulting from increasing population density and concentration of major economic activities, concurrent with the thinning out of the population in regions where there is no such concentration, has led to inequalities in the distribution of goods and services. People and firms are leaving central cities for the future slums of the suburbs. and the lagging regions of the country are not yet able to entice these firms and families to move to their locations (3).

Figure 2-1

12 major urbanized regions
projected by the year 2000 (1)

To alleviate these conditions, a successful urban growth
strategy must go beyond central city enrichment programs.
These efforts have attracted more and more newcomers and
only tend to perpetuate the ghetto (4).  The basic elements
of an overall national urban growth strategy as identified
by Lloyd Rodwin would be (i) to open up the suburbs to
blacks; (ii) to increase the income of the cities and their
residents, to reduce the excessive concentrations and high
densities of the black ghettoes and improve ghetto conditions; and (iii) to establish growth centers in lagging regions (4).

While opening up the suburbs to the blacks is one of the
most controversial and important issues of the day, the
present administration is officially against forcing it (1).
As an alternative, the administration may adopt and implement a strategy of new community development as a more ex-
pedient method for relieving pressures on the central cities.

The Economic Development Administration has already encouraged  urban growth centers in lagging regions, but major
innovations are still needed such as (i) family allowances
or a negative income tax program; (ii) federal sharing of
income tax revenues with states and cities, conditional on
the recipient bodies having acceptable development plans;
and (iii) rent supplements and employment and tax incentives (4).

The Report of the National Goals Research Staff (Toward Balanced  Growth: Quantity with Quality, 1970) recommended the
adoption of policies encouraging dispersal of the population
to areas outside of the major urbanized regions (Fig. 2-1)
by the establishment of growth centers or new communities.
Realization of these policies could be facilitated by legislation that would enable the federal government to assist
state or regional development agencies (similar to New York's
UDC) in assembling land, financing infrastructure costs, and
offering investment credits, tax abatements, guaranteed debenture bonds and deferred loans to developers.  The Housing
and Urban Development Act of 1970, signed into law Dec.31,1970,

52

by President Nixon, however, no longer contains the provisions which would have enabled the proposed national Community Development Corporation to directly engage in the development of new communities. Nevertheless, the act does contain authorizations for increased debenture guarantees as well as loans to cover interest payments.

DISPERSAL STRATEGIES

To achieve a more balanced distribution of the U.S. population, three alternative strategies are identified by the National Goals Staff (1):

1. Spread population by generating growth in sparsely populated areas.
2. Foster the growth of existing small cities and towns in nonmetropolitan areas.
3. Build new cities outside the large metropolitan areas.

The Goals Staff discounts the first strategy (population spread), citing the fact that many economists feel that efforts to promote self-sustained growth in sparsely populated areas generally are doomed from the start, the cost of providing the desired services being simply too great.

Under the second strategy (alternative growth centers), middle-sized communities having the potential for self-sustained growth would be selected and their growth deliberately encouraged. These expanding communities would bolster the neighboring rural areas by providing jobs for their residents, who would no longer have to go to a distant city to find employment.

The potential for using existing small towns as the nuclei of growth centers is indicated by urban growth figures during the period 1960-66 (5). During that period, (i) the total of all major metropolitan areas grew at an average annual rate of 1.7%; (ii) counties in nonmetropolitan areas containing a small city (25,000 to 50,000) and a major highway

53

<u>artery</u> grew at a rate of 1.5% -- only slightly less; and
(iii) nonmetropolitan areas that contained a small city but
no major highway grew at an annual rate of 0.9%. A national
policy aimed at expanding nonmetropolitan areas would, therefore, complement the substantial expansion already occuring
without federal intervention.

The third strategy (new communities) might well save money
in the long run, through efficient design and far-sighted
construction of facilities, while at the same time improving the quality of life.

> Unfortunately, this vision may be very diffi-
> cult to realize. Within the next 30 years new
> communities would not be able to absorb more than
> a small percentage of the urban population simply
> because the rate at which such communities can be
> planned, financed, and built is limited by many
> economic and institutional factors. Such limita-
> tions include the need simultaneously to balance
> the demands of employers for labor; the demands
> of employees for housing, shopping facilities,
> schools, hospitals and recreational facilities;
> and the requirements of suppliers of all these
> services for enough customers to maintain economic
> viability. These limitations generate difficult
> logistical problems. As a major strategy to ac-
> commodate a projected population increase of 100
> million by this way alone, it would require build-
> ing a city the size of Tulsa, Oklahoma every month
> until the year 2000. Even if the lower projections
> of population growth are correct, the number of new
> cities needed would still be beyond our capabili-
> ty...(1)

These observations by the Goals Staff in no way diminish the
need for new communities; the strategies of balanced population distribution that the Staff recommends could each be
seen as a variation of new community design. What they do
make clear, however, is the need for planning and for entre-

54

preneurship.  These ingredients,plus existing and anticipated federal legislation,should prepare the ground for new
communities ventures to gain financial and investment cre-
dibility in the 1972 to 1975 period.

In the more distant future of the 1980's there will be opportunities for new community development to occur in areas
presently considered unlikely for geographical or climatic
reasons.  For example, weather control, which may be feasible in the 1970's, may be applied in the 1980's to modify
the climate (1) in regions of harsh winters.  This would
make such areas more attractive for year-round living;and
new communities could be more aggressively established in
those regions, thus aiding a national population dispersal
strategy.*

Summary of Arguments for
Dispersal of Settlements

1.  Decreasing quality of environment and level of services
    in most metropolitan areas; increased public awareness
    of resulting pathologies and inconveniences.

2.  Increasing crime, alienation and anti-social behavior in
    central cities and suburbs.

3.  Increasing numbers of personal contacts through social
    intercourse and the inverse decrease of quality of
    human relationships.

4.  Realization of communication technologies that enable
    remote access to information and ease of communications
    (e.g., picturephones, CATV, time-sharing computers,
    facsimile reproduction, etc.).

5.  Increased speed and accessibility to remote places for
    reasons of human personal contact by improved transpor-
    tation technologies (e.g., fast transit links, ubiqui-

*It is anticipated that the second and third order ecologi-
cal consequences of weather modification will be understood
more fully in the late '70's than they are presently.

55

tous short-haul VTOL and AGT [automated guideway transportation]).

6. Increased opportunities for sound financial investment in large-scale development resulting from governmental intervention, consumer demand for better living conditions and greater recognition of new community potentials.

## Summary of Arguments for Continued Concentration of Settlements

1. Perceived richness of opportunities for jobs, careers, social intercourse and convergence (male-female contacts).

2. Potential reluctance of public authorities to divert significant sums of money from central city redevelopment.

3. Public and private predisposition to concentrate on short-term problems and payoffs as opposed to recognizing long-term problems and developing approaches with long-term, difficult-to-measure payoffs.

4. Current and past investment risks associated with development of new communities (6).

5. Minority power blocks in central cities viewing their dispersion as inimical to their political forcefulness.

6. In sum, New Towns policy aimed at population dispersal may make little economic or political sense since its impact would be small and its desirability questionable; new towns may, however, provide opportunities for experimentation which could then be applied to existing cities (7).

## HIGH vs LOW DENSITY/ CENTRALIZATION vs. DECENTRALIZATION

Centralization and densities of population affect, and are influenced by, the movement of people, goods and messages between the individual residence, service areas and activity centers. With the emergence of innovative movement and com-

56

munications systems which can move people, goods and messages faster, many new questions arise as to how people may want to live,given access to these emerging technological capabilities, and how people may be influenced to live,given those same capabilities. To what degree can movement of messages be substituted for movement of people assuming high technology in both areas? And to what degree will people want to make use of each medium -- communications and transportation -- for purposes of accessibility? Will highly intense urban areas remain nodes where information is exchanged? Or will decentralization and dispersal of people become possible without disturbing information flows? (9, 10) However relevant and timely these questions are, they are very difficult to answer in precise terms; a more useful approach is to clarify some of the main issues.

## High Density

Some observers of urbanization claim that as previously separated metropolitan areas merge,or as the limits of convenience travel to and from metropolitan centers are reached, overall densities must inevitably increase . At the same time, high densities are needed to provide greater ease of accessibility to a variety of activities, to permit more intensive use of certain key facilities or natural resources, and to permit the conservation of lower intensity use of other areas (11).

Failure to provide for higher densities forces development to spread over much greater areas, increasing travel times and network costs, and increasing problems associated with conservation . When key locations adjacent to attractive activity centers or to an important natural feature such as an outstanding view are occupied by low- or medium-density development, many persons are deprived of the convenience and pleasure of being able to walk to and benefit from those attractions (11).

Areas of high densities, some observers such as Jane Jacobs feel (12), are needed to obtain what many see as the unique values of urban life.  In the words of Margaret Mead,

> ...This value is the value of the freedom of in-
> terchange which follows unexpected routes, per-
> mits individuals to make new contacts, to main-
> tain or break old ones, and brings together in
> face-to-face, multimodal relationships, indivi-
> duals of diverse temperament and vocation. (13)

In summary, the proponents of high densities base their arguments on the following points:

1. Greater ease of accessibility to a variety of local
   activities and local scenic resources.
2. More intensive use of these activities and resources.
3. Allowance for conservation of lower intensity use
   of other areas.
4. Allowance for the possibility of walking to desired
   activities.
5. Stimulation of convergence (i.e., personal exchange,
   random meetings with diverse persons, boy-meets-
   girl opportunities).
6. The fact that high density is, to a large degree,
   a reality that is taking place, dictated by the
   economics of land use and of location patterns.

## Low Density

In contrast to the proponents of high population densities,
there are at this time few strong polemics for the opposite:
low densities.  Forty years ago Frank Lloyd Wright, in his
prophetic The Disappearing City, anticipated the problems of
automobile congestion, environmental pollution and general
societal pathology due to high densities and centralization.
He advocated strategies of decentralization and the achievement of very low densities.  In the meantime, Lewis Mumford
has been building an eloquent case for decentralization.  At
the present time there are those who believe that communications media are substituting for many of the reasons that
people want to be in close proximity to each other.  This

school of thought holds that by exchanging messages in lieu of trips, the density question becomes irrelevant and whether people live in higher or lower densities can be a matter of choice based on factors other than exchange of information (14).

## Centralization/Decentralization

Centralization/decentralization refers to decision making modes as well as to access patterns. Our present society is characterized by decision making mechanisms that are clearly not working. At the community level there has been very little effective decentralized decision making. Often, even when people are in favor of decentralization, it is difficult to put into effect.* As will be noted later, centralization of decision making contributes heavily to alienation, and as such is antithetical to human well-being. Decentralization is, in the words of Goodman,

> ...increasing the number of centers of decision making and the number of initiators of policy; increasing the awareness of individuals of the whole function in which they are involved; and establishing as much face-to-face association with decision makers as possible (15).

*A case in point is the New York school decentralization crisis.

59

## B. GOALS AND OBJECTIVES FOR NEW COMMUNITIES

Aside from the major goal of "The Good Life" for everybody (many might disagree as to what constitutes "The Good Life"), somewhat more tractable goals that most people might agree on are:

1. Every person realizing the fullness of his or her human potential (health and personal capacities for love, and satisfying work and/or leisure).
2. Societal structures that are more responsive to, or congruent with, changing needs and socio-economic conditions.
3. Restoration and maintenance of the presently seriously degraded environment and natural systems.

In terms of community development these three goals may be transformed into the objectives of:

1. Accessibility: High-accessibility to opportunities and choices for education, recreation, shopping, health care, employment and meeting others through improved transportation and/or communication systems and service delivery systems.
2. Participation: Decentralized decision-making mechanisms for local participation in policy-planning and service provision. Expanded opportunities for housing to adapt to multi-family or other new social arrangements.
3. Environment: Selection of industries and municipal and residential hardware that will not pollute or despoil the environment. Favoring of industries and policies that will contribute to restoring and maintaining the environment.

It is the contention of this study that, (i) new communities, as defined earlier, can achieve these broadly based objectives whereas the traditional practices of conventional subdivision development cannot; (ii) these objectives reflect preferences of potential users; (iii) they are, therefore, marketable and potentially highly profitable to entrepreneurs willing to assume the risks and responsibilities of large-scale new community development.  The objectives are individually discussed in the sections that follow.

ACCESSIBILITY

High accessibility to education, work, recreation, shopping, health care and meeting places can mean either having a service readily delivered to the user or the user being able to reach the service more easily.  The two are not mutually exclusive; for example, improved delivery systems for education and health care may not diminish the need for the user to have access to those functions but might increase that need.

"Uniform accessibility" is often advocated as a goal for urban areas.  While desirable, this is not practical by transportation only.  Some areas will be more accessible than others (11).  In the past we have tended to think of accessibility only in terms of movement (walking, bus, car, etc.).  Accessibility can also be thought of in terms of communications (telephone, mail and new media such as picturephones, computers, facsimile reproduction machines, etc.).  With a balanced combination of both movement systems and communications systems the highest degree of accessibility can be achieved.

Almost all of the activities that transpire in an average person's daily urban system can be decentralized into small centers that are within a ten or fifteen minute walk from the dwelling place.  The proximity of activities, services and amenities within walking distance from the dwelling or place of work is only partly a function of access to them; it is also a function of needs for convergence, the multiple acts of the random and planned meeting and greeting of new persons and old friends: proximity facilitates human contact.

61

It should be noted that new communities need not be considered completely autonomous and isolated entities. The community, in one sense, is a sub-set of accounts within a larger set of regional accounts (16); and the importance of its connectivity by various means to other communities and centers of attraction outside of its immediate area must be emphasized. Those main areas of present and future innovation that in the next several years will alter accessibility patterns and how people think about accessibility are discussed in the next sections on communications, movement systems, services and dwelling location.

## Developments in Communications

Communication hardware and methods will be changing radically during the coming decade. The capacity of the communications network will expand so extensively that broadband communications will be as plentiful and cheap as telephone service is now. Picturephones and data transmission by phone, already in limited use, are likely to become widespread. Three-dimensional TV, portable individual telephone  and tape libraries for individual programming of home TV may be in use well before 1980. Such changes will have significant and widespread impacts on education, government, business and family life (1). Some experts believe that new tools of communication can reduce the need for business travel. First, they will be used by businesses; and then, as rates drop, they will expand into widespread home use (17).

From the National Goals Research Staff report:

> Many types of workers may find it increasingly possible to do much of their work at home. This will be particularly true when it becomes economically  feasible to connect home facilities with central computers and [broadband] TV [for what could be called a multi-service communication system]. For example, combining of picturephones, communication satellites, and equipment for re-

62

producing facsimiles of documents and signatures
already make it possible for individuals at many
different points on the globe to converse face-
to-face on a matter, draft final documents and
[exchange] signed copies simultaneously.

Significant educational potentials could be o-
pened through audio-visual tapes for home TV
sets. Much education might take place outside
traditional educational institutions. The cost
of "attending" college courses might be greatly
reduced, while at the same time the quality of
such courses may be raised, since lectures could
combine the powerful educational tools of gifted
lecturers with graphics and pictures. These changes, if they are employed, would require new institutional arrangements (1).

However, despite the profit-making potential of establishing
the world communication networks, some of the main actors,
such as the communications utilities, are hesitating (18).
The full range of consequences of a world-wide hook-up are
not completely clear, but it can be anticipated that several
consequences, such as rising expectations in the Third World
brought about by greater exposure to affluent cultures,
would not be under full control of the originators of the
system.


## Central Data/Information Banks

A major component in the communications network would be the
establishment of a central data bank which would have wide
public access. This would be used for general or specialized
information retrieval primarily in the areas of library, medical and legal data. If this development were to occur it
would probably result in the following impacts (19, 20) in
varying degrees of probability:

63

1. Information overload and the development of new data reduction methods and retrieval systems.
2. Such banks would be used heavily by professionals and could restructure the operations of the professions.
3. Use of home terminals for education -- transformation of the home into a part-time school.
4. Many societal functions such as town meetings would be decentralized.
5. Information storage would become a salable service, resulting in opportunities for widespread revision in business practices.
6. Data would become available to all instead of just the specialists.
7. Individual citizens would become proficient in law and medicine, through easy availability of relevant information in the home.
8. Great privacy problems would be created.
9. Rise of computer-aided or computer-oriented crime could occur.
10. Revolution in library sciences, including greatly improved methods of searching special subjects would occur.

## Self-Supported Dwellings

With the availability of a number of technological developments compatible with sophisticated home-based communications, dwelling units can be free and remote from infrastructure. Compatible developments would be (i) home energy sources such as fuel cells running from bottled gas and (ii) life support systems that recycle water, dispose of solid waste and sewage and provide heating and cooling. If these developments were to occur, they would probably result in the following impacts:

1. Reduction of the necessity for dense settlement patterns for reasons of communication.
2. Location of more settlements and individual dwellings by criteria of agreeable climate, natural

beauty, pure environment and access to attractive
recreational areas.
3.  Reduction of the necessity of short and long dis-
    tance travel for information-exchanging tasks.
    Much business conference activity, education, shop-
    ping, etc. accomplished in the dwelling.
4.  Provision of the basis for the individual dwelling
    place as the nerve center for human activity in
    daily life.
5.  Increase of travel for recreation and pleasure.
6.  Further fragmentation of society unless all citizens
    have access to these technologies (20).

In designing public service systems for a new community,
tradeoffs must be examined between economies and diseconomies of scale.  Take the foregoing examples of waste and
energy systems.  We want to know the proportion of decentralized waste treatment and energy production at the dwelling
versus the proportion of central municipal waste collection
and treatment, and energy production and distribution.  Costs
and benefits of both poles, decentralized and centralized,
depend on a number of factors, some of which relate to the
specific site location and some of which are independent.
In taking a new community out of a locational context, main
factors that will influence the waste and power design are
(i) the density and area of development, (ii) future technologies and (iii) projected future user demand.  These
three are all tightly interrelated.

Other factors being equal, a high density area would have a
high benefit/cost ratio favoring centralized utilities, as
would medium and, to a degree, low density areas.  As small
scale decentralized energy sources and waste treatment methods  become more economical (in the next ten years), however,
low and very low density areas will probably show benefit/cost
ratios for decentralized utilities similar to or higher than
the centralized option.

User demand and emerging technologies interlock in that technologies will certainly be developed to satisfy a market,

but the market may not exist unless the potential user becomes aware that it is highly probable that a desire of his
can be satisfied.

## Evolutionary Automated Movement Systems

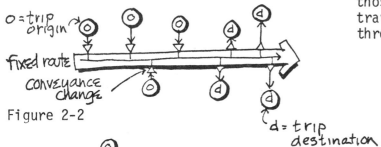

Figure 2-2

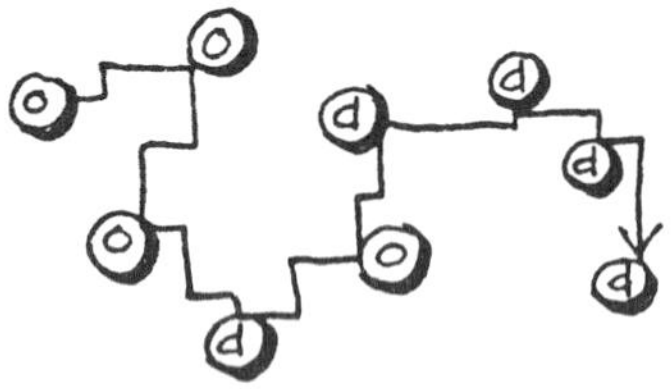

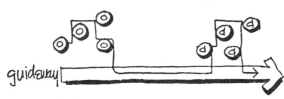

Figure 2-3

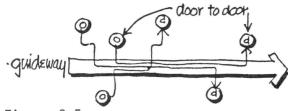

Figure 2-4

Figure 2-5

The successful transportation systems in the future will be
those which conform closely to the user groups' needs and
travel requirements.  It is helpful to think of service in
three classes (21):

1.  <u>Fixed route and schedule</u> (Fig. 2-2)

    Present:  bus
              minibus
              rail mass transit
              monorail
    Future:   VTOL metrobus
              tracked hovercraft
              network cab transit (in transit mode)
              dual mode bus

2.  <u>Fixed route and guideway -- demand-actuated</u>

    Present:  network cab transit (in demand mode)
    Future:   Cablecar

3.  <u>Door-to-door demand-actuated</u> (ubiquitous*)

    Present:  private automobile
              taxi
              Dial-A-Bus (Fig. 2-3)
    Future:   VTOL metrotaxi
              dual mode Dial-A-Bus (Fig. 2-4)
              dual mode car (Fig. 2-5)

---

*Streets are assumed to be ubiquitous.

66

General observations that can be made on these three classes of service are:

1. Fixed route and schedule systems (i) require a large number of common trip origins and destinations (OD) and (ii) are not found to be a significant substitute for automobiles (22).
2. Fixed route or guideway demand-actuated systems are (i) better than rigidly-scheduled systems for time but poorly serve OD desires; (ii) presently limited to high density population corridors and workplace concentrations*; and (iii) an improvement over conventional transit service in demand response.
3. Door-to-door demand-actuated systems (i) are fastest on time and shortest on distances for OD; (ii) are an acceptable substitute for automobile trips; (iii) where automated, achieve cost and time savings; and (iv) provide capacities equal to rapid transit while retaining advantages of the automobile.

The best class of service, door-to-door demand-actuated, is not likely to be available for all people since (i) there are many who do not own or drive a car and cannot afford taxi service; (ii) parking is unavailable or costly; and (iii) overloaded channels discourage some trips.

Of the various methods and modes of innovative movement systems currently being proposed, mass rapid transit systems, while having many advocates, usually require high conveyance charges, outdoor waiting, and do not satisfy door-to-door demand. Similar observations can be made about conventional buses running on exclusively franchised lanes. In the long run, completely automated guideway transportation (AGT) systems with dual mode vehicles (DMV) could best satisfy the widest range of needs while greatly increasing channel capacities and reducing parking requirements in

---

*This would not be a limitation if capital and operating costs are a small fraction of present systems as is expected in the future.

activity centers by routing empty vehicles to remote parking facilities.

Of the currently proposed systems, the two most likely generic types for in-town use, in the near future, are (i) Dial-A-Bus (DAB) and (ii) Network Cab Transit (NCT).* The two possess very different operating characteristics, in some cases serving very different types of demands, but in other cases performing well in unison (both individually have great advantages). While Dial-A-Bus has the capability to adapt to changing configurations of NCT guideways, only NCT has strong evolutionary potential. Consider the following:

1.  The strong contenders for line haul NCT systems today are: Dashaveyor, Alden and several others. These systems consist of captive capsules on their own automated guideways which follow a loop or a fixed-line route and are demand-actuated.

2.  Ford and American Motors are actively interested in the future of guideways (so that they can market their next generation of vehicles). They see the future of guideways as not being exclusively closed systems, but being able to accept dual mode vehicles (able to run on streets under their own power and also on automated guideways). Ford sees this capability as being developed in the late 1970's.

3.  With the large automobile manufacturers viewing automated guideways as channels for their vehicles, decisions in the early stages of community design need to be made on standardization of vehicle track width and profile, and power distribution so that present proprietary guideways can adapt easily to highly probable future systems being actively developed by the large automobile manufacturers. This is an area where federal intervention could be helpful and should be encouraged.

---

*Each of these generic systems, and proprietary systems of each type, are discussed more fully in Part III, Section B-1.

## Staging Strategy

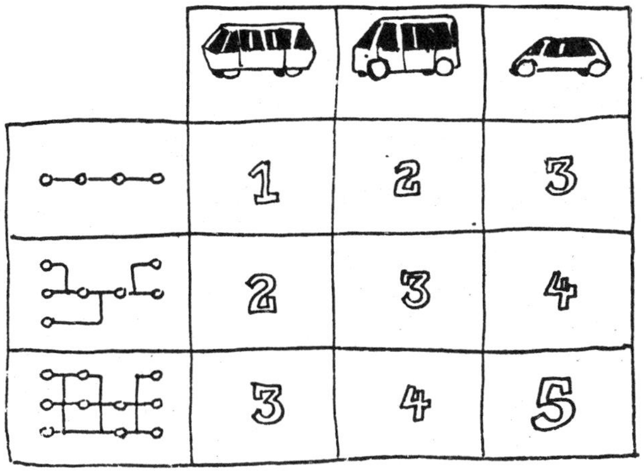

Figure 2-6

Staging Strategy

Richard Schackson, Assistant Director of Transportation Planning at Ford, views the staging strategy for attaining full AGT as a nine cell matrix (Fig. 2-6). The rows are evolutionary stages of the guideway network, (i) line haul link, (ii) tree, (iii) full network; and the columns are the vehicle modes, (i) network cabs (linked together at peak hours for transit mode, separated at off-peak hours for demand mode); (ii) dual mode bus; and (iii) dual mode automobile.

The target system is the bottom right hand cell: dual mode cars operating on full network. Ford's timing is for the realization of NCT by 1974, dual mode bus a year later and dual mode cars four years after that (1979). The realized system would no doubt be localized in a few central cities and larger new communities around the country and would not become generally operational at the nationwide scale until the mid to late 1980's.

Many benefits could be offered by automated guideway transportation. Among them are:

1. The social cost savings in noise and nitric oxide and other pollution from a quiet, non-polluting system.
2. Channel capacities expanded by a factor of four to ten.
3. Capital cost and maintenance expenses saved by reduction of number and width of streets required to serve settled area; consequent addition of land area available for other non-transit uses.*
4. Capital cost and operating expenses saved from parking lots and garages made unnecessary in highly attractive activity centers or service areas.
5. The possibility of cars being leased (rather than owned) on a large-scale basis.
6. Service extending to previous non-users (i.e., handicapped, children, aged and other non-drivers).

---

*New York City, for example, has 42% of its land area covered by streets and pavement (including parking).

## Changes in Future Demand

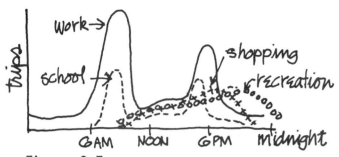

Figure 2-7

Hourly trip distribution, 1970

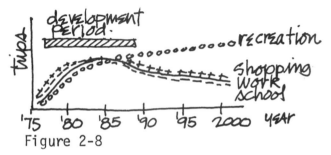

Figure 2-8

Projected trips by year 1985
within new community

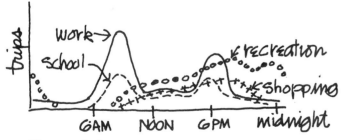

Figure 2-9

Projected hourly trip distribution,
1985

Transportation network design, vehicle selection and channel capacities are based on estimated trips to various attractions such as work, school, shopping and recreation, with a view to minimizing transportation loads. The distribution of average trips per person during weekdays (Fig. 2-7) shows work trips to be highest, with shopping and recreation trips lowest and school trips in between. In planning innovative, evolutionary movement systems for a new community, two projections for 1985 would tend to alter the present distributions:

1. Fifty per cent of the nation will be wired for CATV (Community Antenna Television) by 1980 (23).
2. A thirty-two work week or less will be in effect for the majority of the work force.

The impacts of CATV and compatible communication systems for those who have access to them could reduce the need for trips to work, school and shopping by as much as 50% by 1985. Also, an increase in leisure time of 20% and an increase in personal discretionary income may increase trips to recreational and entertainment facilities by 20% (Fig. 2-8). The hypothetical trip distribution for 1985 would then show, in contrast to 1970, a general change in demand from work trips to recreation trips (Fig. 2-9). Two other assumptions must be made in order to establish the total expected transportation load in a community by 1985.

1. The population will stabilize with a fertility rate of around 2.11 for near zero population growth (1).
2. Through automation there will be an increase in previous non-driver use of movement systems.

The net result of these assumptions is that (i) in 1985, there will be a reduction of trips by previous users by 30%; (ii) this excess will be absorbed by previous non-driver use of the system for a transportation load roughly equivalent to 1970 levels; and (iii) trips for recreation and entertainment will dominate trips to work, school and shopping. This would be a more typical case in new communities than in existing cities since a new community could be planned initially to offer the availability of both innovative communication and movement systems.

Before any system can be evaluated, these general assumptions on future trip destinations and transportation loads must be viewed in reference to the community macroform and spatial organization.

## System A: Centralized or Single-Purpose Activity Centers

> multiple locations of distinct large aggregated functions separated in space (i.e., industry, education, commerce, recreation, etc.) (Fig. 2-10)

## System B: Decentralized or Multi-Purpose Activity Centers

> containing a mix of functions (i.e., employment, education, commerce, recreation, etc.) located in (i) neighborhood scale service areas or (ii) central public function areas (Fig. 2-11)

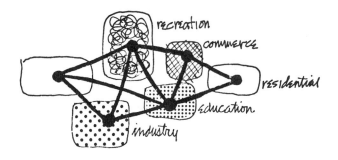

Figure 2-10

Single-purpose activity centers
(System A)

Figure 2-11

Decentralized activity centers
(System B)

What will the cross impacts between these systems of spatial organization and any movement system be over time, given the trip dynamics stated above?

System A (single-purpose activity centers): Home, work, schools, shopping and recreation are separated in space, and journeys to them are quite often made by separate channels and even by separate movement systems (Fig. 2-12).
At a future time the attraction to some service areas will diminish and,to others will grow (Fig. 2-13), causing radical load shifts on the channels as well as on the physical plant requirements of the facilities. The movement systems should be able to adapt easily to this shift.

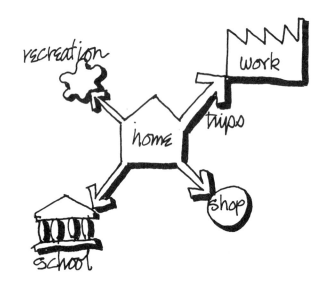

Figure 2-12

Present trip-facility relationship for single purpose activity centers

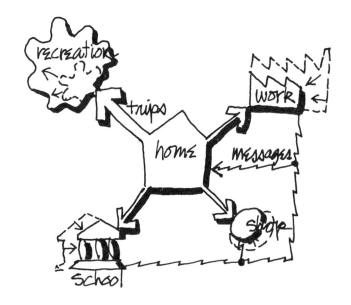

Figure 2-13

Future trip-facility relationship for single-purpose activity centers

System B (multi-purpose activity centers): Work, schools, shopping and recreation are in single locational units and separated from the home (Fig. 2-14).* At a future time the journeys to the activity center will remain the same,but the trip purpose will be altered (Fig. 2-15),causing radical shifts in the physical plant requirements of the facilities but having minimal impact on the movement system channels (except that trips for recreation may have less extreme peaking characteristics than trips for work).

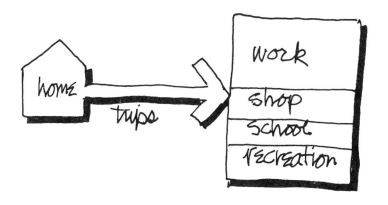

Figure 2-14

Present trip-facility relationship
for multi-purpose activity centers

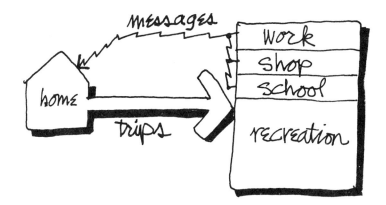

Figure 2-15

Future trip-facility relationship
for multi-purpose activity centers

*Even though walking can be considered as a mode of linkage in both systems,this analysis is primarily for movement systems.

These are both highly simplified models, and most urban organization  exhibits examples of both simultaneously.  There
are, however, apparent advantages in System B over System A.
They are that B (decentralized activity centers):

1.  relates better to walking scale.
2.  causes minimal strain on the movement system, requir-
    ing less need for adaptability.

That system B would require highly adaptable facility structures may seem a disadvantage, but the pressure for structures
to adapt to changing functions may actually be advantageous.
The lack of that pressure, produced by decreasing trip ends,
means a loss of customers or users for a single-purpose facility and a consequent reduction of economic vitality.

## Macroform

The macroform of the community will highly influence the selection of the most appropriate movement system.  The following is a rough list of the preconditions of the form of
the settlement required in order to exploit the unique characteristics  of various movement systems.

1.  Conditions for selecting guideways:

    a.  Where high density residential areas and/or
        strongly attractive activity centers are
        placed in a linear or loop configuration.
    b.  Where requirement for line capacity is high.
        Limited to areas where it is highly likely to
        be used in the future.
    c.  Where need for connecting links from other
        guideway lines to strongly attractive activity
        centers exists.
    d.  Where the bulk of travelers are within a three
        to five-minute walk or 1/4 mile distance in
        the early stages prior to dual mode.

2.  Conditions for selecting Dial-A-Bus:

74

a. At areas of low population density and/or large areas of heavy trip origin or destination.

b. Where a maximum of through streets and a minimum of cul-de-sacs exist, with the dwellings moderately close to the streets.

c. Where many strongly attractive activity centers exist in a dispersed pattern not easily serviceable by an efficient guideway configuration.

3. Conditions for selecting fixed route and schedule bus:

a. Where moderately attractive activity centers with common trip origins and destinations are evenly distributed for efficient routing.

b. Where the bulk of travelers are within a three to five-minute walk or 1/4 mile distance.

## Service Delivery Systems

Social services have hertofore been very much of a producer-oriented activity. With the trend toward a larger service sector in the economy and increasing consumerism, it is important to reconsider the delivery systems for social services.

Service delivery systems will be changing from supply-centered to user- or demand-centered as users become more knowledgeable and influential in the processes by which service systems are provided. The services here fall under the categories of health care, education, child care, human potential, government, employment, job training, welfare, fire prevention, law enforcement, recreation, culture, counseling (legal, tax, financial, consumer, marital) and home services and maintenance.

Today everyone receives services in many of these categories and often takes them for granted, since decisions on the level of service to be provided are usually remote. In addition, the delivery systems are diffuse and not always clear to the user, and the services are uneven in their coverage. For example:

1. Some services are available to some groups in society and not to other groups which could also use them, such as child care and human potential expansion.
2. Some services -- welfare for example -- are in many instances administered in a cursory, inconvenient or degrading way.
3. Some services are available in better quality or quantity for some groups than for others, such as education, law enforcement, fire prevention and health care.
4. Some services that could be used by some or all groups in society are not generally available, such as home services and abortion.

In designing health, education and other social service systems for a new community, the following guidelines have been suggested by Michael Joroff (24):

1. A realistic set of objectives for the composition of the population and their schedule of arrival.
2. A community service system which will be comprehensive in scope and use of regional resources.
3. Program budgeting based on all funds potentially available from the different sectors of the community, including individual residents.
4. The inclusion of citizen involvement in planning activities as soon as new residents begin to arrive and, prior to that time, the broadening of the focus of the developer and government officials beyond their own interests and goals.
5. A method for the transition of the public-private coalition into a viable administrative mechanism which will consolidate rather than further proli-

ferate the jurisdictions which will have continuing responsibility.

The improved delivery of social services in new communities centers around several questions:

1. Given the socio-economic state of a new community
   and of the larger community -- district, state
   and nation -- in which it is placed; what range
   and level of services are feasible now and in the
   future?
2. What range and level of services will various user
   groups want, now and in the future?
3. How are expanded and improved services to be paid
   for? (i.e., user charges, taxes, block grants,
   bonds, etc.)
4. How can the user's awareness of his options for
   new or expanded services be widened, in keeping
   with an enriched range  of services?
5. How can effective provision of services be used to
   strengthen the sense and reality of community,
   while safeguarding individual independence and
   avoiding a "big brother" paternalistic flavor that
   a comprehensive, integrated delivery system might
   impart?
6. In which ways are new communities particularly well-
   suited to the institution of effective social service delivery systems?

While all of these questions are not intended to be dealt
with in detail within the scope of this report, some observations can be made on innovative concepts of service delivery.

The "community of solution" concept, first proposed by the
National Commission on Community Health Services, is a possible model for general application.  The concept purports
to (i) identify the exact demographic group which will use
the service and which must be worked with in order to solve
the delivery problem; (ii) determine for each service the
area to be served and the available and future resources; and

(iii) determine with the users the best combination of options, quality, convenience and least cost. The "community of solution" notion fosters the basic principle that no design for a service system can ultimately be successful until all parties with an interest in the results come together to participate in the decision process.

Access to services is a strong consideration for the users and, as such, the locations for dissemination of information and the making of arrangements for services should be as convenient as possible for the entire population of a community, consistent with economies of operation.

· One concept is the multi-service center, either one main, conveniently located center or several smaller centers that contain major service activities and information on all other services (the "little City Hall" programs recently instituted in New York and Boston are prototypes of this concept).
· A second concept is the dispersed "marketplace of services" (25) with main service vendors intimately mixed within activity centers that contain employment, education, shopping, etc.
· A third concept is that of bringing information on services and many of the services themselves to the individual dwellings via a multiservice cable communications system (see Appendix A for an inventory of services that could be provided in this way).
· A fourth concept combines elements of the first three. Such a concept would be appropriate for a community that is experiencing the addition of a multiservice cable communication system. While some members of the community (because of income level or personal inclination) would be able to take advantage of this kind of home-based system right in their dwelling, other groups in the community would not. Access to services for the entire community would originally occur through multiservice centers, the service marketplace or a combination of both. As a multiservice cable communications system became generally available, small commun-

78

ications rooms serving several households could be installed as part of dwelling clusters where the individual householders would share in the benefits and expenses of the installation.

With rising disposable income levels projected for most socio-economic groups in our society and with the probable lowering of costs for CATV-computer utility systems through wider distribution and economies of scale, it can reasonably be anticipated that all but a very few groups will eventually benefit from the multiservice cable communication concept of service delivery. While multiservice centers could effectively serve present and short-term future needs for all class and income groups, the importance of a physical center for services would diminish with the rise of cable access. These centers could gradually be converted to recreational, cultural or other uses.

PARTICIPATION

The dominant characteristics of the Post-Industrial Society which should predominate in the U.S. by 1980 are (26):

1. Employment -- mostly in the tertiary sector (service)
2. Main technology -- information dissemination and processing
3. Main occupational structure -- professional, technical, science
4. Time orientation -- future, change-oriented
5. Axial principle -- centrality of theoretical knowledge.

With these conditions prevalent, the emergence of a technocratic-managerial elite is likely to occur. While there exists some disagreement on the likelihood of such an elite gaining a formal power base in society, there is general agreement about an extremely strong trend toward a symbiosis of knowledge and power (19) and further centralization. With the growth of these elite groups, there will also be a strong growth of the counterculture (27) representative of all groups in society, but dominantly youth-based, heavily critical of technology, but at the same time using it (mostly computers and electronics) to their own ends which are humanistically oriented. As a consequence of this trend, changes are bound to occur in the traditional notions of representative and participatory governance; and if technocratic elites with a power base do emerge, a major question becomes: who will control them (19)?

It is foreseeable that alienation, which increasingly characterizes men and women in contemporary mass society, will grow in proportion to increasing centralized decision making since alienation is rooted in the impersonalization of centralized structures.

<u>Alienation</u>

Alienation is a poorly understood but almost universal affliction of people in mass society and, as such, is important to understand by those concerned with environmental design and management.

A precise definition of alienation is difficult since the term is used to describe a very broad range of problems. Generally, "alienation lies in every direction of human experience where basic emotional desire is frustrated." (28) There are four main sources of alienation (29): (i) lack of commitment to values; (ii) lack of conformity to norms; (iii) lack of responsibility in roles; and (iv) lack of control of facilities. Alienation is evidenced in:

1. Self Alienation (30)

   ·Suppression of or distance from inner needs
   ·Objectification of self and of the projection of
    personal powers
   ·Over-incorporation into society

2. Work Alienation (31)

   ·Overspecialization of the work task

·Inability to put personal mark on work
·Inability to realize direct pecuniary profit from product of work

3. Social Alienation (30)

   ·Isolation and estrangement from individuals or groups that are different
   ·Estrangement from norms and values held by society
   ·Violative behavior

4. Environmental Alientation

   ·Inability to manipulate the environment to one's own ends
   ·Environmental insult or misuse

Causes for various kinds of alienation can be traced to:

1. Division of labor into overspecialized roles that require uncreative, mechanical, rote work.
2. Increasing aggregation of specialized social functions for the reasons of "economy of scale", e.g., the educational park, the multiversity, the assembly line factory, the industrial park.
3. Increased predetermination and fixity of environmental components, e.g., an over-planned park for children that is seldom used (they are found playing on the street) or a lot that the community wants for a park, but is denied to them for various reasons (The People's Park, Berkeley).
4. Centralized decision making for services and facilities that directly affect people outside of the decision-making process.
5. Increasing differentiation of specialized social functions for reasons of common interest and in

some cases the ease of marketability *-- e.g.
"sunset" communities, "swinging singles" communities, artist communities, middle class suburban
communities, lower class or minority group urban
ghettos, and intentional communities.

Within existing cities and suburban subdivisions there does
not seem to be a strong, continuing movement to reduce alienation  aside from attempts of limited effectiveness to
create and make operable tenants' councils, local community  development corporations, little city halls, and participation programs (the latter almost exclusively limited
to the Model Cities and OEO programs).**

--------------------

*This does not suggest that alienation exists within these
 communities; it is intended to indicate alienation between
 the communities and the components of society external to
 them.  The concept of special purpose communities, large and
 small (from town size to commune size), can be valid.  Variations have been suggested,such as the Vacation City, the
 Government City, the Religious City (32), etc. as prototypes.  It would seem that the special-purpose community's capacity to prevent social alienation is a function of the permeability of the boundaries in (i) allowing
 activities, groups and individuals alien to the special
 purpose easy access to the community, and (ii) stimulating mobility, or the ease to come and go out of the community, for the residents.  Gans (33) writes of the desirability  of "block homogeneity" (a kind of special pur-
 poseness) together with "community heterogeneity".  The "block"
 here is a kind of sub-culture unit in a very traditional sense
 (blocks being divisions that we are all familiar with).

**A notable exception to lackluster participation programs is
  the recent experience in Brooklyn where about 180 residents
  participated in a planning procedure called a "charette" for
  the design of a 12-block, $70-million educational center.
  (John Darnton, "Residents and Architects Plan Local Center
  in Brooklyn," The New York Times, January 6, 1971.)

Continued "disorder and disequilibrium as well as an increase in the alienation and impersonality of urban life" are foreseen by some observers for the future (19). However, "in an effort to dispel frustration and alienation and to regain citizen support, city governments may become reorganized to improve civic services and devise better feedback mechanisms for the discovery of citizen attitudes." (19) Instituting these mechanisms within the set structures of existing cities will be a difficult task that will exact high costs. The following is a list of possible ways of combating the phenomenon of alienation in a new community context:

## New Community Capabilities for Reducing Alienation

1. Screening of industries and businesses attracted to the community for worker-alienating characteristics. Encouragement of those individual industries and combinations of industries which tend to serve worker-involving purposes and community goals.
2. Planning of disaggregated and dispersed functions integrated into the community: community clinics, day-care centers, schools, industries and commercial facilities, craft and skill enterprises, recreational facilities, etc.
3. Designing areal configurations to accept subculture units of various sizes ("living group" to "neighborhood") that can accommodate special interests or purposes.
4. Designing easy access in and out of the subculture units.
5. Planning for inclusion of alternate life styles (e.g. site and housing adaptability for living groups).
6. Establishing a surrogate constituency (such as by a continued sampling of target group user preferences) and a set of community goals in the early stages of a new community before the users are large enough in number to assume control.
7. Establishing mechanisms in the delivery system of housing for buyer-user participation in the design

of their own dwellings.

8. Establishing mechanisms in the planning process for user participation in the planning and management of community facilities, and for control of local decisions.

9. Establishing community forums for participation in local government and planning decisions, in effect, "little city halls".

10. Establishing TV programs, broadcast to homes to describe local governmental and planning decision alternatives. Possible instant feedback for remote referendum and ratification.* Use of this method for social accounting and to monitor user satisfaction with services and environmental quality. Use of local CATV channels for citizen originated and run programs.

11. Increasing the awareness and understanding of complex municipal and natural systems and their interactions (e.g. transportation, waste collection, municipal government, etc.). This can be done by (i) designing the system (where man-made) for high legibility and transparency, and (ii) displaying continuously changing system dynamic flow charts in prominent places. Prototypes: TV weather forecasting maps, Pentagon war room and Energy Utilities Company power control rooms.

The costs of these innovations cannot be examined closely here. In most cases there would be no additional cost to the community, as the innovation would be a variation or would have a different degree of emphasis on procedures carried out under ordinary circumstances. If these innovations were to be effective, the savings in the social cost of alienation could outweigh any direct dollar costs that would be associated with them. In any event, they would be far easier

*The combination of 9. and 10. into a decentralized public forum via two-way CATV has been suggested by Betrand de Jouvenal who calls it a "surmising Forum". A further refinement of this would be through the use of T. J. Gordon's "D Net" or remote instantaneous iterative poll-taking.

to bring about in the tabula rasa of a new community than
in an existing city and could contribute heavily to the inventory of attractions that a new community can offer to
people which no other alternative presently does.  It is
important, however, that these innovations dealing with
participation in decision-making be sincere attempts by the
developers and planners to establish genuine, effective, decentralized decision-making mechanisms, not devices for co-
option, tokenism or attempts to induce decision-making ma-
nipulatively.  If the latter is attempted the community will
inevitably perceive the strategy and react unfavorably.

## Mechanisms

The primary basis for participation in decisions in new communities has, in the past, been through the use of a Homeowners or Taxpayers Association.*  This is usually a nonprofit corporation which assumes management control of recreational  and other non-revenue producing community facilities.   An example of this is the Columbia Parks and Recreation Association (CPRA).  The initial capital investment and management in the facilities comes from the developer
who recaptures the cost by a combination of its distribution
in the sales price of the dwelling units and by taxes, or
what is known as "betterment assessments".  Representation
in the management of CPRA is weighted toward the developer
until the level of assessments is sufficient to cover the
Association's debt service obligations (a function of population size for the most part).  At that time, majority representation  will shift to the community.  With forms of oc-
cupancy such as leasehold, cooperatives and condominiums, becoming desirable for new communities, additional organizations such as tenant management and/or ownership corporations could, together with a homeowners association, form
the basis of full user participation in community decision
making.

---

*There are some still unresolved legal questions of the use of
 real property as a basis for political participation, (possible violation of constitutional equal protection clauses).
 (34)

85

## Evolving Social Structures

Social organization and personal social relationships are changing now more rapidly than at any other time in recent decades. Increasing divorce rates give evidence of the decline of the nuclear family as the basic element of society. New or revived institutions appear to be gaining strength and legitimacy, such as those variously called "communes," "intentional communities," "extended intimacy groups," "non-kinship extended families" and "living groups." The precedents for these living groups lie in the American tradition of Brook Farm, Oneida, New Harmony and others. On the scale of the smaller unit, the precedent is in the kinship-extended family common even today among some lower class ethnic minorities in central city areas.

This life-style was revived most recently in the 1960's by the "hippies." Since then many of its important features have been accepted by a wide range of people (including professionals and middle class, non-hippy elements from every age group). (35)

The size and strength of this trend is difficult to estimate, lacking definite social indicators. It is probably less than 1% of the total population. However, it is not the size of the trend, but its strength of conviction that is important to recognize. This strength is considerable and seems to be growing, not as a movement, but as a response to unfilled societal needs to which existing institutions do not respond. Those forming commune groups could be said to be the positive strain in the counterculture of today. With some exceptions they are trying to reestablish values they feel mass society has lost: values such as love, intimacy, sharing with others, and raising children outside of a restricted nuclear family. This life-style does not generally disavow the dyadic (two-person) relationship; there are, in fact, claims of strengthening it. Moreover, new forms of relationships are emerging. Among those are (i) "corporate marriages" of more than two partners and (ii) group sexual experience.

Whether the majority of people accept these new cultural directions as legitimate variations in a pluralistic society,

Figure 2-16

Private and communal areas
in traditional housing

Figure 2-17

Separated activity spheres

Figure 2-18

Overlapping activity spheres

or whether they view them as aberrations is still to be seen.
But more of the under-thirty age group and those whose life-
style represents what Charles Reich calls "Consciousness III"
(27) actively or tacitly accept these variations; and in the
present "supersensate" culture it is more likely that trends
in new life-styles, mostly revolving around group relations
for reasons of common interest, will grow among all groups
in society.

At this moment it cannot be predicted with any kind of accuracy whether living groups will become a significant trend
relevant to new communities of the kind that would be built
by large entrepreneurial interests (though one such community that is being preplanned by the Cambridge Institute (36)
will be able to include such groups). However, there would
seem to be a potential market here for multi-family dwellings especially designed around large, commonly-shared facilities, especially responding to needs of working mothers
who haven't the time nor the inclination to devote a great
deal of attention to nuclear family child-raising and daily
cooking chores.

In traditional single-family attached or detached dwellings,
space is separated between private and communal areas (shown
respectively in white and in shade in Fig. 2-16). In living
group agglomerations, varying degrees of privacy and individual or diadic autonomy, together with group identity and
sharing, may be controlled by design. Individual spheres of
activity ordinarily separated between dwellings (Fig. 2-17)
can be overlapped to create shared information space which
for the most part generates good feelings for all parties involved (Fig. 2-18) (37). Various configurations (Fig. 2-19)
would generate quite different kinds of private/shared relationships; a through d are focused relationships with strong
public/private definition, e is basically afocal with
both private and public spaces that flow together.

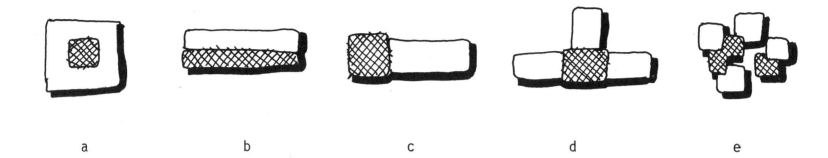

a           b           c           d           e

Figure 2-19

Alternate living group housing,
diagramatic configurations

Enlarging the concentric plan (Fig. 2-19-a) it can be seen
how growth could occur successively in stages (Fig. 2-20)
as new private units are added and the central shared spaces
enlarged.  Private entrances are indicated by small arrows.
Dormitory characteristics of this strategy can be avoided by
people joining together, not by assignment, but by natural
selection.

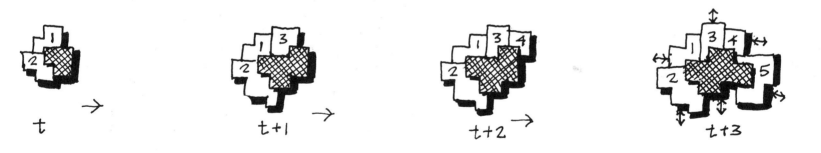

Figure 2-20

Staging strategy for living group
housing growth

88

Additive and subtractive capability for change could occur more easily by the utilization of (i) mobile home type of units, (ii) modular box units and (iii) pneumatic or inflatable structures.

The inflatables are well suited for the shared communal spaces as they have an expansive translucent quality and can be altered with little difficulty. Various shared areas could accommodate such group functions as socializing, cooking, meal taking, recreation and child care as well as special functions such as multi-media communication and entertainment facilities, art and craft facilities, etc. Since densities are moderately high in these agglomerations, a generous portion of the site could be relegated for the exclusive use of the members of the living group with space for ball courts, swimming pool, vegetable gardens, nature areas, etc. The availability of living group housing and the active inclusion of special purpose living groups in a new community would be responsive to social needs that are presently unfulfilled and do much to take what has been to now the almost exclusive middle class, suburban, Bermuda-shorts image off the community. For the present, the trends in living groups and other new life-styles are worth close observation.

ENVIRONMENT

Ecology, it is pointed out by Karl Deutsch, is not a qualitative science but a quantitative one. The question is not whether to cause pollution and destruction or alteration to ecosystems or not; but rather to what degrees do our actions, in affecting the biosphere, alter it for better or worse, given objectives of global and individual welfare now and in the future. The freedom of science and technology to be ethically and morally independent is now being questioned in most quarters, including the scientific community itself. The accountability of technology to anticipate the ethical consequences of its actions is now a major world issue.

Unanticipated deleterious results that have come about from the unconsidered use of the environment are becoming better known.  For example, in fresh water bodies there has been:

1. Cumulative lake eutrophication (death) produced by runoffs of salty brines from irrigation and salt treatment of roads during the snow season, or industrial discharges and untreated municipal sewage.
2. Lake and river pollution produced from industrial and municipal sources.
3. Fish containing high levels of mercury from runoff of wheat field fungicides.

Pesticides alone are a major contributor to imbalance.  Laboratory studies of mammals revealed that some pesticides increased the incidence of cancers, birth defects and genetic mutation (38).  By chemical control of fungus and pests, the fungicides and pesticides such as mercury compounds, DDT, aldrin, dieldrin, 2-4-5-T, lindane, benzene hexachloride (BHC) and others have been shown to be harmful to human health, either directly or indirectly through the food chain (38).  As an alternate to chemical control of pests, biological control shows promise.  An integrated biological control program would utilize (39):

1. Habitat management (e.g., strip crops, etc.)
2. Predator management (e.g., introduction of predator insects, birds, etc.)
3. Food breeding (e.g., use of corn hybrid that corn borers reject but humans enjoy)

René Dubos has demonstrated the delayed reaction on human health from environmental sources.  Bodily insult from the immediate environment, produced by high noise levels or crowding as well as air pollution, substandard drinking water, toxic food and nuclear radiation, can cause mental and physical disorders in years after initial exposures.  The delayed reactions, previously unanticipated but presently recognized, should provide major stimulus for radical action.

## Elimination of Pollution

For significant reductions of levels of pollution and sources of bodily insult, the following actions would have to be considered on a national scale (39):

1. Reallocation of between 4 and 10% of the G.N.P. toward pollution abatement (from a recent O.E.C.D. analysis).
2. Attainment of zero-rate population growth
3. Establishment of monitoring mechanisms for understanding total system dynamics and the second-and third-order impacts of the application of technology on the environment. These would act as "early warning" systems.
4. Establishment of control mechanisms for policy making and execution of sound environmental practices.
5. Influencing the emergence of a less materialistic society with emphasis away from consuming and product orientation toward developing personal growth potential and life process orientation.

Before the poor of society can be convinced of this last measure, they will first need some level of material commodities commensurate with their "shadow values"* of the classes above them. The mechanism for material equity may well lie in housing. Housing can be delivered to the poor through direct subsidies, such as a food stamp program or cash grants as well as by indirect subsidies, such as the present federal 236 housing program (40).

---

*This term is used by Elliot Liebow in Tally's Corner to denote the tendency of the lower classes to assume, to a large measure, the values of their overclass. Hyman Rodman has also recognized this in what he terms "value stretch." David Riesman's notion of the "standard consumer package", that universal commodity bundle held in esteem by most societal groups, is a similar idea.

91

The impacts of these five actions would probably lead to a slower rate of economic growth (viewing fiscal 1970 as an exception to the present long-term growth trend) which the rich and politically powerful of society may not be willing to accept. The implications of these actions and their impacts are:

1. Less "affluence"
2. Less "opportunity" (limited careers and career growth)
3. Improved natural "amenities"
4. Improved physical and mental health

Numbers one and two will be unacceptable for the poor of society until more equitable circumstances occur. Contrary to the commonly held view, there is strong evidence that the poor presently support the rich in society to the same extent that the rich support the poor,since the system is in virtually a steady-state or what Ecologist Frederic Smith calls the "Ecology of Poverty" (39). Structural poverty or how the poor support the rich in society are evidenced in the following:

1. Wealth is self-perpetuating (it is itself a source of income).
2. High "risk" people (poor) pay higher interest rates.
3. Poor people are not informed. They are often victims of induced charge accounts (18% interest or more on loans).
4. Foreclosures and repossessions are commonplace among the poor; and the middle class is often able to purchase such repossessed items, hardly used, at reduced cost.
5. Utility rate scales favor large users with smaller proportional rates.
6. Economic stratification exists between tax units (townships). In poor towns lower personal incomes generate higher proportional taxes or alternately induce lower levels of service.
7. Sales taxes and other constant percentage charges are higher (as a proportion of disposable income) for the poor.

Forces tending to reduce such inequities are:

1. Graduated income tax.
2. Differential reallocation (e.g., subsidies, welfare).

The point that slow economic growth is a precondition of the process of attaining high environmental quality is debatable. Some argue that whole new industries can emerge based on restoring and maintaining the environment. Others contend that these kinds of industries, while potentially profitable for those involved in them, would not be of such a volume as to offset the reduced economic growth that they see as equatable with reduced pollution. The President, while strongly backing environmental quality as a key issue of his administration, has urged higher levels of economic growth. The two may be incompatible.

## The Role of New Communities

The issue of new communities lies right in the middle of these debates. The defenders of low economic growth are very conscious of scarce resources and their allocation and contend that the rational approach is toward conservation: to rebuild our existing cities. The diverting of resources, especially monetary, from central city and suburban needs, they maintain, will be intolerable to the populations of those areas. On the other side, the defenders of balanced growth contend that existing cities are partly to blame for the decreased environmental quality. They are the main sources of environmental deterioration; and while they should be improved, the mechanisms for doing so, because of the social and political complexities of central cities, are bound to remain fragmented and slow to produce noticeable change (41). This latter school of thought wants to relieve the population pressures on central cities as a step toward renewed environmental health, and new communities are part of the plan. The zoning and other constraints designed to keep

*Professor Jay Forrester of MIT's Sloan School presented an argument for this incompatibility in his testimony to the subcommittee on Urban Growth of the House Committee on Banking and Currency on October 7, 1970.

93

the poor out do not exist a priori in new communities and as such, the building of new communities is seen as one major strategy to provide the nation's poor with needed housing (42).

New communities themselves can contribute to a better basic quality of environment by:

1. Strong consideration for natural systems in land use planning.
2. Performance zoning, established with criteria for waste discharge and natural resource utilization.
3. Self-monitoring. Establishing input-output monitoring on major municipal components.
4. Efforts to attract industries that are non-polluters and at the same time vital and potential contributors to economic development.

The following industries might be considered, subject to (i) labor skill level availability, (ii) proximity of raw materials and (iii) demand and proximity of market:

·Media: publishing, films, TV

·Computer associated industries: research, management and control, teaching machines, automatic language translators

·Non-polluting transportation components: Linear Induction Motors (LIM), electric batteries, fuel cells

·Organic farming: agriculture and aquaculture, handcraft and art industries, clothes, works of art, furniture

·Global communications: language translators, international mutual aid and information exchange,

·Leisure industries: sports, skills, knowledge, games

·Medical research technology: prosthetic devices,

biomedical research and production, therapy, drugs, technical devices, chemistry, human behavior, chromosome typing, aging control, disease research (cancer, coronary, etc.)

·Electro-optics and optics:  laser television, facsimile printer, cartridge television, micro-optics, fiber optics - holography

·Cryogenics:  cryogenic surgery, electron beam welding and cutting

·Energy conversion:  fuel cells, fluidics

·Pollution control:  electrostatic precipitators, solid waste reclamation

Solid waste reclamation and its supporting systems, since it could be part of the workings of the community itself, is considered in the following section.

## Solid Waste Reclamation

Of the various methods of waste treatment considered in the section "Technological Forecasting" in Part III,* pyrolysis and the CPU-400 system appeared to be most immediately promising.  Both of these systems can consume the waste to produce energy.  These are both disposal concepts.  A new concept

---

*The conventional methods of sanitary landfill and municipal incineration were not examined since the focus here is on innovative developments.  Both methods are inadequate to handle increasing volumes of waste.  Close-in areas suitable for landfill are being depleted.  Eighty thousand acres per year are currently being filled 6 feet deep with solid waste (43).  However, large amounts of so-called marginal lands could be used;but each case must be examined for economic feasibility and ecological impact.  Burning  currently accounts for only 10% of solid waste disposal (39) and is a major air pollutor.

95

that is gaining support with heavy federal backing (38) is
that of <u>recycling</u>: mechanically sorting and marketing of
waste products as raw materials.

The processing of solid waste can be disaggregated into collection and treatment. Treating solid waste at its source,
that is, in the dwelling or other source, by smokeless incineration or more advanced methods, reduces and could eventually eliminate the need for collection services. For now,
non-combustibles such as bottles and cans etc., through
household sorting, can be substantially reduced in volume
by residential trash mashers* for less frequent pick-up.
The use of quiet trucks that are now available for the pickup operation would considerably reduce noise pollution.

Several innovative methods in solid waste collection appear
promising for multifamily housing and commercial facilities,
especially in medium or high-density areas. The first component in the series is the Automated Vacuum Collection
(AVAC) tube system. This is reputed to be cost effective at
around two mile lengths from sources of waste to collection
points (44) and can handle solid waste up to 20" in diameter.
At the collection point the waste can alternately be (i)
trucked out; (ii) ground up, mixed with water to produce a
"slurry" and piped out; (iii) compacted and exported; or
(iv) finally treated at that point.

### ·Trucking vs. Piping

It has been shown (44) that piping the waste out (the
Pneumo-Slurry system) looks promising as a substitute
for vehicle transport of solid waste if the treatment
plant is over twenty miles distant from the point of
collection.

---

*The first versions of these are currently being sold success-
fully by Whirlpool and Sears Roebuck (at approximately $220
retail, $150 wholesale). Major developers such as Beacon
Construction Company of the Boston area, already include them
as standard equipment in their multi-family housing units.

### ·Treating at Point of Collection

If the treatment plant is located at the terminus of
the AVAC system, no further means are needed to move
that portion of municipal waste collected by that system.  But the plant would also be receiving additional
low density residential waste via trucks; and the con-
tribution to traffic load produced would argue for a
plant location outside of, or at least adjacent to, the
dense area.

### ·Compacting and Exporting

An intermediate means of reduction of the bulk of the
waste could be introduced,such as methods similar to
the Prepacked Refuse system which receives, compacts,
and sends the material on to the plant.  In this case,
it could be transported by conventional trucking or by
a network cab transit vehicle, if that system were also
designed into the community.  The substantial cost savings  become  particularly significant when alternative
uses for the freed municipal funds are balanced by dimin-
ishing  operating cost savings over a twenty-year period.

### ·Final Treatment

In a new community, a potentially profitable and socially
relevant industry would be a municipal waste recycling
plant.  The old stigma of waste handling would not be
connected with such an operation; rather it would be
looked on as a community and environmental benefit.  In
an urban design context the plant could have high comparative visibility and centrality of location commensurate with considerations of efficient connectivity,as
mentioned above.

## Future Parallel Developments

1. Paper currently amounts to 40-50% of all solid waste. Facsimile printout capability in the dwelling may potentially reduce the amount of newsprint stock in the cycle.

2. Public pressure will increase; and government legislation prohibiting the manufacture of disposable, non-biodegradable products (e.g., plastic cups, plastic and metal containers) may be forthcoming.

3. Prices will increase on commodities packaged in the new degradable containers which, in effect, would penalize the lower income groups most heavily, since they would be the least able to afford an increase in price in packaged staples.

4. Increase in "alternative" styles of merchandising (e.g. a growing trend in natural food stores selling organically grown foods and in which some attention is paid to packaging).

5. A re-emergence of food cooperatives which inexpensively merchandise natural foods in bio-degradable packaging.

6. Chain supermarket reaction to food cooperative competition by adopting similar techniques.

Since solid waste management is a national, rather than local issue, federal policies establishing the correct balance of (i) tax on waste products, (ii) investment credits for manufacturers to produce products of longer useful life and (iii) easier reclamation processes, have been theoretically demonstrated to produce the best long-term results in terms of (i) minimizing draining of natural resources, (ii) minimizing pollution and (iii) maximizing the standard of living (43).

98

## C.  ALTERNATE FUTURE SCENARIOS

Plausible alternate scenarios of future life could be described if we better understood the deep psychic images of the environment that people carry with them from early childhood.  The early images and reveries that are sometimes stimulated by storybooks often become the subjective criteria by which we as adults gauge the satisfaction of an environment.

If from their childhood memories and later experiences, the home buyer and the members of his family have an image of their ideal dwelling as a castle on a rock crag, a pavillion in Elysian fields, or a cottage in an enchanted forest, it may not be possible for those images to be realized  except by the economic feasibility made possible through the application of emerging technologies (the enchanted part is not guaranteed, however).

The dwelling of the future may well be the nerve center of daily life.  Much business, education, shopping and entertainment, as well as participation in community decision making and voting will be possible in the home.  This capability, together with economical home energy and waste utilities, raises serious questions about the need for social distance and the need for proximity to municipal pipelines and wires of various kinds.

The two scenarios below describe fairly opposite poles of how people will want to live (and will be able to live) in the future.  On the one hand, close to nature, its beauty and tranquility; on the other, close to one another, to manmade structures and the excitement of the city.  Somewhere in the middle is suburbia or its contemporary equivalent , the new communities like Columbia.

99

## NATURE FIRST

A not unreasonable scenario would picture many householders of the future as wanting to get close to natural beauty and to an unspoiled environment and placing a high premium on scenic values and privacy from their neighbors. They would be able to experience through all of their senses the natural ecosystems of the area. They could accomplish these objectives where the land would be sufficiently inexpensive, yet still maintain contact with the world through their communications system and cars. A new community with very low density of one dwelling unit per acre or four acres (or over) would be organized with transportation network patterns being a secondary consideration and the siting of the dwelling or dwelling group and its relation to natural systems being the primary concern.

This community would be decentralized; and while there would be some activities within walking distance of most dwellings (schools, convenience shops), there would be a strong centralized activity center that is highly urban and that attracts the people in the community when they feel in need of direct human contact or exposure to random experiences of a more urban quality.

## THE "URBAN CITY

The opposite scenario is the highly urban image: the Hanging Gardens of Semiramis, Babylon, the Tower of Babel, the Mediterranean hill town, the Greek island towns (45). These are places where the action is, where residents value close social proximity. Agglomeration patterns of the dwellings are dense and complex. Individual dwellings themselves have a high degree of privacy and amenity, including small quiet gardens, but can be grouped so that some common element is shared by several dwellings for Living Group arrangements. When one steps out of the dwelling he is in the midst of urban activity and the excitement of the city. The zoning is multi-use so that there are layered zones of activity that cover the site.

Servicing this configuration are networks of utility channels

that are grouped in horizontal and vertical utility tubes
and in some places physically integrated with the automated
transportation guideways.  Every dwelling is within easy
walking distance of an activity center that contains most
of the services used on a daily or weekly basis.

This is a sensual city.  The touches, sounds and smells
unique to cities are experienced in walking from home to
activities.        The automated movement system mainly
serves the purpose of allowing fast access to a variety of
activity centers.

THE NEW OPTIONS

Most dwellings will have sophisticated communications equipment which will be used in varying degrees by different individuals but will almost universally be used to transact
business, do shopping and gather information.  Local walking trips as well as trips outside of town will be made for
activities that could be accomplished through the communications system, but for which the individual feels the need
for direct human contact or exposure to random experiences.
The promenade will be reestablished, where people will come
together for no other purpose than to meet each other.
The main reason for trips out-of-town will be for special
recreational purposes or for cultural, political or religious mass gatherings,of which there will be many.

It may be submitted that Ebenezer Howard's original ideal of
combining  the best of the urban with the best of the rural
has never been realized, although suburban and early new
efforts hoped to do just that.  The real possibilities that
now seem to be opening up through advanced technologies,
potential legislation   and user demand are for communities
to exist which are similar to the ones described in the
scenarios:

    1.  Highly diffuse, decentralized and nature-oriented,
        but with services at hand.

101

2. Highly compact, dense and urban-oriented with integrated services.

For either or both of these prototype communities to occur,
highly efficient and responsive public service systems are
required; this condition, in turn, requires an uncommon degree of entrepreneurial management and design skills -- as
well as a high degree of commitment from both public and
private participants in the community development process.
It is from this basis that our search effort has been directed towards technological and programatic innovation in
the provision of public services for large-scale, or new,
comuunity development.

REFERENCES

(1)  National Goals Research Staff, <u>Toward Balanced Growth:</u>
     <u>Quantity with Quality</u>, Washington, D.C., 1970.

(2)  Edward Banfield, <u>The Unheavenly City</u>, 1970.

(3)  Jean Gottmann, <u>Megalopolis</u>, New York, 1962.

(4)  Lloyd Rodwin, <u>Nations and Cities, A Comparison of Stra-</u>
     <u>tegies for Urban Growth</u>, Houghton Mifflin, 1970.

(5)  "Population and National Goals," <u>Science News</u>, Vol 98.,1970.

(6)  Edward Eichler and Marshall Kaplan, <u>The Community</u>
     <u>Builders</u>, Berkeley, 1967.

(7)  William Alonso, "The Mirage of New Towns," <u>The Public</u>
     <u>Interest</u>, No. 19, Spring 1970.

(8)  John Kenneth Galbraith, <u>The New Industrial State</u>, New York,1967.

(9)  F. W. Memnott, "The Substitutability of Communications
     for Transportation," <u>Traffic Engineering Journal</u>,
     February 1963.

(10) T. J. Healy, "Transportation or Communication," <u>IEEE</u>
     <u>Transactions on Communication Technology</u>, VOl. Com. 16,
     No. 2, April 1968.

(11) Barton-Aschman Assoc. Inc., <u>Guidelines for New Systems</u>
     <u>of Urban Transportation, Vol. I: Urban Needs and Poten-</u>
     <u>tials</u>, HUD, 1968.

(12) Jane Jacobs, <u>Death and Life of Great American Cities</u>, 1961.

(13) Margaret Mead, "Values for Urban Living," <u>The Annals</u>,
     November 1957.

(14) Paul Baran, Martin Greenberger, <u>Urban Node in Informa-</u>
     <u>tion Network</u>, RAND.

(15) Paul Goodman, <u>The Radical Papers</u>.

103

(16) Z. Hirsch, ed., <u>Elements of Regional Accounts</u>, Baltimore, The Johns Hopkins Press, 1964, pp.175-209.

(17) R. M. Fano, "The Computer Utility and the Community," <u>IEEE International Convention Record</u>, Part 12, 1967.

(18) Don Benson, "Neurone Cluster Grope," <u>Radical Software</u>, No. 2, 1970.

(19) Raul de Brigard and Olaf Helmer, <u>Some Potential Societal Developments: 1970-2000</u>, Institute for the Future, 1969.

(20) Theodore J. Gordon and Robert H. Ament, <u>Forecasts of Some Technological and Scientific Developments and their Societal Consequences</u>, Institute for the Future, 1969.

(21) Daniel Brand, <u>Dual Mode Transportation Systems: Analysis of Demands and Benefits in Urban Areas and Development of Performance Requirements</u>, Urban Systems Laboratory, MIT, June 1970.

(22) Thomas Domenich, "Estimation of Urban Passenger Travel Behavior: An Economic Demand Model," <u>Highway Research Board Record No. 238</u>, Washington, D.C., 1968.

(23) NCTA News Release, March 25, 1970 as quoted in <u>Radical Software</u>, No. 2, 1970.

(24) Michael Joroff, "New Style Health, Education and Social Services," <u>New Communities: An American Institute of Planners Background Paper</u>, No. 2.

(25) Louis Alfeld et al., <u>Planning for New Communities: A Systems Approach</u>, unpublished paper, Urban Systems Laboratory, MIT, 1969.

(26) Daniel Bell, "Notes on the Post-Industrial Society," <u>The Public Interest</u>, No. 6, Winter 1967.

(27) Charles Reich, <u>The Greening of America</u>, New York, 1970.

(28) Lewis Feuer, "What is Alienation? The Career of a Concept," Sociology on Trial, ed. Maurice Stein and Arthur Vidlich, Englewood Cliffs, New Jersey, Prentice-Hall, Inc., 1963, p.142.

(29) Marvin B. Scott, "The Social Sources of Alienation," The New Sociology, ed. Irving Louis Horowitz, New York, Oxford University Press, 1964, pp.239-252.

(30) Irene Taviss, "Changes in the Form of Alienation," American Sociological Review, February 1969.

(31) Robert Blauner, Alienation and Freedom, Chicago, 1964.

(32) John McHale, Future Cities -- Notes on Typology.

(33) Herbert Gans, The Levittowners, New York, 1967

(34) "Democracy in the New Towns: The Limits of Private Government," University of Chicago Law Review, Winter 1969.

(35) Carol Burke, Kellner-Oshrey Associates, Boston, Mass.

(36) James Morey, Director of New City Project, Cambridge Institute, Cambridge, Mass.

(37) James Tackaberry McCay, Beyond Motivation, Northern Electric Laboratories, 1970.

(38) Environmental Quality: The First Annual Report of the Council on Environmental Quality, The White House, 1970, p.114.

(39) Frederick Smith, Professor of Ecology, Graduate School of Design, Harvard University, in lecture series, Spring 1970.

(40) Frederic W. Demind, Special Assistant to the Secretary of HUD in seminar on housing strategies, MIT, January 20, 1971.

(41) U.S. President's Committee on Urban Housing, A Decent
     Home (The Kaiser Report), a report of The Presidential
     Committee on Urban Housing, 1969.

(42) Charles Haar, Professor of Law, Harvard University, in
     seminar on housing strategies, MIT, January 27, 1971.

(43) Jorgen Randers, The Dynamics of Solid Waste Generation,
     unpublished paper for The Systems Dynamics Group, MIT,
     1971.

(44) Iraj Zandi and John A. Hayden, "Are Pipelines the Answer
     to Waste Collection Dilemmas?", Environmental Science
     and Technology, Vol. 3, No. 9, September 1969.

(45) "Megastructure for Renewal," Architectural Forum,
     June 1967, p.58.

# III. TECHNOLOGICAL AND PROGRAMMATIC INNOVATIONS

Since a new community development is staged over a length of time of 10, 15 or 20 years or longer, it is essential to the design and planning processes to have a clear idea of the community service systems which may be available in the years to come (insofar as we can rationally project future developments). Part II dealt with the demand side of an equation which must ultimately attempt to balance the requirements of a community's residential and industrial populations with the services installed as part of the community infrastructure. The purpose of this part is to identify the components of the supply side of the equation; in particular, we have attempted to describe innovations in technology and programmatic mechanisms which comprise a community's public service network.

In recent years, new institutions and new methods have emerged with the specific purpose of exploring the future. Since 1964, starting with Helmer and Gordon's now classic study for the RAND corporation, "Report on Long-Range Forecasting Study," many specific forecasts have been undertaken and made public. In the early forecasts, some conservatism is now notable; for example, in the 1964 RAND study, automated guideway transportation was not expected at the earliest until 1985. Now, six years after that study, with new evidence, guideways look promising for the late 1970's.* In reviewing the body of forecasting work, it has

---

*See the "Staging Strategy" in the section on "Evolutionary Automated Movement Systems" in Part II for the strategy being followed by the Ford Consortium. Also, in Japan, the Ministry of International Trade and Industry, together with Tokyo University, are jointly developing a $51 million guideway construction test program. Vehicles are small, two-  (Cont'd)

been our task to bring the forecasts into focus for their
direct application to new communities.  Some descriptions
included here are broadly future-based, such as the section
on nuclear energy; and some are descriptions of specific
developments that are now, or will soon be, available.  The
descriptions range over invention, innovation and diffusion.

In this part, the ranges of public service and hardware innovations explored during the research are identified and
summarized in reference format.  It is intended that these
summaries serve largely as descriptors to acquaint the reader
with current efforts aimed at improving the quality and/or
reducing the costs of urban public services or individual
hardwares.  A source list for each of the services discussed
is included to enable the reader to locate more detailed
information about any specific service in which he might be
particularly interested.

---

*(Cont'd)   passenger, rubber-tired, battery-powered,
computer-controlled, demand-actuated "city cars".  The
guideway network, with projected channel capacities of
14,000 cars per hour, is  arranged in a one-kilometer grid
of high-speed guideways with a 100-meter grid of low-speed
guideways.  See Asahi Evening News, October 17, 1970 and
the Japan Economic Journal, October 27, 1970.

## A. TECHNOLOGICAL FORECASTING (PRODUCT INNOVATION)

Technological developments can be predicted by linear
extrapolation, envelope curve analysis and other methods.
Although none of these techniques was explicitly employed
here, the descriptions of technologies noted in this report
(both present and future) are, with very few exceptions,
taken from actual research and development activities and
reports of those activities which often utilized predictive
techniques.  This is not to suggest that all relevant R & D
activity that would affect new community design is covered
or that we have exhaustively explored all potential areas
of information on innovations.  Indeed, the proprietary
nature of much of the current research and the lack of
centralized information sources preclude the achievement
of complete documentation.  It should also be noted that
projections of the kind in this section are basically optimistic and implicitly exclude such possible future events
as thermonuclear war, ecological disaster, etc.  There will
be, in all likelihood, unanticipated occurrences which will
have major impacts on technology and society and which will
modify many previous projections (i.e., breakthroughs such
as the discovery of zero gravity potential and other even
less expected events).

For descriptive and reference purposes, the technological
innovations described in this section are listed within the
following major categories:

- Movement Systems*
- Energy Systems**
- Communications Systems

*In view of the vast number of relevant experiments in trans-
portation, we have limited our discussion here to innovations
in relatively advanced stages of development.  Hence,

·Waste Management: Sewage
·Waste Management: Collection
·Waste Management: Treatment
·Miscellaneous Utility Systems

_____

*(Cont'd)
analysis is not included of numerous systems which, although significant and innovative, are either of such
long-range character or present usage as to be beyond
the possible length and adequate description of this
study.  Examples of the first category would be: air-
cushion vehicles, gravity vacuum tube transit, tunnel-
ing technology and transport ramifications, aerotrain,
linear induction motor, magnetically levitated high
speed ground transportation, or electric urbmobiles
(rentable and private); of the second category, moving
sidewalks, exclusive bus rights-of-way, or helicopter
ambulances and other specialized usages.  For a more
complete description of the range of transportation innovations currently being explored, the following general references provide further sources on other particular transportation systems:

1. Makofski, R.F., ed., Technical Evaluation of Advanced
   Urban Transportation Systems, The Johns Hopkins University Applied Physics Laboratory, Silver Spring,
   Maryland, prepared for the U.S. Department of Transportation, June 1970.

2. U.S. Department of HUD, Tomorrow's Transportation:
   New Systems for the Urban Future, U.S. Government
   Printing Office, Washington, D.C., May 1968

**Similar to the multifarious innovative situation in trans-
portation, the following emerging energy technologies are
some which have not been found possible to discuss: air or
wind power, wave power, coal conversion to gas, the solar
cell dish, direct solar heating and cooling of enclosed
space, non-contact power transmission.  The same pattern of
omission certainly applies to the other technological systems categories.  There is no attempt at total comprehensiveness.

STAGE OF DEVELOPMENT

R & D is completed at the MIT Urban Systems Laboratory on the CARS project. Dial-A-Bus service can be installed in the early 1970's. (The generic Dial-a-Ride will be called Dial-A-Bus in this report.)

OPERATING CHARACTERISTICS

This is a door to door demand-actuated system that is programmed for computer. Small buses would follow flexible routing instructions radioed to the driver from a computerized central scheduling point. To summon a bus, passengers would telephone. The computer would then relay the pickup location to the central computer which would compute the most efficient routing. Appropriate vehicle size is the 12 to 20 passenger minibus. Advantages are:

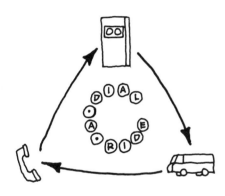

·carries trips not well served by conventional transit
·no special rights-of-way
·has peaking characteristics similar to auto and taxi
·substitutes for auto trips
·provides feeder service to rail or bus lines
 adaptable to off-peak hour and weekend service
·provides special shuttle service
·services institutional trips: schools, hospitals, airports
·services circumferential trips: community-to-community

SCALE CHARACTERISTICS

·services lower density areas than conventional transit
·it should be economically feasible at less than 10% of the population needed for a fixed route bus service -- depending on the trip generating potential of the area
·it should be economically feasible at 20 trips per square mile per hour

·where demand is too low to support Dial-A-Bus, taxis
 are the most economical form of transit
·where demand along a corridor can support fixed route
 of service, such service will generally be more economical than Dial-A-Bus

REFERENCES

Edwin Porter et al., Summary Report: Dial-A-Bus System
Design, Urban Systems Laboratory, MIT, July 1970.

Edwin Porter et al., Economic Considerations for Dial-A-
Ride, Urban Systems Laboratory, MIT,  Summer, 1971

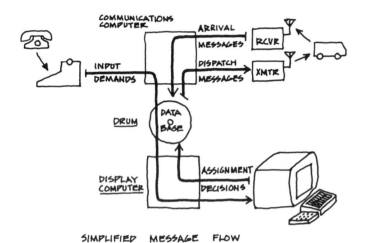

SIMPLIFIED MESSAGE FLOW

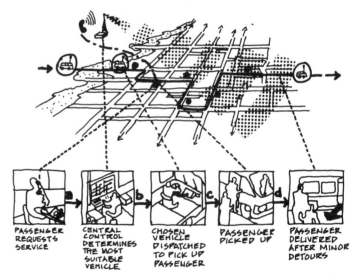

● INDICATES OTHER PASSENGER PICKUP AND DELIVERY POINTS

SEQUENCE OF DIAL-A-RIDE OPERATIONS

MOVEMENT SYSTEMS

COLLECTION/DISTRIBUTION

ALDEN CAPSULE TRANSIT SYSTEM

STAGE OF DEVELOPMENT

The system's main problem is lack of sufficient computer software programming for system management and control (1).

OPERATIONAL CHARACTERISTICS

This system by Alden Self-Transit Systems Inc. of Bedford, Mass. is a rubber-tired vehicle operating in a tracked guideway at cruise speeds of 15-40 miles per hour and maximum speed of 60, capacity of 15 persons,and operating headways of 1.6 seconds.  At 15 miles per hour it is designed as a demand-actuated system (1).

SCALE CHARACTERISTICS

It has application as a Network Cab Transit system for localized guideways in high density areas and has excellent guideway potential for dual mode capability.  The system has a central computer with onboard switching equipment (2).

REFERENCES

(1)  Robert A. Maokfski, Technical Evaluation of Advanced Urban Transportation Systems: Summary Report, Applied Physics Laboratory, Johns Hopkins University, June 1970.

(2)  "StaRRcar System Description and Application Notes," Alden Self-Transit Systems Corporation, Bedford, Mass.

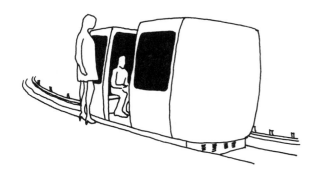

DASHAVEYOR

STAGE OF DEVELOPMENT

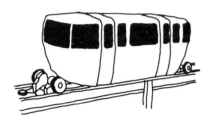

For simple shuttle applications, Dashaveyor is an essentially state-of-the-art system offering no major technical problems other than those normally associated with the introduction of new equipment.  It is presently undergoing extensive re-design, concentrating on vehicle control, suspension and the propulsion subsystem (1).  Dashaveyor is being put into operation for the Dallas-Fort Worth Regional Airport transit system.

OPERATIONAL CHARACTERISTICS

The system by Dashaveyor Corp. of Los Angeles is a pneumatic-tired system designed to operate on a dual-rail guideway at speeds of 30 miles per hour, with capacities of from 30 persons at headways of 35 seconds (1).

SCALE CHARACTERISTICS

It has application as a Network Cab Transit system for localized guideways in high density areas, and has good evolutionary potential for dual mode vehicles, providing that the present generation guideway would accommodate standard vehicle track widths.  The system has a central computer with on-board switching equipment.

REFERENCES

(1)  Robert A. Makofski, Technical Evaluation of Advanced Urban Transportation Systems: Summary Report, Applied Physics Laboratory, Johns Hopkins University, June 1970.

MINIRAIL

STAGE OF DEVELOPMENT

Operational

OPERATING CHARACTERISTICS

This is a small rail-under (similar to ALWEG) system.  The vehicle rides on a double I-Beam, powered by electricity collected from the rail.  They carry 4 to 12 passengers each and have cruising speeds of 12 to 20 miles per hour. Switching is slow (10 to 15 seconds).

SCALE CHARACTERISTICS

It has application as a Network Cab Transit system for localized guideways,but because of switching problems can only operate in the transit mode of stopping at all stations.  It has highly limited guideway evolutionary potential for dual mode vehicles.

REFERENCES

Universal Mobility Incorporated, Salt Lake City, Utah.

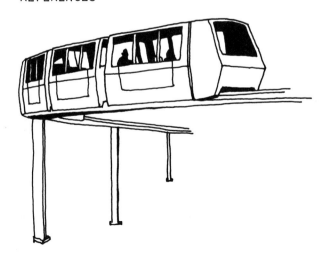

SKY CAR TRANSIVATOR SYSTEM

STATE OF DEVELOPMENT

Several developments are required in the system, including communications and control facilities, lateral stress, resistance of the guideway and supporting pylons (as to crosswinds and centrifugal forces), and switching time under the short headways (1).

OPERATIONAL CHARACTERISTICS

This is pneumatically-tired vehicle suspended from a steel-beam monorail with a cruising speed of 15 miles per hour (maximum: 60) and 12-passenger capacity operating on 5-second headways (1).

SCALE CHARACTERISTICS

It has application as a Network Cab Transit system for localized guideways in high density areas, but has highly limited guideway evolutionary potential for dual mode vehicles.
The system has wayside control and guideway-located switching.

REFERENCES

(1)  Robert A. Makofski, Technical Evaluation of Advanced Urban Transportation Systems: Summary Report, Applied Physics Laboratory, Johns Hopkins University, June 1970.

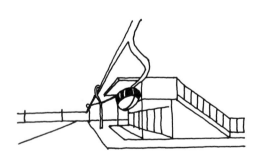

STAGE OF DEVELOPMENT

Working prototypes of this system have been demonstrated as low speed vehicles. Additional computer software development is necessary before the system can be operational. Considerable development effort on the advanced component technologies is prerequisite to practical implementation (1).

OPERATIONAL CHARACTERISTICS

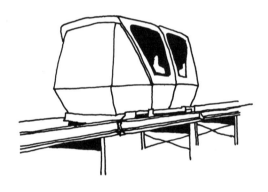

This system, by Transportation Technology, Inc. (TTI), of Madison Heights, Michigan, is a six to twelve passenger, 20 to 60-mile-per-hour tracked air cushion system with headways of 3 to 10 seconds. It operates with the linear induction motor and air cushions and makes use of "docking" technique at stations, in which individual cars move laterally off and onto the main line at designated stops. Cars can move at will to and from stations -- providing "random access" to system-routes -- limited only by the number of available "docks" and not by presence of other vehicles in a station (1). The system has central computer and on-board switching equipment.

SCALE CHARACTERISTICS

It has application as a Network Cab Transit system for localized guideways in high density areas. The guideway potential for dual mode capability is unknown.

REFERENCES

(1)  Robert A. Makofski, Technical Evaluation of Advanced Urban Transportation Systems: Summary Report, Applied Physics Laboratory, Johns Hopkins University, June 1970.

STAGE OF DEVELOPMENT

Development is required in the unit's command and control system, vehicle-guideway dynamics and on-board switching (an "arm" in the vehicle reaches out to a new track to effect change of direction, rather than a switch mechanism in the guideway moving the vehicle to a new track).

The primary problem is vehicle control. Varo envisages a series of simplified blocks, similar but on a smaller scale to railroad systems; with each vehicle automatically slowing when its headway, measured in blocks, is decreased, then accelerating when the headway is increased. This would cause too much "pulsing" (deceleration-acceleration) with headways of just a few seconds. Varo is now undergoing redesign (1).

OPERATIONAL CHARACTERISTICS

This is a six-passenger vehicle suspended from above by rubber tires riding in an inverted U-channel monorail with a cruise speed of 34 miles per hour, top speed of 68 and headways of from three to seven seconds. The Varo system is one of the "people movers" under testing for the Dallas-Fort Worth Regional Airport (1). The system has wayside control and on-board switching equipment.

SCALE CHARACTERISTICS

It has application as a Network Cab Transit system for localized guideways in high density areas, but has highly limited guideway evolutionary potential for dual mode vehicles.

REFERENCES

(1) Robert A. Makofski, <u>Technical Evaluation of Advanced</u>
<u>Urban Transportation Systems: Summary Report</u>, Applied
Physics Laboratory, Johns Hopkins University, June 1970.

STAGE OF DEVELOPMENT

There is potential communications interference resulting from electrical noise generated by propulsion and power collection equipment still to be resolved (1).

OPERATIONAL CHARACTERISTICS

This system by Westinghouse Electric Corp. is similar to Pittsburgh's Transit Expressway "Skybus" system. The vehicle rides on rubber tires over a concrete guideway, and has a capacity of from 25 to 35 persons, headway of 40 to 60 seconds, and cruising speeds of 45 miles per hour (1). The system has wayside controls and guideway-located switching equipment.

SCALE CHARACTERISTICS

It has application as a Network Cab Transit system for localized guideways in high density areas, and has excellent guideway potential for dual mode capability.

REFERENCES

(1) Robert A. Makofski, Technical Evaluation of Advanced Urban Transportation Systems: Summary Report, Applied Physics Laboratory, Johns Hopkins University, June 1970.

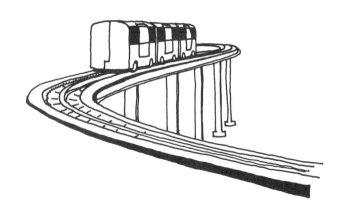

MOVEMENT SYSTEMS

INTER-URBAN

V/STOL AIRBUS SERVICE

STAGE OF DEVELOPMENT

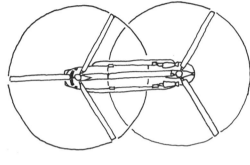

BOEING-VERTOL 157 HELICOPTER

EXTERNAL - FLOW   JET - FLAP  STOL

1970's  VTOL fare levels reduced to 2.5¢ per passenger mile,
        same as ground bus (1)
1980's-1985  V/STOL craft used for 90% of air travel (2)
1980's  (middle-late) proliferation of small private VTOL
        aircars

Vertical and Short Take Off and Landing systems (V/STOL)
linking activity centers of communities have recently been
studied at two levels of network coverage, (i) short haul
inter-city links in the range of several hundred miles (3)
and (ii) intra-urban systems with stage lengths between
20 and 50 miles (4).

Two vehicle concepts for the intra-urban VTOL system are
the 40-80 passenger "metrobus" and the four or five passenger "metrotaxi."  Helicopter and tiltrotor VTOL lift modes
were considered for the vehicles (4) of both concepts.  STOL
could also be applied to the metrobus network.  The metrotaxi would be an origin-destination, demand-actuated service where the vehicle would reach a small vertiport or
minimally developed landing area nearest the passenger
within a few minutes of a telephone call (4).

The short haul inter-city system was found to be potentially
feasible for development in the 1970's while the intra-
urban system was found to be not feasible in the 1980 to
1985 period.

Presently, the holdups from realizing these systems lie in
the political area.  Some experts consider that the government should view transportation as a quasi-public utility,
not as a private enterprise; and VTOL systems in particular
should be considered as common carriers (5).

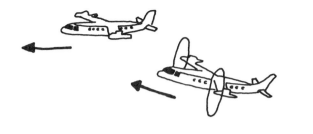

TILT ROTOR CONFIGURATION

Some VTOL craft under development are:

<u>Helicopter Skycrane</u> - Sikorsky
<u>Compound Helicopter</u> - Lockheed

    CL-1026  30 passengers - preliminary design
    CL-1090  95 passengers - under study

Other lift modes include:

<u>Tiltwing Propeller</u> - LTU XC-142, Vought-Hiller-Ryan XC-142
<u>Tiltrotor Propeller</u> - Bell X-22, Curtiss-Wright X-19
<u>Stowed-Rotor</u> - Sikorsky, Lockheed, Boeing-Vertol
<u>Lift-Fans</u> - North American Rockwell, Hawker-Siddeley,
    Ryan XV-5A
<u>Lift-Jets</u> - North American Rockwell, Lockheed XV-4A.

Two STOL aircraft under development and in current applied use are:

DeHavilland DHC-4 Caribou (32 passenger, 185 mph
    cruising speed, 1185 feet takeoff distance)
McDonnell-Douglas 188E - American versions of French
    Breguet 9415 (80 passenger, 300 mph cruising
    speed, 500 feet takeoff distance).

OPERATING CHARACTERISTICS

The intra-urban system study concluded that batched passenger public urban systems could not compete with individual systems like the automobile for the total mass market, but must attract a much reduced travel volume consisting of trips between local areas surrounding stopping points. This would lead to alternate conveyance access and egress times with the air system of around 1/2 hour, greatly reducing its time advantages, especially for short trips (4). However, with highly efficient metroport terminals and movement interface systems it can be foreseen that the negative feasibility could change in favor of intra-urban VTOL systems for trips of twenty to fifty miles and more.

Total systems economies would come from designing the terminals as highly efficient transportation exchanges or "mode mixers," where a number of conveyances such as rail, private and rental automobiles, bus, water transportation, and automated guideways can interface, so as to minimize the trip time and ease the process of conveyance change for the traveler. This facility should be one of high image quality, as train stations were at the turn of the century. Terminals can be modular, starting with two pads and adding increments as the demand increases.

The dominant problem in implementing an urban air system is community acceptance of the metroport, and the prime concern here is the noise factor. VTOL noise pollution is the system's present major social cost; rotary wing, or helicopter, is the least noisy in the present array of lift modes. The FAA and IATA have been remiss in not issuing criteria for community noise levels as yet. A peak noise level of 85 Pndb (perceived noise in decibels) at 500 feet is suggested as acceptable, based on experience with 70 heliports in the Boston Area (4). Studies have shown that acceptability is dependent on both Pndb and the frequency of occurrence. Doubling the time of exposure of a given noise is equivalent to about a 3-db increase in noise annoyance. Community noise criteria would include factors other than peak noise, such as frequency of occurrence, background (masking), noise levels, number of persons listening, etc.

From Frontiers of Technology, by North American Rockwell Corp:

> Helicopter rotor noise is dependent on the number, diameter, and area of the rotor blades, the weight of the vehicle, the blade rotational speed, and the proximity of the rotating blades to the fuselage. The two important aerodynamic parameters are the disk loading (the ratio of the weight of the vehicle to the disk area of the rotor), and the blade loading (the ratio of the weight of the vehicle to the total blade area in the rotor systems).

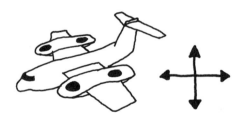

LIFT FAN CONFIGURATION

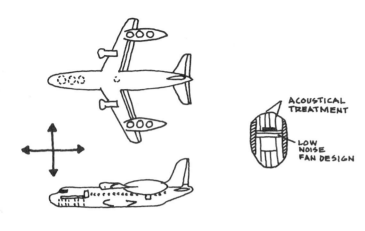

ACOUSTICAL
TREATMENT

LOW
NOISE
FAN DESIGN

LIFT — FAN   BLOWN-FLAP   VTOL   CONFIGURATION

It is unlikely that major technological breakthroughs will result from additional research on noise generation, nor can significant relief from the predicted noise levels be expected from additional research on noise controls. Rather, the available noise prediction techniques must be used in the planning and design of the overall transportation system including the ground facilities as well as the aircraft (6).

With most cities, it is quite possible to site metroports where approach zones can be over areas less important for quiet control, such as bodies of water, industrial areas, or railroad yards. But this does, to a degree, restrict their siting.

SCALE CHARACTERISTICS

The strongest impact of a V/STOL airbus system on a new community in the '70's would be in its influence on the aggregation of a number of modes into a central transportation exchange. It is likely that in the '80's, with a proliferation of lighter, smaller craft, capable of vertical takeoff and landing, one central facility, because of aircraft queuing delays, may disaggregate into a number of dispersed locations around the community. The central facility would handle the commercial traffic and dispersed facilities would handle the private traffic.

Given the existence of a good inter-city VTOL and/or STOL system a priori, it could play a strong part in determining the location of a new community within a given region. VTOL may prove accommodating to emerging freight transportation patterns which favor rapid delivery at rates increasingly competitive with truck and rail. Improved regional access by VTOL can provide stimulus to industrial location and effective labor market use, fortify leisure activities and related service industries as an integral part of economic development, and assist in the development of new communities marked by beneficial urban-rural balance.

124

COST INFORMATION

It has been shown by a MIT study group (3) that short haul air transportation systems can be developed in urbanized regions in the 1970's that would operate at fare levels of around 5¢ per passenger mile over stage lengths of 100 miles. Leading cost reduction incentives which favor the implementation of VTOL and/or STOL are the comparatively small investment required for terminal and land acquisition and the flexibility for inexpensive growth and network change. Operating costs are not decisive between VTOL, STOL and CTOL but the indirect costs of siting and terminal costs favor VTOL over the others (3).

REFERENCES

(1) Getler, "Way to Plan Airway?", Space/Aeronautics, Vol. 51, No. 5.

(2) J. Block, "Airport Planning: For a Place in the Future Environment," Futures, Vol. 1., No. 4, June 1969.

(3) Robert H. Simpson, et al., A Systems Analysis of Short Haul Air Transportation, prepared by MIT for the U.S. Department of Commerce.

(4) Concept Studies for Future Intra-city Air Transportation Systems, prepared for NASA by MIT Department of Aeronautics and Astronautics, 1970.

(5) Robert H. Simpson, Professor of Aeronautics, MIT.

(6) North American Rockwell Corp., Frontiers of Technology, Vol. II Survey, HUD, 1968.

STAGE OF DEVELOPMENT

ROCKET BELT BY BELL AEROSYSTEMS

1971  operational
1980's  (middle-late)  general acceptance

Recently, personal methods of flying -- such as Bell Aerosystems flying belt and Williams Research Corporation's flying platform -- have been undergoing intense R & D.  Both
systems are operational.  The Williams flying platform operates on a small gas turbofan engine weighing about 60 lbs.
and having about 430 lbs. of thrust.  It carries fuel for
about 20 minutes of flight.

The flying platform, once fully developed, would very likely
be first introduced as a military, then as a sports item.
With the probable increasing recreation and sport consciousness in the near future, it is likely that it could be successfully marketed sometime in the late 1970's.  Giving it
ten years to catch on and be refined, owners would very
likely be using them in the cities for uses other than
sports (providing they would not be inordinately noisy); and
while doing so, uncovering voids in indemnification and re-
gulatory mechanisms.  Giving these mechanisms and a fad for
flying platforms another five years to develop, it would
seem reasonable that by 1985 this method of transportation,
together with air taxis and extensive VTOL networks, will
all be realities.

OPERATING CHARACTERISTICS

The capability of personally safely and comfortably flying
through the air to any destination that one wants to reach
may be one of technology's ultimate realizations.  Whether
this would be more practically done in a small vehicle the
size of an automobile or small aeroplane, or whether it
would be done in an even smaller conveyance depends on many

FLYING BEDSTEAD BY ROLLS ROYCE INC.

SCALE CHARACTERISTICS

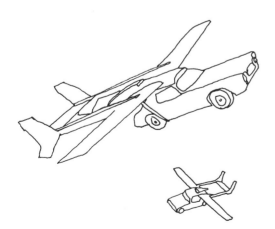

factors, including technology. With every person having the capability to fly, enormous problems would arise of (i) air traffic control; (ii) the "locust effect",* or visual pollution of the skies with thousands of vehicles hovering and passing their shadows over people on the ground; and (iii) safety.

With advanced sensor and computer technology, existing today in aerospace, air traffic control would not seem to represent a major hurdle for this development to occur. And application of soft air bags and automatic parachutes would increase safety levels considerably. The locust effect might be a major problem, given the equivalent of automobile size vehicles. With this development, the sky would need to be zoned. Areas of overflight would need to be defined; and those areas where no overflight would be allowed (wilderness areas, some non-metropolitan residential areas, etc.) would have to be determined. Stratified layers of movement or airstreams would have to be defined for (i) commercial and private planes, commercial VTOL, and private air cars, and (ii) compass directions of travel for the VTOL craft.

Predictably, an extension of air-rights application would occur over existing throughways and other major roads, where flight patterns could be ordered and potential hazards reduced. Such possibilities might lead to second-order effects, involving the easing of overcrowded ground level transportation and the reduction of capital investment in transportation networks. Vertical access zones or chimneys that would allow access in and out of the strata or air streams would need to be determined. All things considered, for this innovation to be fully realizable for society at large, there would have to be many regulations and controls with the result that the idea of omnidirectional, free personal air travel might not result in the full freedom of the skies as originally conceptualized.

---

*This term is suggested by Dr. Sigfried Breuning for the proliferation of small VTOL machines in the air.

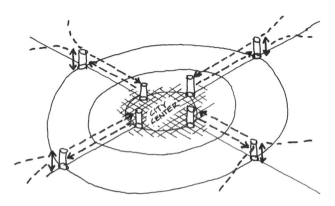

VERTICAL ACCESS 'CHIMNEYS' AND HORIZONTAL
TRAVEL STRATA NETWORK

However, there might practically be several levels of this kind of movement, including at the first level the personal flying platform that would substitute for short trips by walking and other methods of transportation to destinations between 1/4 and 1 mile distant. Here the speed would be relatively slow, and visual contact would be maintained for control.

At the second level, there would be the personal or family-size VTOL aircar that might have to be restricted to vertical and horizontal channels of movement. It might require that it not take off directly from the dwelling (unless it were situated in a very low density area)* but that it would have to travel by ground to a vertical access chimney in order to reach the horizontal travel stratum.

At the third level would be the batched passenger VTOL craft which are presently operational or in advanced R & D stages. The smaller air taxi VTOL are well within the realm of the foreseeable future (1). The personal, or family-size VTOL aircar is an extension of practical VTOL common carrier service and advanced command and control technology. And the personal flying platform would seem to be an inevitability given the state of general technological sophistication and the market for new gimmicks.

CONSEQUENCES: The personal flying belt will more than likely not be able to accommodate the very young (under 12 years of age), the very old, or the handicapped. In its first decades of introduction, it will probably be met with some skeptical or timid resistance. For the users of this mode, it would redefine the concept of the community in terms of walking distance. But this would not eliminate

---

*Alternatively, if reduced speed or other means were employed to make direct access to the individual dwelling possible in high density areas, a major design consideration would have to be given to the residential structure's roof and **to** the entrance/exit patterns of living units.

the walking distance scaled community. Today, analogous
ground-based vehicles such as bicycles and motorcycles are
used with little effect on the need for having activities
within walking distance.

REFERENCES

(1) <u>Concept Studies for Future Air Transportation Systems</u>,
    prepared for NASA by MIT Department of Aeronautics
    and Astronautics, 1970.

LEONARDO'S 'TENT OF LINEN'

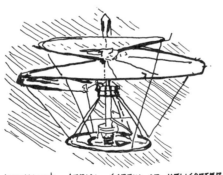

LEONARDO'S AERIAL SCREW OR HELICOPTER

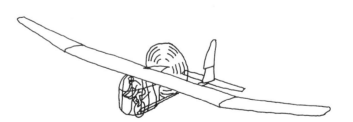

MAN-POWERED FLIGHT

STAGE OF DEVELOPMENT

1980   all-underground systems in urbanizing areas (1)

New transmission channels actively being developed are (i) cryogenic resistive conductors, (ii) compressed-gas-insulated cables, and (iii) superconductors.

Prospects for superconducting cables using liquid helium look dim.  The helium is rare and expensive and refrigeration and insulating procedures are difficult or costly.

Power distribution has been going and will continue to go underground.  While underground transmission in suburban areas is practically nil at the present time, the demand for undergrounding is expected to increase markedly as load growth requires large blocks of power to be brought into or through settled areas.  The two main reasons for this trend are (i) increasing competition for surface land over which transmission lines are located, and (ii) increasing interest and concern for the protection of scenic values.

SCALE CHARACTERISTICS

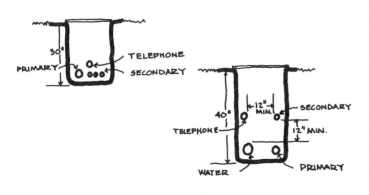

Nationally, underground lines comprise less than 1% of the transmission system but nearly 100% of the transmission is in dense areas.  The economics of future routing may favor passing through a developing area to reach large load centers and where this is the case, an increasing proportion of lines may be put underground for either land economics or visual reasons (1).

The integration of the new high conducting lines into a utilador in dense urban areas would be a likely prospect, and the trend toward underground transmission provides supporting justification for utilador use.

130

## COST INFORMATION

Presently, underground high power transmission is accomplished with oil-paper insulated cables, the cost of which ranges from 5 to 25 times the cost of equivalent overhead lines. Cryogenic resistive cables using liquid nitrogen would reduce the cost by decreasing the loss through more effective materials utilization: this would cut costs by 50% (2). Compressed gas lines in aluminum housings, using sulfur hexaflouride, look most promising at present (2).

## REFERENCES

(1) Herbert H. Woodson, "Underground Power Transmission: A Report to the Federal Power Commission by the Advisory Committee on Underground Transmission," April 1966.

(2) Herbert H. Woodson, "Applications of Superconductivity and Cryogenics in Electric Power Systems," unpublished paper, MIT.

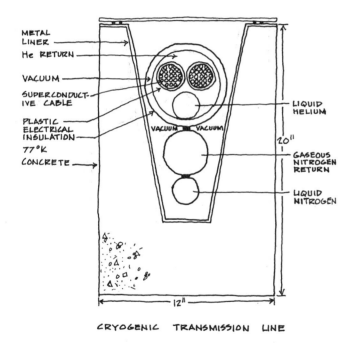

METAL LINER
He RETURN
VACUUM
SUPERCONDUCT-IVE CABLE
PLASTIC ELECTRICAL INSULATION
77°K
CONCRETE
LIQUID HELIUM
VACUUM  VACUUM
20"
GASEOUS NITROGEN RETURN
LIQUID NITROGEN
12"

CRYOGENIC  TRANSMISSION  LINE

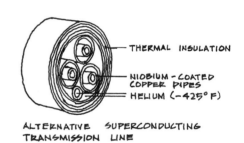

THERMAL INSULATION
NIOBIUM-COATED COPPER PIPES
HELIUM (-425°F)

ALTERNATIVE  SUPERCONDUCTING TRANSMISSION  LINE

STAGE OF DEVELOPMENT                      Operational

OPERATIONAL CHARACTERISTICS              The total energy concept (all natural gas) is being marketed
                                         by the gas companies in the form of gas turbines equipped
                                         with regenerators and "waste head" recovery boilers.  Fuel
                                         cells would figure into this equation in the future.  The
                                         total energy concept has proved economical in certain appli-
                                         cations.  Maintenance economies, as well as possible com-
                                         munity ownership of plants, are possible.

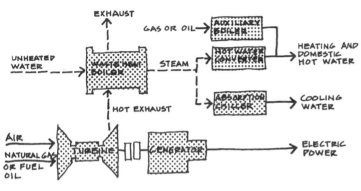

                                         The total electric concept being marketed by the electric
                                         utilities involves configurations of central plants, heat
                                         pumps, and other systems adapted to the specific require-
                                         ments of the community.

TOTAL ENERGY SYSTEM USING TURBINE

SCALE CHARACTERISTICS                    Individually determined for each community.

COST INFORMATION                         A recent comparison of total energy and electric systems
                                         for Fort Lincoln New Town revealed that the two were com-
                                         petitive in cost given that local rate structures are de-
                                         signed to be competitive.  The study recommended that both
                                         systems be employed in the community (1).

REFERENCES                               (1)  Norman Kurtz, Fred S. Dubin and Assoc., "Comparative
                                              Energy Source Study," Appendix K, Developing New Com-
                                              munities: Application of Technological Innovation, HUD.

132

STAGE OF DEVELOPMENT

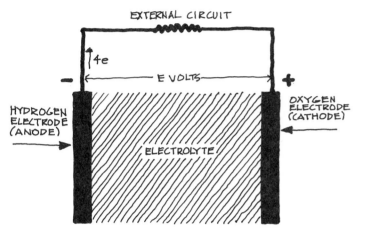

OVERALL REACTION
$$2H_2 + O_2 \rightarrow 2H_2O$$

DIAGRAM OF HYDROGEN-OXYGEN CELL
ADAPTED FROM M.A. SULKIN, ET AL, NORTH AMERICAN
ROCKWELL CORP.; FRONTIERS OF TECHNOLOGY STUDY, VOL. III,
PREPARED FOR U.S. DEPT. OF HUD, LOS ANGELES, 1968

OPERATIONAL CHARACTERISTICS

1972  field trial
mid-1970's  fuel cell availability on the commercial market
1984  extensive use of fuel cells (1)

LONG RANGE DEVELOPMENTS:  Fuel cells operating on deliverable bottled fuels.

The TARGET program at Pratt and Whitney, the largest fuel
cell program in current progress, is developing technical
and economic data on fuel cell power plants (2).  Pratt and
Whitney research is being sponsored by the "energy distribution community" of the franchised utilities (gas and electric) and the national pipeline companies (3).  Their Comprehensive Installation Plan, to be completed in 1972, will
test fuel cell installations in single-family and multi-
family dwellings, remote facilities, small commercial and
small industrial establishments.

Even though their plan proposes to feed the fuel cells
with piped gas, large fuel cell power plants are being considered by electric utility interests for generating capability at the substation level.

The developers feel that the units will be owned and operated by the utility companies, who will sell a service in the
same way as they do now.  In that case, the capital and operating  costs must be such that electricity provided by a
fuel cell installed on-site could be sold competitively with
electricity provided by existing generation and distribution
techniques (3).

Technical problems still have to be worked out.  Past indications are that operating temperatures and pressures may

133

lead to safety hazards.  Fuel cell operating parameters vio-
late boiler codes in many residential districts (4).  The
types of fuel that could power a fuel cell could conceivably
be wide-ranging and eventually include deliverable bottled
fuels.  The TARGET program, sponsored as it is mainly by
the gas companies, is continuing with natural gas, from which
the fuel cells of their design will generate electricity by
extracting hydrogen from the gas and combining it with oxygen from the air.  Meanwhile, work is continuing over much
of Europe in fuel cell development (5); and fuel cells using
alternate fuels can be foreseen emerging in the future.

SCALE CHARACTERISTICS

This more decentralized power source will place less demand
on the large energy producers such as fossil fuel and nuclear power plants, and fuel cells free of gas piping will
aid in the decentralization and dispersion of dwelling units
and other facilities.

COST INFORMATION

When developed and marketed they are projected to be competitive with other energy sources.

REFERENCES

(1)  Nigel Calder, "Summing Up," World in 1984.

(2)  William F. Morse, Director of Research, Columbia Gas
     System Service Corp.

(3)  William H. Podolny, Chief Engineer, Advanced Power
     Systems, Pratt and Whitney Aircraft.

(4)  Robert A. Bell, Director of Research, Con Edison.

(5)  Herbert H. Woodson, Professor of Electrical Engi-
     neering, MIT.

STAGE OF DEVELOPMENT

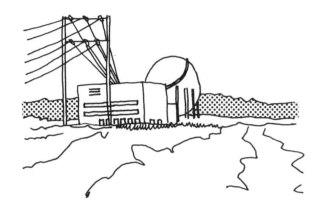

1990's  (middle)  nuclear power surpasses fossil fuel power
        generation (1)
1980's  High Temperature Gas Cooled Reactor (HTGR)
        Heavy Water Moderated Organic Cooled Reactor (HWOCR)
        Light Water Breeder Reactor (LWBR)
        Agro-Industrial Complexes with new communities as a part
1980   fusion reactor prototype plant (2)
1990   Liquid Metal Cooled Fast Breeder Reactor (3)
1990's  fusion power production (2)

The two most promising reactors being developed are the
fast breeder reactor and the fusion reactor.  Breeder reactors would be able to produce more fissile plutonium than
they consume.  Under ideal conditions they have a 7-year
doubling time (the time required to produce as much excess
fissionable material as is needed in the initial loading to
achieve critical mass).  Since more fuel is created than is
consumed, an energy source theoretically lasting forever
would be achieved.

Optimistic projections for fusion reactors suggest they will
be operational in the '90's.  Their fuel would be extracted
from water in the form of heavy hydrogen (deuterium), and
they would therefore have a cheap fuel source.

OPERATIONAL CHARACTERISTICS

Present boiling light water reactors are only 34% efficient,
the high heat of conversion causing what has been called
thermal pollution.  The AEC's back-up reactor program, due
for results in the late '70's, will produce plants with
roughly the equivalent efficiency of fossil fuel plants (about
40%), so there will be a negligible difference in efficiency
between types of plants.  In some present plants, radioactive emissions occur beyond the limits set by the AEC (4).

135

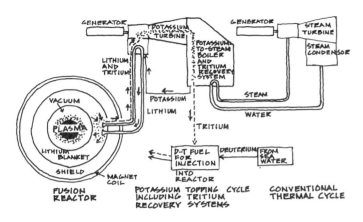

DEUTERIUM-TRITIUM FUSION POWER PLANT
ADAPTED FROM AEC DIVISION OF RESEARCH: WHY FUSION?,
CONTROLLED THERMONUCLEAR RESEARCH PROGRAM, 1970

Since the effect of strontium 90 on human and animal bones is destructive, no tolerable limits can be set. Recognizing this, the biopoly of reactor manufacturers, G.E. and Westinghouse, have announced a "zero emission" nuclear plant design which bottles and ships the nuclear waste (5). How it can be finally disposed of is still unclear and that may present an ultimate environmental problem with respect to nuclear energy production.

The "thermal pollution" problem inherent in the relatively inefficient present generation of fission reactors upsets marine ecosystems in lakes and rivers that are otherwise stable at lower temperatures. Nonetheless, this waste heat can be diverted for practical and useful purposes such as fish farming; municipal heating/cooling systems (5) and for year-round heated recreational swimming areas. The first of these purposes is currently being profitably practiced in Texas (6).

SCALE CHARACTERISTICS

With increasing energy demands, the power grid is likely to grow to include nuclear plants about 100 miles apart (6). For undeveloped desert coastal areas, especially in developing countries, large agro-industrial communities based around nuclear energy plants are an extremely likely prospect for the '80's and '90's (7). The capital investment for these centers would be in the neighborhood of 1/2 to 1 billion dollars. The complexes may become units in a world-wide power grid, capable of power distribution via satellites, microwaves, laser beams and superconductors. The AEC has preliminary plans (8) for the possibilities described.

In addition to generally increasing energy demand trends, the highly probable proliferation of electrified automated guideways in the '80's will place an even higher demand on the energy producing community than has been anticipated. However, a good portion of this unanticipated demand may be relieved by the emergence of fuel cells as decentralized, ubiquitous energy producers.

REFERENCES

(1) Robert A. Bell, Director of Research, Con Edison.

(2) Amasa Bishop, Assistant Director of Controlled Thermonuclear Research, AEC.

(3) John Bewick, "Decision Analysis in the Public Sector: An Analysis of the Atomic Energy Commission's Civilian Power Program," unpublished paper, Harvard Business School.

(4) Rochester Committee for Scientific Information, "Industrial Radioactive Waste," Bulletin No. 3, 1968.

(5) Hilary W. Szymanowski, Director of Research, Research and Development Center, Westinghouse Corp.

(6) Herbert Woodson, Professor of Electrical Engineering, MIT.

(7) Nuclear Energy Centers Industrial and Agro-Industrial Complexes Summary Report, Oak Ridge National Laboratory, 1969.

(8) Glenn Seaborg, Chairman of the U.S. Atomic Energy Commission.

STAGE OF DEVELOPMENT

The future of this type of energy production is unclear at the moment.  Practical engineering problems exist, such as the provision of duct materials to withstand the high temperatures.  After some initial research, it has been dropped by Westinghouse as by the British and French in government-sponsored projects.  Russia and Japan are still developing MHD.  The AEC sees MHD integrated with nuclear power plants so that the units would operate from the waste reactor heat.

REFERENCES

Hilary W. Szymanowski, Director of Research, Research and Development Center, Westinghouse Corp.

Lawrence Lessing, "New Ways to More Power with Less Pollution," Fortune, November 1970.

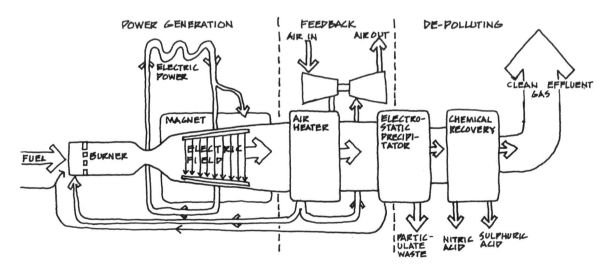

MAGNETOHYDRODYNAMIC   POWER:   SUPERSONIC  FLOW  OF  IONIZED  GASES

STAGE OF DEVELOPMENT &          Tidal power plants such as those at Passamaquoddy and Se-
SCALE CHARACTERISTICS          vern Barrage are examples of applied tidal energy.  Lunar
                               tides appear to be the only opportunity on a world-wide
                               basis, since solar tides are discernible at only a few lo-
                               cales.  An inconvenient characteristic of the power which
                               retards its use is its periodicity (its uneven performance
                               over the monthly cycle).

COST INFORMATION               Costs are as little as 1.0¢ per kwhr.

REFERENCES                     Richard L. Meier, Science and Economic Development, New
                               Patterns of Living.

TIDAL POWER PLANT AT INLET

STAGE OF DEVELOPMENT &
SCALE CHARACTERISTICS

Operational in very special locales.

The internal heat of the earth is most easily tapped through hot springs and fumarellos (steam spouts in volcanic areas). These sources are employed for power purposes mainly in Italy but they are less significant over the whole earth than tidal power.

REFERENCES

Richard L. Meier, Science and Economic Development, New Patterns of Living.

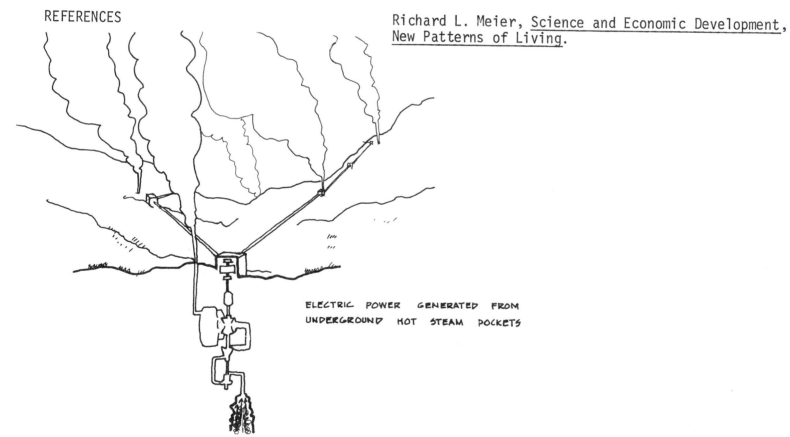

ELECTRIC POWER GENERATED FROM
UNDERGROUND HOT STEAM POCKETS

SOLAR ENERGY

STAGE OF DEVELOPMENT

Theoretical

OPERATIONAL CHARACTERISTICS

This would be accomplished by stationary synchronous orbiting satellites receiving the sun's rays on twenty-five square mile solar cell collectors, converting and beaming it down to receiver stations on earth via microwave. One advantage is that the heat of conversion takes place in outer space.

SCALE CHARACTERISTICS

One satellite could provide power for a city the size of New York.

REFERENCES

Dr. Peter Glaser, head of Engineering Sciences, Arthur D. Little.

Lawrence Lessing, "New Ways to More Power with Less Pollution," Fortune, November 1970.

SATELLITE SOLAR POWER STATION TO PRODUCE $10^7$ KW

ADAPTED FROM PETER E. GLASER, "A CONCEPT FOR A SATELLITE SOLAR POWER STATION," ARTHUR D. LITTLE, INC., CAMBRIDGE, 1970

141

## STAGE OF DEVELOPMENT

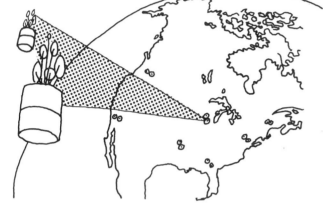

MULTI-PURPOSE SYNCHRONOUS SATELLITE SYSTEM

1973  eight-city picturephone network (1)
1974  data network installed on private line basis (1)
1970's (late) commercial broadband service linking most
       major U.S. cities
1980's (early) pervasive use of picturephones with low
       toll charges in the U.S.

The deployment of additional communications satellites will
enable global hook-up of local systems in the 1980's and
1990's.  These local systems of coaxial cables will tie individual homes and offices into the network.  A single cable
might supply a home or office with as many as 26 commercial
and educational channels, picturephone and time-sharing computer access.  Individual channels for each subscriber to
the system for personal TV can be developed by the application of state-of-the-art switching technology.

## OPERATIONAL CHARACTERISTICS

Long-haul digital carrier systems operating over coaxial
cables, microwave channels, and waveguides will provide enor-
mously increased channel capacities and data speeds.  Digital transmission will enhance data communications (the fastest growing aspect of the telephone industry) and will be
used for voice and video messages.  Waveguides will be an
important element in the network.  They are 2" copper-lined
steel pipes for carrying high-frequency millimeter waves long
distances.  Straightness and minimum curvature of channel
(similar to the constraints of an automomobile expressway)
are essential to the operation.  Waveguides are planned to
be buried 4' underground, encased in a protective conduit.
In all likelihood, they will prove adaptable to utiladors
for short runs in high density urban areas.  The system can
send the equivalent of a 24-volume set of encyclopedia in
1/10 of a second.

SCALE CHARACTERISTICS

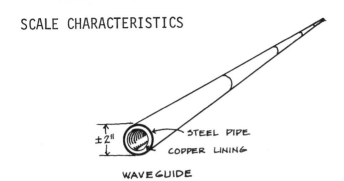

WAVEGUIDE

REFERENCES

(i) Reduction of the necessity for dense settlement patterns for reasons of communication, (ii) reduction of the necessity of short and long distance travel for information exchanging tasks, business, education, etc. (2), (iii) provision of the basis for the individual dwelling place as the nerve center for human activity in daily life, and (iv) location of many settlements    by criteria of access to recreation, agreeable climate, and natural beauty (3).

(1)  H. I. Romnes, Chairman of the Board, ATT, Third Quarter Report, 1970.

(2)  John Pierce (Bell Labs), "Private Television Instead of Travel," in World in 1984, Vol. 1, Nigel Calder, ed.

(3)  Paul Baran, Martin Greenberger, Urban Node in the Information Network, RAND.

STAGE OF DEVELOPMENT

1971  operational
1980  will serve 40% to 60% of the U.S. population

There are presently approximately 2400 community antenna or cable television systems operating in 49 states and the Virgin Islands.  These systems serve about 3900 communities. Estimated annual revenues are approximately $300 million. Approximately 60,000 people are employed in the operation of CATV systems, service and equipment supply (1).

Average system size: 1900 subscribers.

People served:  Estimating 3.3 persons per home (service to 4,500,000 homes), CATV systems relay television signals to almost 15 million viewers, or about 7% of the U.S. television audience.  In addition to the approximately 2400 operating CATV systems, there were, as of January, 1970 approximately 2100 additional communities where CATV applications were pending before local governing bodies.  Industry leaders have estimated that, assuming reasonable regulation, the CATV industry will in 10 years serve 30 million homes, or over half of the nation's population (2). This will be through around 7500 systems and have annual revenues of $3 billion, a building investment of $5 billion, and will directly employ 750,000 people (2).

OPERATIONAL CHARACTERISTICS

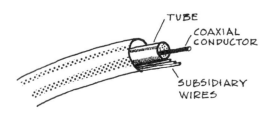

TUBE
COAXIAL CONDUCTOR
SUBSIDIARY WIRES

Cable television or CATV is a superior way of receiving television pictures.  Broadcast signals received on sensitive antennae at a specially selected site, are fed through a network of coaxial cables to the homes of individual viewers (1).

The cable hook-up consists of:

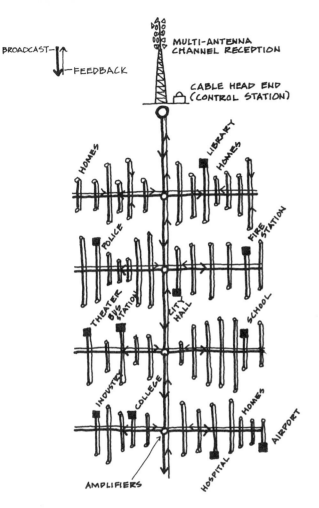

BROADCAST

FEEDBACK

MULTI-ANTENNA CHANNEL RECEPTION

CABLE HEAD END (CONTROL STATION)

HOMES

LIBRARY HOMES

POLICE

FIRE STATION

THEATER BUS STATION

CITY HALL

SCHOOL

INDUSTRY

COLLEGE

HOMES

HOSPITAL

AIRPORT

AMPLIFIERS

30-PLUS CHANNEL VIDEO CABLE DISTRIBUTION WITH LIMITED, NARROW BAND RESPONSE CAPACITY

SCALE CHARACTERISTICS

1. Tower selected for good reception.
2. Antenna system so that there are separate anten-
   nas for each channel to be received (sometimes
   distant signals are relayed to the tower by one or
   more microwave transmitters).
3. "Headend", a small control station at the foot of
   the tower where signals are brought up to maximum
   strength and clarity.  (Here, some of the signals
   may be rechanneled, i.e., cable systems put UHF
   stations on empty VHF channels.)
4. Amplifiers, placed at distances of 1500-2000 feet
   along the trunk line into town to keep signals
   strong.
5. "Feeder" lines, "tapoffs" and "housedrops" which
   carry the signals from the main cable to individual
   homes (1).  This is essentially a tree system.

Coaxial cable consists of:

1. Copper wire in the center like lead in a pencil.
2. Insulated by polyethylene foam (the major part of
   the diameter in cross-section).
3. Coated with a tubular shield of braided copper or
   seamless aluminum sheath.

When a current or signal is introduced into the cable an
electromagnetic interaction takes place between the center
wire and the surrounding sheath.  The interaction prevents
currents from radiating off the cable.  This is the secret
of the cable's key characteristic -- its immense capacity
for carrying electronic signals, data and information (3).

Personal channel CATV broadcasting capability is possible
from the home but has special technical problems given the
tree-structured distribution system.  Upstream transmission
can be accomplished by frequency or time multiplexing which
would require new types of switching; or it can be accomplished by rediffusion which requires a special two-way

145

cable-pair plus special switching gear. With a point-to-point switching capability developed, such as now exists to connect telephone subscribers to each other, a rediffusion system could approach a TV-bandwidth (4).

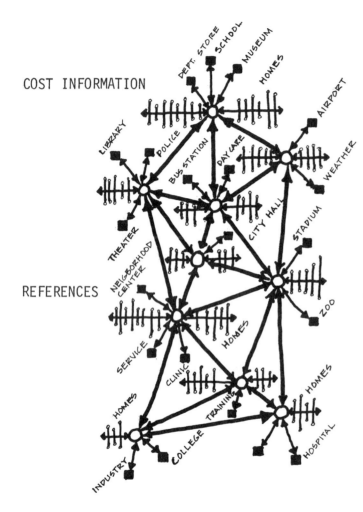

COST INFORMATION

REFERENCES

30-PLUS CHANNEL BROADBAND NETWORK WITH TWO-WAY LIMITED SWITCHING CAPABILITY

The installation fee usually runs from $10 to $20, and the monthly service charge is about $5.

"...One of Cable TV's great potentials is its inherent ability to end the economy of scarcity on which the power of the present TV broadcasting oligarchy is solidly based." (3) Many new CATV rigs are being built for twenty-channel reception. San Jose, California is installing one for 42 channel capacity. Experts believe that the cable could carry as many as 26 channels with present technology (4).

(1)   "Cable," Radical Software, No. 2, 1970.

(2)   NCTA News Release, March 25, 1970 as quoted in Radical Software, No. 2, 1970.

(3)   Ralph L. Smith, "The Wired Nation," Nation, May 18, 1970.

(4)   John E. Ward, unpublished paper, MIT, 1970.

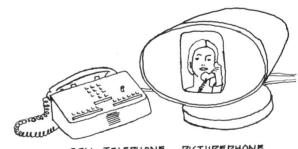

BELL TELEPHONE   PICTUREPHONE

146

STAGE OF DEVELOPMENT

1971  basic technology
1980's  basic world-wide hook-up

The technology exists today to provide every person on earth with a direct electromagnetic audio-visual communications channel to every other person.  IT&T is technologically ready to produce computerized, battery powered, hand-held, touch-tone video-phones (1).

The technology has also been developed to plug these wireless videophones into film printers, audio-visual recorders, xerox and linotype machines.

OPERATIONAL CHARACTERISTICS

The video portion of the call can be presented on a thin plastic screen containing microscopic bubbles of three different gases (one for each of the basic colors) which will provide a high definition color picture according to the variations of electrical potential across each bubble.  This is being called a "plasma screen".  Everything ever published will eventually be available as will the collective information of all individuals within the hook-up (1).

SCALE CHARACTERISTICS

Local and world-wide.

COST INFORMATION

The basic charge for a wireless video-phone could be about fifteen dollars per month.  The cost of a three minute call via stationary overhead satellite to anyone anywhere in the world could be as little as one dollar.  The procedure required to initiate a call with a videophone automatically would alert the local billing center which would keep an accounting of calls for all subscribers.

REFERENCES

(1)  Don Benson, "Neurone Cluster Grope," Radical Software, No. 2, 1970.

DICK TRACY created by Chester Gould, Copyrighted 1971, Chicago Tribune-New York News Syndicate.

STAGE OF DEVELOPMENT

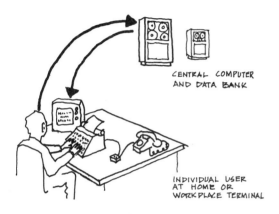

CENTRAL COMPUTER
AND DATA BANK

INDIVIDUAL USER
AT HOME OR
WORKPLACE TERMINAL

1975-1980  limited application
1980's  widespread application

Time-sharing computers as a public service system and major community resource are technologically possible now.  Even though public demand for this service is not great at this time, it is bound to grow as more people are exposed to the usefulness of computers and as computer technology itself becomes more useful through the development of "naive languages", pattern recognition, voice translation, and increasing use of graphic displays (especially cathode ray tubes), all of which are forecast for development for more common use in the middle and late '70's.  If present trends continue, virtually everyone in the United States will have access to a computer by 1980 (1).

Institutional constraints present the major hurdles to the realization of this service (2).

1.  Decisions from FCC are needed on CATV as a common carrier or a network-owned venture.
2.  Federal legislation on privacy protection is needed to insure public confidence, together with hardware that can be developed that is foolproof and tamper-proof to unwanted access to private data.

Entrepreneurial skills are acknowledged to be the major missing ingredient in this service.  This requires a party who is willing and capable of organizing the system and bringing the interests together (2,3).  Risk-sharing through a consortium of the municipal agency supplying the service and one or several large corporations such as Sears and Roebuck has been suggested as one way to start the program.

Initially, large-scale public computer utilities will occur in education as teaching aids and in consumer purchasing as illustrated data files at stores made available through their marketing budget. Presently, project INTREX at MIT provides the equivalent of a remote-access library where through a typewriter keyboard and cathode ray tube display, a user can quickly search through the archives by subject sets and call up the summaries of several documents covering one topic or a full document itself -- page by page. As part of the system, pages of special interest can be retrieved by a microfilm and xerox process.

OPERATIONAL CHARACTERISTICS

Uses of the home computer link would initially be for computing taxes, teaching aids for children's homework, access to central data files for encyclopedic information (analogous to a library) and retrieval of hard copy, answering the telephone and communicating when the family is out. Some similar systems are already in use commercially in department stores and banks (3).

Further, the computer could be used for keeping inventory accounts of household supplies, doing the shopping and ordering supplies, assisting in business activity, teaching aid for ongoing education for all members of the family, and recreation and games.

SCALE CHARACTERISTICS

(i) Reduction of the necessity for dense settlement patterns for reasons of communication, (ii) reduction of the necessity of short and long-distance travel for information-exchanging tasks (Business conferences, education, shopping can be done in the dwelling), (iii) provision of the basis for the individual dwelling place as the nerve center for human activity in daily life, (iv) location of settlements by criteria of access to recreation, agreeable climate, and natural beauty (3).

COST INFORMATION

As more people become exposed to these services, more demand will be generated for them to be installed in dwellings, given reasonable cost (2). The average household cannot afford several hundred dollars a month for such a system; something more in line with typical monthly phone bills is more realistic. This sets the base cost of the user charges at very roughly 15 to 30 dollars per month. Included in this cost would be the home terminal (4) and in all probability some minimum amount of computer time.

REFERENCES

(1) Earl Joseph, "Towards a Fifth Generation," Science Journal, October 1970.

(2) R. M. Fano, "The Computer Utility and the Community," IEEE International Convention Record, Part 12, 1967.

(3) Paul Baran, Martin Greenberger, Urban Node in the Information Network, RAND.

(4) Dr. Ralph Gomory, Director of Research, IBM.

COMMUNICATIONS                          VIDEO CASSETTES

STAGE OF DEVELOPMENT                     Operational and being marketed by CBS, RCA, Sony, Hitashi
                                        and others.

OPERATIONAL CHARACTERISTICS             Video cassettes enable the individual viewer to utilize tapes
                                        of his own choosing, whether of his own making or from a public
                                        or private library.

SCALE CHARACTERISTICS                   It is capable of integration into local community TV broad-
                                        cast and network facilities, educational, library and cen-
                                        tral data bank resources.

COST INFORMATION                        CBS EVR system presently costs $795; CBS predicts it will
                                        cost about $300 in two years.  RCA expects its system to
                                        market for less than $400 in 1972.  Sony's $400 Video-
                                        cassette system, which will allow the owner to tape and
                                        play back programs he receives on his TV, will be avail-
                                        able in late 1971.

REFERENCES                              Boston Globe, August 14, 1970; Time Magazine, August 10,
                                        1970; Wall Street Journal Editorial Staff, The Innova-
                                        tors, 1968.

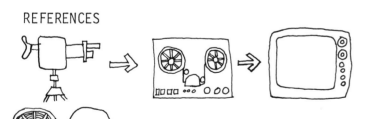

IMAGE    SOUND
FILM/DISC/TAPE/  ⇒  RECORDING AND  ⇒  VIEWING
HOLOGRAPHIC         PLAYBACK
TAPE/EXPOSURE

STAGE OF DEVELOPMENT

1971  availability
1980's  general use in the U.S.


OPERATIONAL CHARACTERISTICS

The Japanese newspaper Asahi Shimbun has been licensed
to transmit facsimile newspapers into homes by radio.  A
receiving set was developed in cooperation with Toshiba E-
lectric Co. and produces in 5 minutes a newspaper page 12
1/2 by 18".  RCA is also developing a facsimile reproducer.


SCALE CHARACTERISTICS

Facsimile records of all kinds can be available in the home.
The necessity for dense settlement patterns for reasons
of communication and data exchange will be reduced.  Information access and flow will expand.


COST INFORMATION

A receiving set can be supplied under mass production for
$50 to $100.  Like the television receiver, this device
could be expected to drop increasingly in price after the
initial marketing.  Presently a large part of the costs of
this service is in the price of the paper (.05 to .10 a
sheet).  This price could also be expected to drop through
the application of more advanced paper and machine technologies.

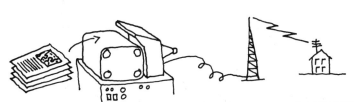

ORIGINAL → SCANNER/PRINT OUT → BROADCAST → DESTINATION

FACSIMILE AND PHOTOGRAPHIC PRINTOUT

STAGE OF DEVELOPMENT

1971  operational
1970's (late)  general application

OPERATIONAL CHARACTERISTICS

Holographic Signs and graphics can be displayed without being supported by physical structures.  The image is projected by tele-optics devices and appears to hang in mid-air.  R & D is in process of current application to highway signs. Display can be read in all light and weather conditions (1). Images can be easily changed.  Projected uses:  highway signs, outdoor and point-of-sale advertising signs, visual information aids for use in the city (direction, time, events).

Recent concepts of "soft architecture" or "responsive environments" such as those of Warren Brodey, could be achieved by this technology.

LONG RANGE DEVELOPMENTS:  Three-dimensional architectural or sculptural light forms projected in the cityscape that can be (i) programmed for change and (ii) dynamically changed to be responsive to, and interact with, the users' psychological needs in real time through sensor pickup and processing of user psycho-physiological data (1990's).

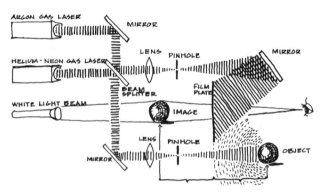

ILLUSTRATION OF HOLOGRAM PRINCIPLE: DIAGRAM OF THREE-COLOR HOLOGRAM MADE FROM BEAMS FROM TWO LASERS (ADAPTED FROM "GETTING THE WHOLE PICTURE FROM HOLOGRAPHY," FORTUNE, SEPT. 1971)

SCALE CHARACTERISTICS

(i) A reevaluation of the definition of architecture as being static and solid to include dynamic and non-solid elements; (ii) more immediate communication and exchange of information with individuals, groups and mass crowds out of doors; and (iii) reduction of cultural importance of built-form for structural-esthetic reasons.  Increase of importance of image-form for information reasons.

HOLOGRAM AS CIVIC ART/DRAMA

154

COST INFORMATION

Unknown.  Projection equipment may trade off with sign structures.

REFERENCES

(1)  Harry Forster, "Holosigns," <u>Traffic Engineering</u>, April 1968.

PROJECTED   HOLOGRAPHIC   SIGNAL

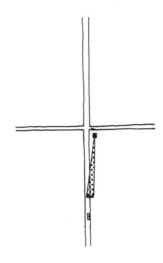

STAGE OF DEVELOPMENT

1972  laboratory demonstration
1980's  operational (1)

State-of-the-art is capable of projecting a static 3-D picture on a large holographically etched screen (1).  Color 3-D movies are predicted for laboratory development in 1972 (2).

LONG-RANGE DEVELOPMENTS:  Instantaneous TV broadcast of full color, 3-D, high-resolution image to dwellings and offices.

OPERATIONAL CHARACTERISTICS

Given stereo information from two conventional video cameras, it is possible that a laser projector in combination with a holographically etched screen could produce 3-D stereo projection video without the use of polaroid glasses or other physical encumbrances.  This technique is presently possible with a laser projector.

SCALE CHARACTERISTICS

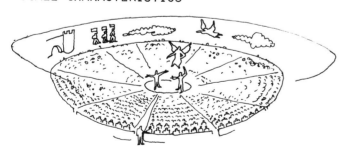

HOLOGRAPHIC  THEATER-IN-THE-ROUND
WHO ARE THE AUDIENCE ?  WHO ARE THE ACTORS/HOLOGRAMS ?

Using a 360° pickup system with a conventional Vidicon camera system, and a 360° overhead laser  projector scanning the recorded video onto a circular wall, viewers would receive a complete 360° view of the camera's environment over a vertical angle of 60°.  The viewer would be standing or seated in a large circular room seeing in all directions and having difficulty determining the reality of the environment (3).

REFERENCES

(1)  Dr. Dennis Gabor, CBS.

(2)  Dr. Harper Q. North, TRW.

(3)  Lloyd G. Cross, "The Potential Impact of the Laser on the Video Medium," <u>Radical Software</u>, No. 2, 1970.

HOME VACUUM SEWERAGE (LILJENDAHL SYSTEM)

STAGE OF DEVELOPMENT

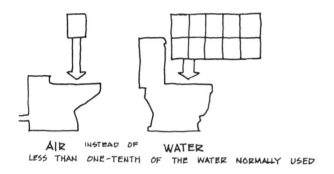

AIR INSTEAD OF WATER

LESS THAN ONE-TENTH OF THE WATER NORMALLY USED

Even though this system has been tested and proved reliable and economically feasible in Sweden and in the Bahamas it is currently experiencing difficulty being accepted in the U.S. for the following reasons (1):

1. Specification Code restrictions.
2. Acceptance of this innovative system by unions and tradesmen is objectionable in some locations.
3. Each installation must be engineered for pumps and disposal lines.
4. It is thought that the existence of pumps in the system would require the availability of maintenance personnel more than conventional systems would.
5. Royalties on the Swedish patents are considered high.

The system has been installed in a large elementary school in Lafayette, Indiana; and according to the developer, it is living up to all best expectations (2).

OPERATIONAL CHARACTERISTICS

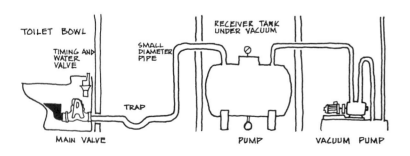

TOILET BOWL

TIMING AND WATER VALVE

SMALL DIAMETER PIPE

RECEIVER TANK UNDER VACUUM

TRAP

MAIN VALVE

PUMP

VACUUM PUMP

This is an advanced sewerage system for use at the point of collection. It uses air in lieu of water for sewage evacuation, and separates black water (toilet waste) from gray water (other liquid wastes). The black water from the special water closet is conducted by vacuum piping to a collection or treatment facility, whereas the gray water is evacuated by gravity, as in standard installations.

The system is a water saver. For each toilet flush, a standard system consumes five gallons of water. The Liljendahl system uses less than 1/2 gallon. This water is mixed with 20 gallons of air for the flushing action. A greatly reduced volume of effluent is discharged (40%) and consequently, the aerobic process can be employed with increased efficiency. Since the gray water is separated from the black, it can be recycled for non-household purposes or purified and recycled for household purposes. To make a recycling system feasible without costly treatment equipment, detergents with phosphates and other nonbiodegradables would have to be avoided in original water use. Such avoidance is now a major trend in public environmental policy actions.

The system avoids the use of vent pipes. It also uses 2" soil pipes from the toilet, instead of the conventional 4" pipes. This characteristic is a source of some plumbing code difficulties which flatly specify 4" as a minimum size soil pipe.

SCALE CHARACTERISTICS

For the Liljendahl system to be economical several of the above drawbacks would have to be overcome. An installation of between 100 and 200 units is considered minimum to achieve economies of scale.

REFERENCES

(1) Robert J. Wentz, Chief Product Design Engineer, Eljer Plumbingware Division, Wallace-Murray Corp.

(2) J. Fred Harless, Vice President and General Manager, Lafayette Division, National Homes Corp.

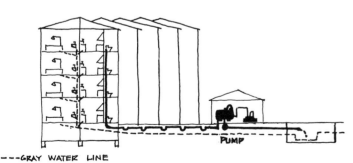

- - - GRAY WATER LINE
—— BLACK WATER LINE
    APARTMENT COMPLEX       VACUUM PUMP   CONVENTIONAL WASTE TREATMENT EQUIPMENT

PUMP

GRINDER PUMP/PRESSURE SYSTEM

STAGE OF DEVELOPMENT

Westinghouse Corporation, General Electric Corporation and several other companies are developing and marketing portable sewage systems for multi-family and individual dwellings.

OPERATIONAL CHARACTERISTICS

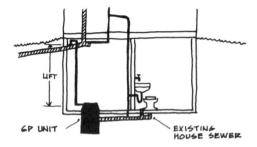

The sewage collection system by the Environment/One Corporation is a small unit the size of a trash can and is located in the dwelling. It receives sewage from a standard soil line, grinds it into fine particles and distributes it under pressure to either a septic tank or a community sewerage line. This can be accomplished against gravity or in hilly terrain where a gravity sewer cannot be used. This method is especially applicable to dispersed dwelling units.

SCALE CHARACTERISTICS

Individual home units 4' by 15' can serve eight persons. Multiple dwelling unit installations can serve up to 50 persons.

REFERENCES

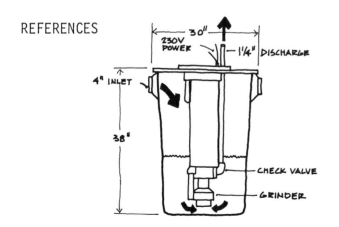

Urban Hydrology Research Council, ASCE.

WASTE TAMER

STAGE OF DEVELOPMENT

Operational

OPERATIONAL CHARACTERISTICS

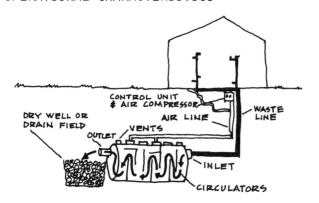

An improved commercial home sewage treatment unit, manufactured by Environmental Services, Inc. and marketed under the name of Waste Tamer, is a chambered underground
tank that receives sewage, pumps air through it to speed the
aerobic digestive action and drains the effluent into a
dry well or field drain.  The control unit housing the air
compressor and system controls is about the size of a win-
dow air conditioner and can be placed in the garage or service core of the dwelling.  The system is said to reduce
biological oxygen demand and solids up to 90% compared to
30% for standard septic tank systems.

SCALE CHARACTERISTICS

For individual and multi-family units.

COST INFORMATION

$2500 to $2700 installed for an individual Waste Tamer
home system.

REFERENCES

Arnold P. Consdorf, "The Great Garbage Gap," Appliance Manufacturer, October 1970.

161

MUNICIPAL SEWAGE TREATMENT (UNOX SYSTEM)

STAGE OF DEVELOPMENT

Operational

OPERATING CHARACTERISTICS

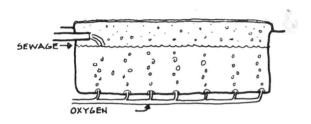

Unox is a process for municipal sewage treatment marketed by Union Carbide Corp. (1). It is essentially an updated version of the "activated sludge" process which exposes a mixture of raw sewage and sludge to the air, causing aerbic digestion of the waste. Oxygen is bubbled through the waste water in enclosed tanks, thereby speeding bacterial action. This cuts down the time needed to hold the waste water in the tanks and speeds the entire process.

REFERENCES

(1) "Treating Waste in Greater Haste," Business Week, November 7, 1970.

AUTOMATED VACUUM COLLECTION (AVAC)

STAGE OF DEVELOPMENT

The Envirogenics Division of Aerojet General Corporation is the United States' outlet for the A.B. Centralsug vacuum solid waste collection system of Sweden.  Swedish installations have been tested since 1961 and include laundry and trash systems for hospitals as well as large residential trash collection systems.  Six of these installations are presently operating in Sweden and 12 additional ones are under contract in several European countries.  The company claims to be installing two miles of the AVAC system piping in the Walt Disney World of Florida (1).

OPERATIONAL CHARACTERISTICS

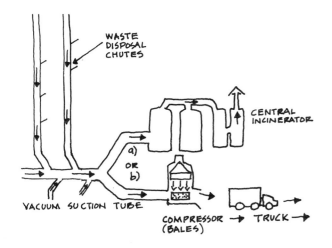

WASTE DISPOSAL CHUTES

CENTRAL INCINERATOR

a) OR b)

VACUUM SUCTION TUBE

COMPRESSOR (BALES) → TRUCK →

The operation is simple: refuse from dwellings and other buildings is collected by vacuum through 16"to 24" steel pipes to a transfer station for further processing such as grinding, compacting or disposal.

Waste material can be either bagged or left loose.  The system operates smoothly with no history of clogging. Air velocities are 10,000 CFM for a 20" pipe (approximately 60 miles per hour).

COMPATIBLE SYSTEMS:  The AVAC system is very compatible (i) with the Utilador concept, (ii) set up with slurry waste collection, and (iii) with Prepacked Refuse.  The last two depend on distance to the point of final treatment.

SCALE CHARACTERISTICS

AVAC claims to be cost-effective in high density environments where large quantities of solid waste are generated;

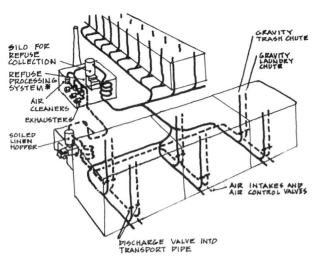

SILO FOR
REFUSE
COLLECTION
REFUSE
PROCESSING
SYSTEM *
AIR
CLEANERS
EXHAUSTERS
SOILED
LINEN
HOPPER

GRAVITY
TRASH CHUTE

GRAVITY
LAUNDRY
CHUTE

AIR INTAKES AND
AIR CONTROL VALVES

DISCHARGE VALVE INTO
TRANSPORT PIPE

* INCINERATOR SHOWN HERE.
ALTERNATIVES CAN BE COMPACTOR
OR GRINDER.

AVAC SYSTEM SERVING HIGH-RISE BUILDING CLUSTER,
DUAL REFUSE AND LAUNDRY SYSTEM IN NEAREST BLDG.

REFERENCES

and for medium-to-long range lateral transfer or for centralized collection from multiple gravity chutes such as would be the case in vertically-organized multiple dwelling units, hospitals and offices (1). A maximum two mile distance from points of generation to point of collection is considered economical (2).

BENEFITS:

- capital cost of collection trucks saved
- operating cost of trucks and collection personnel saved
- time saved in handling refuse for householder and office personnel
- noise pollution from barrel handling and truck compacting avoided
- overall community trip times shortened by the avoidance of collection truck interference in traffic

(1) Peter H. Luiten, Manager of Marketing, Pneumatic Transport Systems, Envirogenics Co.

(2) Iraj Zandi and John A. Hayden, "Are Pipelines the Answer to Waste Collection Dilemma?", Environmental Science and Technology, Vol. 3, No. 9, September 1969.

STAGE OF DEVELOPMENT

An investigation supported by a Public Health Service re-search grant was conducted at the University of Pennsyl-vania carefully examining this system (1).  The study con-cluded that (i) grinding and shredding all kinds of muni-cipal waste is practical with a Wascon Pulper and a Dorr-Oliver Gorator set up in series; (ii) when converted to a slurry (as high as 12% by weight) by the addition of the sewage, the shredded waste has qualities conducive to pipe-line transport; and (iii) from a comparative study of cen-tral Philadelphia the discounted costs and benefits of the system over a fifty-year period showed the Pneumo-slurry system to be cheaper than truck collection for a 50-mile-distant disposal site; and, with improved technology, com-petitive with truck collection for a 20-mile-distant dis-posal site (1).

OPERATIONAL CHARACTERISTICS

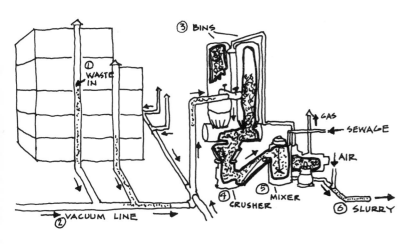

① WASTE IN

② VACUUM LINE

③ BINS

④ CRUSHER

⑤ MIXER

⑥ SLURRY

GAS

SEWAGE

AIR

Essentially, this is a system for complete pipeline trans-port of solid waste from origin to point of final treat-ment (1).  The process is two-stage: (i) pneumatic col-lection from source of waste by the AVAC system and (ii) grinding, shredding and conversion to slurry at a transfer station and subsequent piping to final processing point for disposal or recycling.

For final treatment this system would be compatible with many of the traditional processes and newer process such as wet oxidation (the cost effectiveness of this system is still unknown).

A strong trend in solid waste treatment is toward recycling. Since reuse systems utilize crushers, it is possible that

165

crushing of solid waste for pipe transport will be the first
step of a recycling process. It is unclear what effects
the mixture of sewage in the waste would cause in the sorting process. For reclamation purposes, the initial mixing
may have to avoid black water as the transport material.

SCALE CHARACTERISTICS

The addition of the Slurry pipe system to the AVAC system
is economically warranted when the transport distance is
more than about two miles, and/or when the total volume
of waste handled by the pipe is excessive. By contrast,
a water slurry pipeline becomes less expensive per ton-
mile as the haulage distance and volume increase (1).

REFERENCES

(1)  Iraj Zandi and John A. Hayden, "Are Pipelines the
     Answer to Waste Collection Dilemma?", Environmental
     Science and Technology, Vol. 3, No. 9, September 1969.

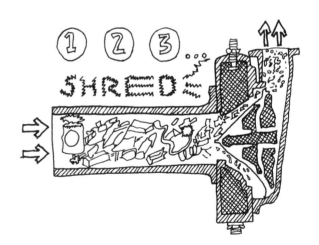

SHREDDER: ALTERNATIVE FIRST STEP IN
PIPELINE TRANSPORT - INSTEAD OF CRUSHER
AND MIXER

PREPACKED REFUSE COLLECTION SYSTEM

STAGE OF DEVELOPMENT

Operational in England.

OPERATIONAL CHARACTERISTICS

This system receives collected solid waste at a central transfer station and by mechanical action compresses it into a cartridge approximately seven feet in diameter by 21 feet long for conveyance to the point of final processing.

REFERENCES

Developing New Communities, Report to HUD, prepared by David Crane et al., 1968.

① WASTE COLLECTION

② COMPRESSION

③ CARTRIDGE

④ TRUCK TO DISPOSAL

WASTE MANAGEMENT

COLLECTION

GARCHEY COLLECTION SYSTEM

STAGE OF DEVELOPMENT

Operational

OPERATIONAL CHARACTERISTICS

This system receives and temporarily stores solid waste in an undercounter unit. Upon demand the refuse is washed through a waste tube pipe to a central collection chamber. Then the waste may be removed by compacting it and trucking it out, or by a number of other ways.

SCALE CHARACTERISTICS

Multi-family dwellings.

REFERENCES

Flats and Houses, Her Majesty's Stationery Office, 1958.

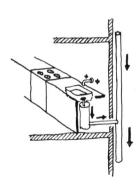

WASTE MANAGEMENT

TREATMENT

PYROLYSIS DISPOSAL SYSTEM

STAGE OF DEVELOPMENT

Operational

OPERATIONAL CHARACTERISTICS

Pyrolysis involves destructive distillation in an inert or oxygen free atmosphere, usually carried out in batches.

Among the advanced methods of refuse processing the pyrolysis system ranks high in terms of economic feasibility. However, the outputs of this process result in char, liquids, gas and some ash; and unless a use can be found for these intermediates, except for the gas, they constitute another disposal problem. It appears doubtful that any significant credit can be obtained from the sale of these pyrolysis products (1).

But with application of higher temperatures (1000° C) all that results is gas and ash. The economics accrue if the energy generated in the process is used to produce power. Present estimates show a strong possiblity for the process to be self-supporting (2).

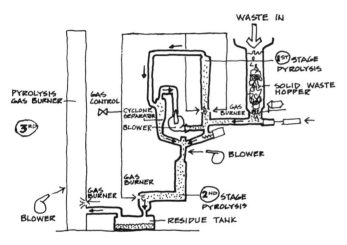

PYROLYSIS-COMBUSTION UNIT (DEVELOPMENTAL) FOR PROCESSING SOLID WASTES

SCALE CHARACTERISTICS

Municipal

REFERENCES

(1)  Adel F. Sarofim, "Pyrolysis," Summer Study in the Management of Solid Wastes, Urban Systems Laboratory, MIT.

(2)  Environmental Quality: The First Annual Report of the Council on Environmental Quality, The White House, 1970.

CPU-400 DISPOSAL SYSTEM

STAGE OF DEVELOPMENT

This system under development by the Combustion Power Company of Palo Alto is said to be a promising concept in solid waste management (1).

OPERATIONAL CHARACTERISTICS

A fluidized-bed incinerator burns solid waste at high pressure, which produces hot gases, which power a turbine, which in turn drives an electric generator. The generator whould provide 10% of the power requirements of the community providing the refuse. The system can utilize the vacuum produced by the gas turbine to draw refuse to the incinerator through transport lines as long as six miles.

SCALE CHARACTERISTICS

Municipal

REFERENCES

(1) Environmental Quality: The First Annual Report of the Council on Environmental Quality, The White House, 1970.

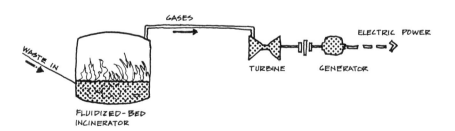

WASTE MANAGEMENT
TREATMENT

COMPOSTING DISPOSAL (BIOSTABILIZATION)

STAGE OF DEVELOPMENT

Operational

OPERATIONAL CHARACTERISTICS

Inorganic materials such as metal and glass are separated; the remainder is converted through composting to a peat-like organic fertilizer and soil conditioner to be sold commercially. This method has not yet proved successful, but cannot be ruled out on the basis of economics at the present stage of investigation (1), even though it does not appear promising at this time.

SCALE CHARACTERISTICS

Municipal

REFERENCES

(1)  C. G. Golueke and P. H. McGaukey, Comprehensive Studies of Solid Waste Management, Sanitary Engineering Research Laboratory, College of Engineering and School of Public Health, Berkeley, January 1969.

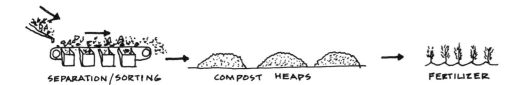

SEPARATION/SORTING          COMPOST HEAPS          FERTILIZER

ANAEROBIC DIGESTION

STAGE OF DEVELOPMENT

Experimental

OPERATIONAL CHARACTERISTICS

This is a process of disposal of all solid wastes through the application of sewage sludge and anaerobic action in a central processing plant. This treatment is still experimental but appears to take a considerable amount of time for processing. Some materials such as wood are for all pracical purposes inert to the action (1). This system does not appear promising at this time.

REFERENCES

(1)  C. G. Golueke and P. H. McGaukey, Comprehensive Studies of Solid Waste Management, Sanitary Engineering Research Laboratory, College of Engineering and School of Public Health, Berkeley, January 1969.

172

STAGE OF DEVELOPMENT

1971   home solid waste treatment capability
1976   recycling water systems for commercial use (2)
1980's   recycling water systems for dwellings
1980's   integrated waste, water and heating and cooling
           systems for dwellings

Research and development in home waste treatment concepts, and in commercial and domestic water recycling concepts is being or has been recently undertaken by several companies.

1.  Grumman Aerospace in an Operation Breakthrough Type B proposal outlines a system based on two spin-offs from their aerospace R & D.  The system balances household flow patterns.

    Excess heat from household appliances that is ordinarily dissipated within the dwelling or vented to the outside (such as through conventional flue furnace) is used in an evaporator-condenser for water reclamation and building heating.

    Water consumption is reduced by purifying gray water (water from the lavatory, bath, kitchen sink, dishwasher, and laundry) and recycling it for reuse in laundry, shower and toilet.  Heat pumps operating over long periods meet heating and cooling demands by using heat stored in hot water tanks (1).

2.  Westinghouse Corporation is engaged in R & D activity on various components of a complete water and waste treatment system for the individual dwelling, with make-up water provided by rain.  On balance, the dwelling inputs would be fuel, foodstuffs and other commodities and the outputs, non-toxic gas and ash (2).

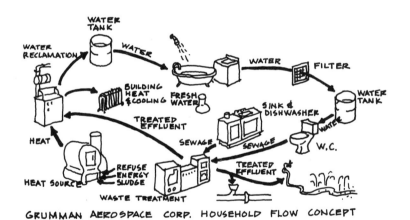

GRUMMAN AEROSPACE CORP. HOUSEHOLD FLOW CONCEPT

3. One company believes that recycling water systems will occur first in commercial applications. This company sees its big customers, within the next five years, as the U.S. Navy (which is committed to federal ecological conservation policies) and large laundries and laundromats, which are consumers of enormous quantities of water (average of 125,000 gallons per day) and are great drains on municipal water supplies. The recycled water could be bacteriologically pure enough to drink but still carry non-biodegradables such as phosphates, which impart a detergent flavor. Filtering out the non-biodegradables would constitute a problem if the water were to be considered potable.

One problem in recycling waste water for drinking purposes is psychological; and for it to ever be considered potable (even though it could be pure), it would take major changes in users' attitudes. However, with the future use of such systems by astronauts on long space missions, public attitudes may alter in the late 1980's.

While R & D into integrated life support systems goes on, the basis exists, through presently available home appliances, for the effective treatment of most domestic solid waste at its source. This can be accomplished at the individual dwelling with three waste appliances: garbage grinders, smokeless incinerators, and compactors. The wet garbage can be ground up and moved into the sewerage line; combustible solid waste (including wet garbage) can be burned and reduced to ash; and bottles, cans and plastics can be compacted and collected on a once-a-month basis.

Smokeless incinerators, manufactured by the Calcinator Corporation, the Martin Corporation and the Warm Morning Corporation have been in use for several years. The units have afterburners that produce an odorless and virtually smokeless condition. They can be placed within the home. In some cases, they are able to provide a 90% reduction in weight and

WHIRLPOOL COMPACTOR BIN
COMPACTS TRASH IN 4:1 RATIO

RESIDENTIAL GAS
INCINERATOR

CALCINATOR

OPERATIONAL CHARACTERISTICS

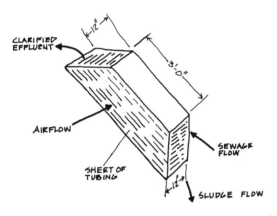

INDIVIDUAL BIOREACTOR UNIT (GRUMMAN)

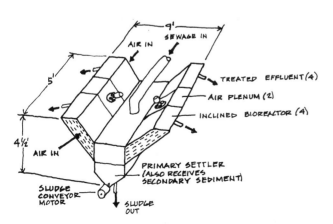

GANGED OXYGENATING BIOREACTORS (OBR'S)

volume of combustible refuse.

The smokeless-odorless claim is not entirely accurate, however. A small percentage of smoke and gas is released into the air. But this amount meets the requirements of the American Gas Association Laboratories under the USASI Z-21-6 Standards. Gas incinerators are currently approved in all but four major U.S. cities: Los Angeles, St. Louis, Philadelphia and Kansas City, Mo. (4).

The Grumman system is not a completely closed loop. There still is sewage water disposal in winter, and the problem of disposal of noncombustibles such as plastics, bottles, tin cans and other such objects. Such a system would thus require the home owner to separate these type objects from refuse for collection (3). Grumman project engineers estimate that winter fresh water requirements of 300 gal/day for a family of four could be reduced to 62 gal/day. Sewage effluent, figured at 70% of daily intake, would be reduced from 210 gal/day in winter to 86 gal/day (3).

In the summer, when water consumption doubles because of landscape irrigation, the daily requirement would drop from 600 gal/day to 181 gal. There would be no sewage water discharged, since it would be used for irrigation which can be done safely with proper precautions (3).

The two basic components of the Grumman system are

1. A sewage treatment oxygenating bioreactor of a kind developed for a life support system for the Mars manned space flight. It is one-fifteenth the size of commercially available units. But because of uneven peak times in household water use, a surge tank would be required which would then amount to a total space requirement similar to a standard septic tank.
2. An evaporator-condensor in which gray water is evaporated and passed through a fine filter which removes

particles as small as bacteria. The vapor is then
condensed and collected in a storage tank for reuse.

SCALE CHARACTERISTICS

CONSEQUENCES: (i) Reduction of the necessity for dense settlement patterns for reasons of economical water-line and
sewerage layouts; (ii) settlements can be dispersed and located by criteria of easier access to recreation, agreeable
climate and natural beauty by application of this system with
compatible systems such as satellite TV broadcast, facsimile
printers, home fuel cells, and computer utility; (iii) more
usable land for each dwelling or dwelling group and more private open space; (iv) because of the greater efficiency of
the sewage process, less clogging of leaching fields would
occur, permitting smaller fields and higher density land use;
and (v) less pollution spread with recycling done on a
decentralized basis.

COST INFORMATION

In the Grumman proposal it was estimated that refuse disposal costs of $4.25 billion annually could be reduced to
$1.20 billion if such a system were installed nation-wide.

Savings in secondary sewage treatment plants, which cities
will need to build to meet projected new home construction,
could be as much as $1.5 billion annually, the report added,
if the integrated system were installed in all new houses (3).

Incineration of all combustible household refuse would reduce
present refuse disposal requirements by a factor of five (3).
Hardware for the system probably would cost twice what present household heating and sewage disposal equipment costs.
Since the savings would be community-wide, a tax abatement
plan might be necessary to encourage the home owner to adopt
the integrated system (3).

In a test case a similar system to that proposed was found
to yield economies at levels of around 150 dwelling units (1).

176

These systems are based on the two innovative components of the oxygenating bioreactor and the evaporator-condenser in series with conventional household appliances.  It would seem that further cost reductions could occur if individual home appliance designs could be modified to operate more effectively as system components in the integrated system.

Cost for a domestic gas incinerator is between $125 and $200.

REFERENCES

(1) Arnold Reed, Environmental Control Engineer, Grumman Aerospace Corp.

(2) Hilary W. Szymanowski, Director of Research, Westinghouse Corp.

(3) Aviation Week and Space Technology, December 15, 1969.

(4) "Can Residential Gas Incinerators Curb the Exploding Garbage Boom?", Gas Appliance Merchandising, December 1969.

STAGE OF DEVELOPMENT

REUSEABLE 'WASTE'

1971  basic technology exists
1973  plant feasibility

Recycling has the most promise of any final treatment method currently being developed.  The Federal Government is
heavily committed to the emerging technology of salvage and
recycling (1).  The Lone Star Organics or the Metropolitan
Waste Conversion Corporation of Houston, Texas is an example of central-station reclamation.  Rubber tires, paper,
glass and metal are separated and the remaining refuse is
composted (2).

OPERATIONAL CHARACTERISTICS

Various human and mechanical coding techniques are being
developed to facilitate high speed disaggregation of heterogeneous refuse.  Methods and equipment nearly ready for
widespread application have been developed for automatically
separating and sorting various mineral and metal portions
of municipal solid waste as it is received.  Sorting techniques being tested are density separation, froth flota-
tion, screening, high intensity magnetic field,and others (3).

SCALE CHARACTERISTICS

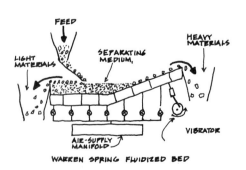

WARREN SPRING FLUIDIZED BED

With solid waste management having become a highly visible
public issue, plants designed for the reuse of waste shed
an entirely new light on waste treatment.  These facilities
can legitimize and even, within limits, glamorize in the
public view the handling of municipal waste so that the
plant could figure prominently in a community urban design
context.

178

COST INFORMATION

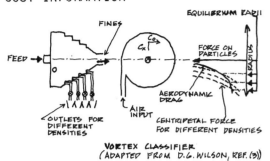

VORTEX CLASSIFIER
(ADAPTED FROM D.G. WILSON, REF. (3))

REFERENCES

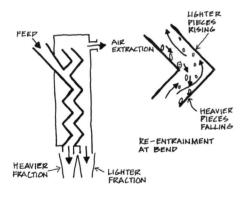

SRI ZIG-ZAG CLASSIFIER

Paper mills will accept clean newspaper, and some bottle manufacturers will use 100% cullet (broken glass) if it is color separated and metal-free. Both materials are profitable for secondary dealers. However, the secondary-materials market is presently an uncertain one. The prices for materials fluctuate widely on a monthly basis, but then for the consumer of secondary materials the source has always been uncertain. The long term future of reclamation is thought to be a bright one (3).

(1)   Environmental Quality: The First Annual Report of the Council on Environmental Quality, The White House, 1970.

(2)   Victor Brown, "Segregation Systems for Processing Heterogeneous Solid-waste Materials for Resource Recovery," Proc. National Industrial Solid-wastes Management Conference, Houston, Texas, March 1970.

(3)   David G. Wilson, "Present and Future Possibilities of Reclamation from Solid Wastes," New Direction in Solid Waste Processing, Technical Guidance Center for Industrial Environmental Control, University of Massachusetts, Amherst, Massachusetts, 1970.

FUSION TORCH RECOVERY

STAGE OF DEVELOPMENT

Theoretical
2000   operating plant

OPERATIONAL CHARACTERISTICS

This proposal for closing the materials cycle is to divert some of the hot plasma produced in a nuclear fusion energy plant to vaporize metals and to recover pure metal from low grade scrap and alloy (1).

SCALE CHARACTERISTICS

Regional

REFERENCES

(1)  Proposal by Bernard J. Eastland and William C. Gough, in The New York Times, January 22, 1970, p.7.

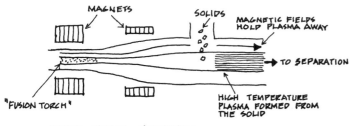

FUSION TORCH SCHEMATIC
(ADAPTED FROM AEC DIVISION OF RESEARCH, THE FUSION TORCH, 1971)

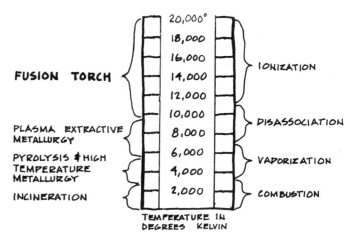

OPERATING TEMPERATURES FOR INCINERATION AND EXTRACTIVE TECHNIQUES

STAGE OF DEVELOPMENT

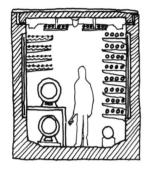 

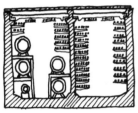

UTILITY TUNNEL TYPES (SINGLE AND DUAL)
MADE FROM PRE-FABRICATED CONCRETE UNITS
(UTILITY TUNNEL DRAWINGS ADAPTED FROM
M.E. POERTNER, REF. (2))

OPERATIONAL CHARACTERISTICS

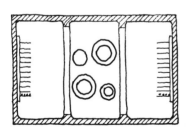

PUBLIC SERVICE TUNNEL IN NEW YORK

1971  basic technology

The American Public Works Association, in their project #68-2, has recently concluded an 18-month investigation on utility corridors.*  The study was conducted by Stanford Research Institute, APWA staff and special consultants and was funded by the Federal Highway Administration and the APWA Research Foundation.

The Planning Department of Akron, Ohio made a feasibility study of utilador tubes in 1966 and concluded that they were feasible in the CBD.  The primary unresolved questions related to construction, ownership and maintenance.  It was suggested that the municipality would build the utility tubes and that the public service department would own and maintain them and lease or sell space to the utilities.  Unresolved conflicts between all interests, including conflicting codes, impeded implementation of the project.  From this precedent, it can be expected that the utilities industries will resist employing utility tubes until it can be shown that it is to their economic benefit.  This would not seem to be a major hurdle (2).

One major conclusion of the APWA study was that utility tubes can provide a main channel for an aggregate of channels for

---

*Grouped utility corridors are sometimes known as "utiladors". That name has been trademarked by RIC-WIL Inc. and they are now variously called utility tunnels (below grade) and utility corridors (above grade).  In this section they will be called utility tubes to indicate the generic category of below-grade and above-grade horizontal and vertical grouped utilities.

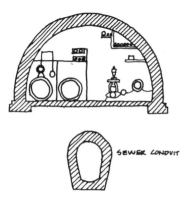

ROADWAY

SEWER CONDUIT

PUBLIC SERVICE TUNNEL IN LONDON UNDER ROADWAY

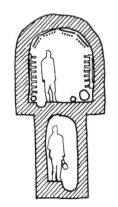

SECTION OF MADRID TUNNELS

electric power, telephone, telegraph, gas, water, sanitary and combined sewers, storm sewers, police and fire alarm lines, steam lines, street lighting and traffic signal lines. They can also accept newly emerging services such as coaxial cables, waveguides, heating and cooling lines, secondary quality water systems, vacuum and slurry solid waste collection lines, snow removal, mail delivery tubes and package delivery tubes. Further, the utility tubes are adaptable to presently unidentified systems developed in the future, with diminished likelihood of interruption of other services or street surface activity.

Combined with a transit system they can be considered to be a total delivery system including delivery of cargo and persons in a multiple-use right-of-way. For example, combined with a guideway, they can achieve major economies. With transportation and utilities both strongly influencing urban growth form, the combination of them makes for an even stronger form determinant.

In its present level of development, utility tube networks are not necessarily compatible with expressway networks; but the potential and benefits of compatibility can be enhanced by combined planning. They are more generally compatible with primary collection and distribution networks and appear to have the highest degree of potentiality in high-density urban areas. In secondary distribution and local street systems they are fully compatible, as every street contains most utilities. However, utility tubes cannot be economically justified for all classes of urban streets; and in secondary street systems, easily accessible small conduits, instead of utility tubes, would offer major long-term economies (1).

Dangers and organization difficulties of combining utilities often cited are (i) ruptures and explosion of gas lines; (ii) leakage of sewer lines and possible resultant flooding, contamination, and short-circuiting of electrical lines; and (iii) conflicts resulting from overlapping maintenance and responsibility. However, with the use of modern materials

182

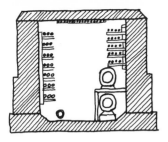

PUBLIC SERVICE TUNNEL IN MOSCOW

and techniques these can be considered to be of an acceptably low probability. This is not to minimize the potential problems of induction problems between power and communications systems, electrical safety, water and, in the future, cryogenic leaks. These problems have been resolved abroad. Cities with utility tubes include London, Zurich, Berlin, Paris, Madrid, Moscow and Kiev. All things considered, utility tubes offer very worthwhile advantages for the dense central public function areas of new communities.

## SCALE CHARACTERISTICS

Utility tubes have potential for application in (i) dense commercial, residential and institutional development situations; (ii) in linear city conditions; and (iii) in combination with vertical displacement such as stairs, escalators and elevators for modularly zoned load centers in areas of vertical development. New communities are seen as one major type of demonstration project in which utility tubes can be tested. With high density as a criterion, a more highly dense new-town-in-town would be an appropriate opportunity for application.

There are several alternatives for utility location, including total underground burial (under street or sidewalk), surface (along curb, sidewalk, street, center strip or greenway) and elevated (along building facades, between light-poles or along transit systems). One alternative deserving particular attention is the elevated location, integrated where feasible with a transit system.

CONSEQUENCES: A combined transit and utility tube system in a visible service spine for public and private buildings; and where laterals are required, they need not be excavated for, but rather made legible and visible. It is possible for some buildings to plug on to this utility/movement service spine and for the spine to pass through some public buildings.

BENEFITS:

.Joint use of right-of-way
·Cost saved in street cuts for installing laterals or new systems
·Cost saved in street deterioration due to street cuts
·Noise pollution from street cuts avoided
·Trip time shortened by avoidance of traffic interference
·Man hours saved and overall efficiency achieved by ease of inspection and maintenance of utilities and aggregation (instead of fractionalization) of administration and maintenance responsibility
·Downtime saved from outages and repairs
·Cost savings in reduction of utilities and services length by means of unifying them in one channel rather than two or more (especially in the case of those utility lines customarily running along both sides of the street)

REFERENCES

(1) Lloyd A. Dove, Assistant Executive Director, APWA, "Feasibility of Utility Tunnels in Urban Streets," paper delivered to AASHO/APWA joint meeting, November 1970.

(2) Herbert G. Poertner, Director of Research, APWA, "Evaluation of the Feasibility of Utiladors in Urban Areas," paper delivered at the conference on "Joint Utilization of Right-of-Way for Utilities and Municipal Services in Urban, Suburban and Rural Environments," July 1969.

STAGE OF DEVELOPMENT                  1970's  (middle)  operational


OPERATIONAL CHARACTERISTICS          A system compatible with the AVAC system and using a simi-
                                     lar technology is the large (24") tube package delivery sys-
                                     tem that can link stores and distribution points with indi-
                                     vidual dwellings or collection points serving clusters of
                                     dwellings.  This system has not as yet been seriously pro-
                                     posed but seems to be practicable for dense urban areas of
                                     multiple dwelling and commercial use.  It can operate compa-
                                     tibly with picturephones and a computer utility for shop-
                                     ping without leaving the dwelling and can in this way expand
                                     the buyer's awareness of options and enable him to receive
                                     goods almost instantly.  It is foreseeable that queuing de-
                                     lays could occur on the pipelines, but these could be dimi-
                                     nished by built-in overcapacity and programming of tube use.

                                     A second-order benefit of this system would be the signifi-
                                     cant decrease in truck delivery traffic and labor cost.


SCALE CHARACTERISTICS                It is quite possible that implementation of this delivery
                                     system can best be achieved by means of applying it ini-
                                     tially to post office service.  This method involves the
                                     distribution of mail and packages from a central post of-
                                     fice facility to branch or neighborhood offices, whence it
                                     could be piped directly to the addressee  or stored temp-
                                     orarily for addressee pickup.

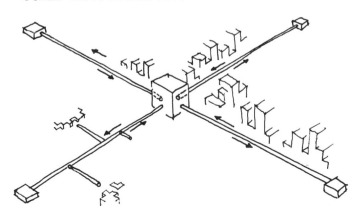

## B.  PROGRAMMATIC FORECASTING (PROCESS INNOVATION)

Because programmatic developments are much more difficult,
and therefore time-consuming, to project than technological
ones, process innovations are not examined in full detail
in this report.  We have, however, attempted to identify
relevant emerging trends in selected areas of major importance: education, health and institutional control.  A
complete analysis of developments in these areas would
start with an examination of actor group values and goals,
and then project how these values and goals would alter
through time in a dynamic process among groups, and how
the actor groups themselves would undergo transformation.
This section does not encompass this kind of analysis;
rather it concentrates on describing process innovations
in the areas listed above which hold potential for meeting
values and goals for improved public services in new communities.  Previous works in the area of forecasting, most
notably those by T. J. Gordon and Olaf Helmer of the Institute for the Future, are suggested as references for
approaches to the problem of projecting values and goals.
Part II of this report, while not attempting to project overall
social goals, does identify several broad categories of goals
and objectives for new communities as well as trends with
which the innovations described here must ultimately be
evaluated.

OPPORTUNITIES FOR HEALTH
IN NEW COMMUNITIES

The World Health Organization defines health as a "state
of complete physical, mental, and social well-being, not
merely the absence of disease or infirmity."  New communities offer an especially strong opportunity to apply
from the beginning the most advanced institutional processes and medical technologies in fulfilling the conditions of
health for their residents.  Through the acceptance of
comprehensive planning responsibilities, the involvement
of public and private health institutions in planning from
the earliest stages and the farsighted acquisition of resources, the new community developer can provide effective
health services which optimize the organizational and technological potentials of innovative programs.  There is
opportunity for superior health service for residents and
for demonstration and attraction of residents by the
developer.

The health service field on the national scale is currently
undergoing great changes in policy, organization and technologies.  In the climate of these and future changes, it
is important to identify what innovations are particularly
applicable to new communities, with what benefits and at
what costs.  Many of the advances described in the ensuing
paragraphs are occuring and will continue to occur in communities of all types, existing and new.  The new community,
however, offers the unique opportunity to (i) assure from
the earliest phases of development the complementary func-
tioning of physical facilities with programs; (ii) integrate
health programs with networks of family, school and employment; (iii) foster the awareness of service availability
in the community; (iv) strategically involve the residents
in health service planning; and (v) merge hardware developments with institutional mechanisms.

The potentials for health service innovations in new communities must be evaluated against three backgrounds: (i) the national climate on health service issues, (ii) emerging and projected health and biomedical technological innovations and (iii) specific programs and process developments in the provision of services.

NATIONAL TRENDS ON HEALTH SERVICE POLICY

The strongest single factor in emerging national trends in health is "the slowly incubating idea that health or access to health is the right of all citizens, regardless of ability to pay."(4) The idea advocates assurance of medical care not as a function of income but of a single, nationwide system of insurance and of a single, uniform method of payment. Consideration of any institutional or technological innovation in health service delivery must recognize this basic trend. The movement follows from the basic pattern established by social security and extended with the passage of Medicare for the elderly and Medicaid for the indigent. It leads inevitably to the guarantees of health security implicit in a single, national health insurance program (4).

The movement toward a national health insurance program is reflected on the national, state and local government levels, from legislative and executive branch origins. In August 1970 fifteen U.S. Senators proposed such a program, which was described as equivalent to Medicare for persons of all ages (not just those over 65) and would cost an estimated $40 billion a year, $10 billion more than is currently being spent. A Health Security Trust Fund similar to the Social Security Fund would finance the program. This bill followed half a dozen similar preceding concepts but offered unprecedentedly detailed proposals on financing.* Former Senator Goodell subsequently introduced a bill for national health insurance with objectives of emphasizing "new types

*New York Times, August 27, 1970.

188

of outpatient, ambulatory and clinic care, thereby assuring
that the entry point to the health care system is readily
available to all Americans"; financing guaranteed equal coverage and access to a single system; and stimulating new institutions and more efficient means of providing health care.
Goodell cited prepaid group practice as an example of the
latter objective.*

On the state and local level, the Lindsay administration in
New York is pressing for major statewide changes in public
and private health care that would:

1. Institute financial incentives to hospitals to provide comprehensive care for families and do away
   with the impersonal assembly-line procedures characteristic of many outpatient departments.
2. Create a new class of health professionals -- physicians' assistants -- to relieve doctors of routine
   chores.
3. Establish a comprehensive program of treatment of
   alchoholism.
4. Consolidate state and city mental health programs.**

An important overall effect of this program, similar to
trends in many other states, would be to increase the standardization and efficiency of access to health care.  The
Nixon administration is expected to introduce early in 1971
health service reforms that would introduce:

1. "A family health insurance plan for low-income
   families that would all but replace the heavily
   criticized Medicaid program...
2. So-called catastrophic medical condition coverages
   for middle-income families...
3. Promotion of the growth of what is known as the
   health maintenance organization, actually a team

*New York Times, September 27, 1970.

**New York Times, November 15, 1970.

of doctors and other health professionals working together as a unit, rather than as individuals to treat disease not only after it begins but also before it starts...

4. A system of negative tax incentives that would all but force employers to raise to a specified minimum health insurance benefits offered employees...

5. Payments to schools to train doctors, dentists and other health professionals, based in part on the degree to which they expand their enrollments...

6. Offering of incentives, by either money or draft exemption, to young doctors who serve in urban ghettos and rural areas that are short of physicians..."*

While seeking to involve the private sector in the provision of health services and while, for the present, falling far short of the Senate proposal, the administration's expected response is symptomatic of the push toward a comprehensive health system. The Office of Economic Opportunity has demonstrated interest in utilization of the private sector in order to provide effective health service delivery to the poor; and to a considerable extent, the OEO Neighborhood Health Center, referred to by OEO officials as a "first generation" vehicle, may provide a model for subsequent programs available to all economic levels. The present administration is reported to concur in principle with nationwide, comprehensive health insurance, but to feel that the time is not politically advantageous to drive through such legislation through Congress.

The American Hospital Association recommends the establishment of a nationwide system for delivery of health services called AMERIPLAN, which revolves around health care corporations set up to provide comprehensive care to specified populations, such as community or neighborhood. Affirming health as an inherent legal right of each individual, the plan would supplant actively both Medicare and Medicaid with

*New York Times, January 4, 1971.

190

a comprehensive program to all and would be financed by
both federal and private funds.*


COSTS AND INSTITUTIONAL CHARGES

Meanwhile, total health costs and public and private expenditures are continuing to rise steeply in absolute terms
and as a proportion of the GNP.  U.S. government spending
on health has tripled in the last five years to an annual
rate of $19.3 billion.  Budget obligations for health
programs (including Medicare and Medicaid) rose from $288
million in 1955 to $15.8 billion in 1970.**

The exponential rise in health care is no secret.  Sixty-
seven cents of each dollar spent for hospital care goes to
employees.  In 1954, 207 hospital employees were required for
the care of each 100 patients; in 1964, 247 were required for
each 100.  With the increase in costs (despite reduced in-
patient hospital time, the proliferation of advanced technical equipment, the increasing specialization of medical
fields and the government-backed efforts to translate the
fruits of biomedical research into practical application),
a major and probably irreversible trend toward centralization has developed.  Centralized hospitals assure that the
necessary specialized materials, equipment and skills are
at hand and reduce the doctor's travel time (3).

The trend toward centralization converges with the move-

---

*New York Times, November 24, 1970.
**Budget obligations to health programs (including Medi-
   care and Medicaid) 1955-1971 (in Billions of Dollars):

| 1955 | 1960 | 1965 | 1967 | 1968 | 1969 | 1970 | 1971 |
|------|------|------|------|------|------|------|------|
| $0.288 | 0.933 | 2,571 | 8,508 | 12,466 | 14,111 | 15,847 | 17,850 |

Source: Charles Schultz, Setting National Priorities,
The 1971 Budget.

191

ment toward a single system of health insurance and care. Within this context, the neighborhood health center can and should grow if considered as a delivery mechanism within and for the overall health system, not as an autonomous and independently financed mechanism.  Currently, over 70% of health services are financed from private sources, with approximately one third of all private expenditures paid by health insurance.  Seventy-five per cent of the cost of health facilities are private expenditures, with the remainder subsidized from tax revenues.  The further multiplicity of health care services is suggested by the existence of both non-profit and profit-making hospitals and other health care institutions, a multiplicity described as "a pluralism with a complicated admixture of governmental (federal, state and local) and private responsibility... an incoherent multiplicity," (16) in which the preventative and curative segments of health care are inefficiently integrated.

THE TREND TO
PREPAID GROUP PRACTICE

Probably the most significant response to this complex and uneven service-network is the emergence of prepaid group practice which stresses preventative as well as curative care and efficience.  This trend has been heavily backed by the Office of Program Innovation in the Medical Services Administration of HEW and is seen by OEO as a fertile field for improving delivery systems to the poor, developed in coordination with private group health cooperative corporations.  Such a marriage of public and private programs may well signal the pattern for future direction.  Prepaid group practice has been developed in numerous locations across the country and advocated by public and private spokesmen at national and state levels.*  Families numbering 200,000 in the

_____
*See, for example, Senator Charles Goodell's proposals, New York Times, September 27, 1970.

state of Washington are enrolled in the Group Health Co-operative of Puget Sound, observed as providing superior service at moderate expense.  Medicaid enrollees numbering 74,000 are served by the Health Insurance Plan of New York, which outperforms more conventional services.  The Kaiser Health Plan delivers excellent, inexpensive health service to 2 million subscribers in several cities, including Oakland, Portland, Denver and Cleveland.  One OEO official observes that for a small increment in subscriber cost, the quality of service provided by Kaiser could be raised even higher to an unexcelled level, still at very reasonable cost.   The Harvard Health Plan in Boston is still another example of a prepaid group practice that performs at efficiency and cost levels far superior to most other systems.

These models are adaptable to existing or new institutions, or combinations of the two and could cover a wide range of diversified health services, i.e., specialized, general, preventive and curative.  One of the most significant innovations undertaken at the new community of Columbia, Maryland was the prepaid health system developed in cooperation with Johns Hopkins Hospital (9), which assures preventive and positive health conditions as well as the traditional diagnostic and cure emphasis of medicine.  It is clear that the new community context of Columbia lent itself advantageously to the introduction of such a comprehensive service.  Such opportunities are evident, although to a lesser degree, in the medical and health programs offered in many of the more special-purpose new communities, such as retirement communities.

PROFESSIONAL TRENDS

Notable within the medical profession is the decreasing role of individual private practice, particularly general practice (10).  The trend most definitely favors the grouping of complementary, specialized health skills in medical partnerships geared to most efficiently exploiting centralized institutional and technical resources.  It should be emphasized, however, that "centralized" does not necessarily imply single-point, geographic concentration only.  Whereas the growth of general hospitals large enough to accommodate a wide range of specialized service and research functions seems likely to continue, it will be accompanied by parallel growth of dispersed systems which effectively tie neighborhood and community health centers to the larger centers according to need.  Prepaid medical partnership and national health insurance programs can prove adaptable to such a network; and professionals -- whether general practitioner, researcher, specialist, surgeon, dentist, etc. -- will find innovative and effective mechanisms for delivery of their services.

In order to increase the number of doctors required and to reduce the redundancies and other inefficiencies in medical education, a strong movement has been in progress to reduce the length of time required in school for doctors.  Senator Edmund Muskie made this recommendation in the Senate in conjunction with proposals for more effective use of military corpsmen returning to civilian life and other paramedical and health-related personnel.*  The Office of Economic Opportunity has also attempted to tap this human resource by advocating the training of health services paraprofessionals.  In the post-industrial context of burgeoning service industry employment, and in the particular context of the expanding health industry, the development of paraprofessional skills will have significant positive impacts on health care for all groups, particularly the elderly, young mothers and infants, mentally ill and retarded, disabled, chronically ill and the in- and outpatients of hospitals and health centers.  In activities such as bedside nursing, midwifery, medical social work, physical therapy or hospital specialization in scores of individual skills, the use of paraprofessionals

---

*New York Times, November 21, 1970.

will certainly strengthen the delivery of medical services, professional and quasi-professional.

EMERGING HEALTH TECHNOLOGY

Developments in health care are evolving in the presence of rapidly advancing technological achievement and applications. The results are seen at the most general level in reduced infant mortality rates and increased life expectancy. Research and treatment technologies (stemming largely from radiology and laboratory analysis during the last 20 years), as well as access to health care by increasing numbers of the population, have played a substantial role in the dramatic reductions of deaths previously caused by a host of diseases (15). A substantial decrease in feeble-mindedness and other inherited abnormalities is occuring and seems likely to continue. Death rates from stroke have been radically reduced due to the development of vascular drugs. The present form of oral contraception, requiring daily administering, will likely give way to a new form of prostoglandin drug taken only once a month;* and artificial fertilization of the female egg cells <u>in vitro</u>, amounting to the implant of the human embryo, appears close at hand.** Organ "banks" have existed for some time for eyes, eardrums and other bodily parts and can be expected, despite the complex ethical issues involved, to increase in number and use to preserve for transfer kidneys, livers and hearts. The use of synthetic organs will also proliferate.

Indicative of the widening of the technological applications is the emergence, especially since the discovery of DNA, of new patterns of productive interaction among disciplines such as physics, mathematics and biomedical engineering. This tendency is reflected in the use of devices and techniques such as the following:

---

*<u>New York Times</u>, September 6, 1970.

**<u>New York Times</u>, October 28, 1970.

Medical engineering:

1. Ultrasonic, electromagnetic and isotope scanning devices.
2. Electronic devices for processing and recording
   electrocardiograms, monitoring cardiac arrhyth-
   mias, analyzing electroencephalograms, etc.
3. Color thermography for tumor-detecting.

Clinical data-handling:

1. Automated cell counters.
2. Multiphasic screening systems.
3. Automated clinical laboratories.
4. Intensive-care unit monitors and diagnostic
   aids.

Therapeutic and prosthetic devices:

1. Artificial organs such as implantable organic
   and artificial hearts and kidneys.
2. Heart pacemakers automatically adjusting rate
a  and timing to meet demand.
3. Hearing aids which act beyond simple amplifi-
   cation to compensate for certain forms of
   nerve deafness.
4. Artificial limbs controlled by nerve or muscle
   signals (14).

Clinical use of the computer has been increasing slowly, its
main uses having been confined thus far to research and to
routine applications such as (i) accounting, (ii) scheduling,
(iii) patient monitoring, (iv) automated laboratories (1).
One doctor points out that there is, as yet, little real application of advanced technology, including computers, to
patient treatment since the organization and human acceptance
of available technologies occurs more slowly than the actual
development of the technologies themselves (12). And no one
expects hospital computers or other technological devices to
substitute for invaluable personal contact in health treatment.

A RAND study of 1964 (7) predicted the following medical developments:

1.  "automated interpretation of medical symptoms" -- 1980 to 1990;
2.  "electronic prosthesis (including radar for the blind, servo-mechanical limbs, etc.)" -- 1980 to 1990; and
3.  "implanted artificial organs made of plastic and electronic components" -- 1980 to 1990.

These developments have been unfolding at a rate much faster than originally anticipated; two of the three have, in fact, already occured.  An Institute for the Future study of 1970 (6) projects the following significant events by 1980:

1.  "Laboratory solution of the foreign body rejection problem.
2.  Development of mass-administered contraceptive agents.
3.  Availability of cheap, non-narcotic drugs (other than alcohol)  for the purpose of producing specific changes in personality characteristics.
4.  Development of immunizing agents which can protect against most bacterial and viral diseases.
5.  Laboratory creation of a primitive form of artificial life (at least in the form of self-replicating molecules).
6.  Laboratory demonstration of artificial generation of protein for food through in vitro cellular processes.
7.  Demonstration of techniques by which the sex of babies may be chosen with 90% certainty.
8.  Laboratory demonstration of chromosome typing for abnormalities in humans within weeks of conception.
9.  Demonstration of implantable artificial hearts with a very long duration power source..."

These developments recently occuring and foreseen are of themselves momentous.  Their impact on health policy, institutions and delivery systems will result in further broadening

197

and complexity of the range of skills and delivery instruments available, both at the major central hospitals and at the smallest local health centers.  The technological innovations must be seen as an important defining element in the design and formation of both national and local health delivery systems.

INSTITUTIONAL INNOVATION
IN HEALTH SERVICES

Implementation of the innovative advances in health technology  cannot take place without the health care network to deliver them.  Whereas technological developments, emerging public health policies and organizational trends will undoubtedly apply in varying degrees to all communities, new communities present an especially favorable opportunity for the merging of new hardware capabilities with new institutional delivery mechanisms.  For example, several innovative technical systems can be identified which may well be made more effective if accompanied by institutional innovations:

·computer-assisted diagnostic services
·multiphasic health screening*
·centralized monitoring of remote outpatients
·helicopter ambulance service
·interactive two-way remote screening and surgery control**

Health care plant facilities can be planned from the beginning to accommodate these services, many of which require special equipment or health plan contract agreements which would be more feasible in a new, as opposed to existing, urban setting.

*For an example of this process, the Kaiser Oakland Medical Center operation is described in Scientific Quarterly, October, 1970.

**Such as practiced by Dr. Kenneth Bird at Massachusetts General Hospital, Boston, Massachusetts

The capability of providing effective, innovative health delivery networks is enhanced in new community situations in a manner similar to the provision of other innovative facilities (such as transportation, communications, education, social services, etc.), because of the opportunity to plan them comprehensively from the inception of the community, to assess continually changing requirements, long-range goals and phasing of the networks and to integrate them with other community networks. In existing cities, particularly large ones, innovative health systems must be superimposed on already present systems not integrally designed. Thus, such systems are often implemented in ways which may seriously reduce their potential for improving the quantity and quality of a community's health services.

The following list enumerates some of the more significant innovative institutional program mechanisms and processes which might be selected for the design of the health service program for a new community.

Institutional programs

1.  Prepaid comprehensive medical program
2.  Dispersed community clinics or health centers (either in form of conventional single-purpose health centers or of multi-purpose community centers, dispensing a wide variety of social, cultural, recreational and informational services in addition to health)
3.  Adaptable hospital or clinic design (acute, extended or nursing care bed and facility adaptability)
4.  Alcoholic, drug and mental disturbance hot line service
5.  Birth control clinics
6.  Abortion clinics
7.  Paramedical personnel training and use in service
8.  Human potential or growth centers with availability of trained professionals, as a component of community

health service*

9.  Paraprofessional dispersed psychiatric consultation services**
10. Programmed involvement and use of elderly persons in child care centers and other socially constructive, participatory community activities (on paid and/or voluntary basis)***
11. Resident involvement in provision of voluntary health services for the indigent
12. Use of field audit teams to monitor hospital and health center network performance in caring for patients****

---

*Warren Bennis asserts that more than 6 million Americans belong to the so-called "human potential movement" of which the Esalen Institute, Synanon, the Casriel Institute and Phoenix Houses are some of the more well-known examples. As one most recent manifestation of psychotherapeutic trends, it is somewhat controversial but will undoubtedly influence future attitudes and techniques in mental health programs, private and public.

**The principles in practice in the so-called "storefront psychiatry" centers in low-income areas may be exportable to other areas. (New York Times, April 21, 1970: "'Storefront Psychiatry' Helps Brooklyn's Poor.")

***Such involvement has been practiced for many years in England as an integral part of comprehensive health care, by which young and old mutually benefit. The Peckham Health Center in London was the progenitor of health service programs implemented in many of the English New Towns. Similar patterns have been used to advantage in Finland, Sweden and Switzerland.

****Medical Services Administration program reported in The New York Times, September 27, 1970.

## Institutional processes

1. Involvement from initial community planning stages of accessible university medical schools or other medical resources in planning, programming and provision of facilities and services.*
2. Provision for special fund for low interest medical loans, probably through prepaid medical program (8).
3. Involvement of community residents in health services planning.
4. Continuing participation of community residents in health services programs.**
5. Provision of attractive professional, research and environmental incentives to encourage location of health personnel in the community.

CONCLUSION

The new community health services plan, like the plans for education, transportation, utilities and all other services must be integrated effectively into the overall planning and development process if it is to be most responsive to the demands it must satisfy. None of the innovative technologies can be considered apart from institutional processes and programs through which the technologies will be applied; none of the processes can be considered for new communities com-

---

*Columbia, Maryland is the precedent for this important innovation. Health systems planning in the U.S., including that for new communities, has generally been deficient. Reston, Virginia adopted a similar program.. Probably it is now standard practice for most new communities.

**The value of resident participation is substantiated by the English New Towns experience, which provided basic models for the community health center and by the OEO experience in poverty areas where resident involvement has resulted in increased outreach, improved morale and more effective cure and prevention rates (11, 12).

pletely separate from policy, institutional and professional trends on the national and local levels. Viewing all considerations together, new communities would provide a fundamental opportunity to implement superior health systems comprised of both innovative and conventional components. The new community health plan can proceed from policy and goal formation to assessment of requirements and resources, setting of objectives, phasing, involving residents through detailed planning and continuously evaluating the program and modifying it as required. A new community would seem to be the best opportunity to combine the most advanced technologies with the most innovative health care processes, thereby increasing the ultimate attractiveness of the community to its prospective residents.

REFERENCES

(1) Dr. G. Octo Barrett: "The Computer's Role in Health-Service Research," Tech Review, April 1970.

(2) Dr. Ivan L. Bennett, "Conditions and Problems of Technological Innovation: Medicine," Tech Review, April 1970.

(3) Dr. Robert H. Ebert, "A Note on the Impact of Technology on the Practice of Medicine," Tech Review, April 1970.

(4) Rashi Fein, "Financing U.S. Medical Care," Tech Review, April 1970.

(5) H. D. Geiger, Seymour S. Bellin, Count D. Gibson, "Impact of Ambulatory-Health Care Services on the Demand for Hospital Beds: A Study of the Tufts Neighborhood Health Center at Columbia Point in Boston," New England Journal of Medicine, Vol. 280, April 10, 1969.

(6) T. J. Gordon and Robert H. Ament, Forecasts of Some Technological and Scientific Developments and their Social Consequences, 1970.

(7) Theodore J. Gordon and Olaf Helmer, Report on a Long-Range Forecasting Study, 1964.

(8) Harold Herman and Michael L. Joroff, "Planning Health Services for New Towns," American Journal of Public Health, Vol. 57, No. 4, April 1967.

(9) Morton Hoppenfeld, "A Sketch of the Planning-Building Process at Columbia, Maryland," American Institute of Planners Journal, November 1967.

(10) Stanley Lesse and William Wolfe, "An Exploration of the Basic Determinants and Trends of Medicine in Our Future Society," American Journal of Psychotherapy, Vol. 20, No. 2, April 1966.

(11) Bruce L. Maliver, "Encounter Groupers Up Against the Wall," The New York Times Magazine, January 3, 1971.

(12) Samuel Moffat, "Promises, Promises -- But Few Wedding Bells," Tech Review, April 1970.

(13) OEO, Catalogue of Federal Domestic Assistance.

(14) ___, "Bibliography (Annotated) of the Comprehensive Health Services Program and Addendum," 1969, 1970.

(15) ___, Office of Health Affairs, "Criteria for a Community Health Network."

(16) Innes H. Pearse, M.D. and Lucy H. Crocker, The Peckham Experiment: A Study in the Living Structure of Society, London, Allen and Unwin, 1943.

(17) Donald J. Scherl, M.D. and Joseph T. English, M.D., "Community Mental Health and Comprehensive Health Service Programs for the Poor," American Journal of Psychiatry, Vol. 125, No. 12, June 1967.

(18) William M. Siebert, "New Technology and New Medical Education," Tech Review, April 1970.

(19) Wall Street Journal Staff, Here Comes Tomorrow!, 1966.

(20) Dr. Alonso S. Yerby, "Health Care Systems: Some International Comparisons," Tech Review, April 1970.

EDUCATION

The program for primary and secondary education in a new community is of critical importance for several reasons:

1. Investments required for construction and operation of school facilities are substantial and may result in the building and location of facilities which present an inherent obstacle to changing educational requirements.
2. Since neighborhoods often tend to be defined in size and boundary locations by the size and placement of schools, the patterns of development in a new community may be a direct reflection of the educational plan.
3. As a marketing tool, the quality of education offered for children of prospective residents of a community is virtually as important as the quality of available housing.

The current emphasis in educational experimentation and reform is primarily directed toward the generally inflexible nature of public school systems-- an inflexibility which characterizes curricula, student-teacher relationships, teacher-family relationships and student interaction (particularly in areas of race relations). While this emphasis is undeniably justifiable, the innovations of concern here are those which are aimed at creating a new relationship between the educational system and the other institutions within a community. In particular, educational experiments which foster the decentralization of facilities and/or their close integration with the overall community structure are described; for it is this philosophy which is likely to have the greatest impact on the cost, placement, and nature of educational facilities in a new community. In turn, the development patterns of the community might be strongly influenced by the adoption of an educational program which departs from the traditional concepts of neighborhood elementary schools, district high schools and even community colleges, all operating on a nine-month basis and whose facilities are used for very limited purposes.

The potential for expanding education beyond the classroom has been articulated by Marshall McLuhan and George Leonard:

> ""Why should I go back to school and interrupt my education?" the high school drop-out asks. His question is impudent but to the point. The modern urban environment is packed with energy and information -- diverse, insistent, compelling (1).

Two efforts which attempt to realize the potential of this "energy and information" for educational purposes are the Parkway Program, currently underway in Philadelphia, and the educational system proposed by Mario Fantini and Milton Young for Fort Lincoln New Town in Washington, D.C. In addition to these innovative programs, several other developments in education, including the tuition voucher system and the use of electronic teaching aids, are discussed in this section.

## THE PARKWAY PROGRAM

The Parkway Program High School (2) in Philadelphia was designed in 1968 as a partial answer to the city's desperate shortage of high school facilities. While the school board was attempting to find ways of securing funds for new school construction, the idea emerged of utilizing the city's cultural institutions (most of which are located within walking distance of each other along the Benjamin Franklin Parkway) as the "facilities" at which instruction could take place. In effect, the capital expenditures for the new school had already been made; and its operating expenses were allocated from the city's school budget, supplemented by a Ford Foundation grant. Although the initial impetus for the Parkway Program was based largely on financial considerations, the two-year history of the program has been characterized by

the identification of new opportunities to increase materially
the quality of high school education. The first of these
opportunities is, of course, the ability to utilize the
facilities, personnel and materials of Philadelphia's excellent cultural resources (Philadelphia Museum of Art,
Franklin Institute of Science, etc.) as the basic resources
of the school. In addition, the participation in the program
of several of Philadelphia's major industries (e.g., General
Electric) and commercial establishments (e.g., theaters and
craft enterprises such as leather shops) has widened the
scope of potential study areas, provided additional meeting
places for "basic skill" classes and encouraged the direct
involvement of businessmen and practicing professionals whose
previous exposure to the educational system was probably
limited to an occasional lecture or a PTA meeting. Of significant importance also is that the departure from a traditional physical environment for education has precipitated
a number of experiments within the program which provide
the students with much greater freedom in course selection
and a much larger role in the teaching-learning process,
even in "basic skill" courses.

As the Parkway Program has expanded in student enrollment
(presently 1000, expected to reach 2400 by 1972) and in the
number and type of participants (now including insurance
companies, television studios, etc.), the transportation
system within the center of the city has virtually become
an integral element of the program as students often travel
considerable distances to attend classes. Indeed, the
availability of an extensive bus and subway network in
Philadelphia has substantially reduced the need for transportation expenses as part of the school's operating budget.

The success of the Parkway Program can be measured in two
ways (3). One is that plans are currently being formulated
(or are in operation) to establish similar programs in Hartford, Kansas City and elsewhere. Secondly, the results thus
far in Philadelphia are encouraging when compared with other,
more traditional city schools with respect to (i) racial in-
cidents (despite the fact that 50% of Parkway's students are

black); (ii) drug and disciplinary problems; (iii) attendance and learning rates; and (iv) student satisfaction. The favorable comparisons between Parkway and other schools become more significant in light of the fact that Parkway students are selected randomly from applicants throughout the entire city.

FORT LINCOLN EDUCATIONAL PROGRAM

The Fort Lincoln New Town project (FLNT) in Northeast Washington, D.C. is a new town-in-town proposal for the development of a 335-acre site formerly occupied by the National Training School for Boys (5). A planning team under the direction of Edward J. Logue (now chief executive officer of New York's Urban Development Corporation) prepared a development program for the site with a target population of 15,500 residents. The plan for the new town's educational system was developed by Mario Fantini of the Ford Foundation and Milton Young of the Travelers Research Corporation in Hartford.

The basic structure of the educational system proposed by Fantini and Young is "...essentially decentralized, but [with] nodes of concentrated educational activity..." (4) located near the transit stations on the community's proposed internal network cab loop. In contrast to the Parkway High School program in Philadelphia, the FLNT program would accommodate primary, as well as secondary, school children in its pattern of utilizing dispersed facilities for general and special instruction. In a manner similar to that in Philadelphia, the instructional facilities will often be those used for other community purposes, including commerce, culture, manufacturing and recreation.

As a potential model for new community planning, the FLNT system is notable for several reasons:

1.  It has been designed for a high degree of integration with other community functions and services.
2.  It is intended to complement the school system

throughout Washington, D.C. by making its facilities and activities available and accessible for
students outside the new town.
3. As was the case in Philadelphia, the innovative
concepts in facility distribution have been accompanied by similarly innovative proposals for
curriculum reform, teaching methods and other
components of the total educational program.
4. Opportunities for continuing adult participation
in both learning and teaching have been imaginatively incorporated in the dispersed facilities
concept.
5. The possibility of using educational facilities on
a year-round basis and for other community activities is an integral component of the proposal.

At the moment, the Fort Lincoln Project remains a proposal
far from realization. Even if the project should be built,
it is questionable whether an educational system so radically different from the existing Washington, D.C. system
could obtain necessary approval from the appropriate city
and federal agencies. Nevertheless, the proposed system is
consistent with a trend toward educational decentralization
which is obtaining greater public acceptance as an alternative to traditional school concepts and which holds particular value for new community planning where innovations in
educational need not be incorporated incrementally.

OTHER MODELS FOR DISPERSAL

The concept of integrating an educational system with the
total range of city activities is by no means new; however,
its application at a scale which permits evaluation and
comparison is a relatively recent, indeed contemporary,
development. One early system which generated a good deal
of interest, apparently short-lived, is the "Random Falls"
(6) model which perceived the city as a total campus and
its activities (commerce, industry, culture, etc.) as
teaching materials. In this proposal, first advanced in
1956, a student's four years in high school would be

carefully and individually planned to make full use of the city's resources to prepare him for meeting his career objectives, to appeal to his interests and to acquaint him with the wealth of information and opportunities available in his community.

Two additional proposals which are based on concepts of dispersal are the British Open University and "Intermix"; the former is an extensive experiment just initiated in England which hopes to provide university education throughout the country on an "extension" basis, while the latter is a concept conceived at Rice University and proposed specifically for new communities. Each of these proposals depends largely on the use of electronics and communications technologies, the Open University making extensive use of nation-wide television and radio linkages and "Intermix" projecting a community information system which, in effect, surrounds community residents with learning opportunities.

## The Open University

In an attempt to extend college-level education to a far broader range of people, the Open University (7) was established this year in England as an extensive correspondence school with programs available to anyone over 21. While permanent facilities for centralized administration and local meetings are presently being constructed, the basic teaching method of the school, in reality, is the use of national television and radio. With a current enrollment of 25,000 (equal to 40% of the number of first-year students entering traditional universities), the University is expected to vastly increase the country's supply of degree-holding, college-educated people.

The use of television and radio for education is, of course, a concept often discussed and even implemented in this country (Sesame Street being a notable example). What is unique about the Open University is its scale of operations coupled with a correspondence program and occasional group meetings (on a local and regional level) which illustrates

210

the vast potential for using electronic communications not as an educational supplement but as the core of an extensive effort to provide educational opportunities independently of locational considerations.

"Intermix"

An even more extensive exploration of the application of technologies to education was conducted at the School of Architecture at Rice University in 1968 (8). Under the supervision of several nationally known educators and architects, proposals for an educational system for a new community included some of the following technological elements:

1. Roving buses containing an assortment of audio-visual devices which would roam neighborhoods in much the same way as ice cream trucks.
2. Information retrieval units scattered throughout the community like telephone booths and which would provide the user with specified information or programmed presentations.
3. Specially equipped transit vehicles and "school buses" which would contain programmed instructional materials.
4. Self-contained "plug-in" cubicles electronically connected to information banks which would be attached to dwelling units.
5. Elaborate shoulder harnasses containing audio-visual and sensory equipment to entertain and educate children anywhere an electronic connection to a central data bank would be located.

Most of the devices studied for the "Intermix" program are highly innovative and unlikely to be fully operational for several years. The value of the exercise conducted at Rice, however, is in describing and illustrating how the creative use of presently available technologies can virtually elim-inate the need for construction of single-purpose educational institutions. The investment in school plant and equipment

in existing cities is sufficient, in itself, to inhibit
experimentation with such devices as alternatives to traditional educational methods.  With no such previous investment in new communities, many of these devices could be
rapidly developed and incorporated into an educational
system which makes much better use of available technologies
and provides the basis for closer interaction between the
process of learning and range of  activities which constitute community life.

## TUITION VOUCHERS

One additional development in education which may have
significant implications for new communities is the tuition
voucher system currently being explored by the Office of
Economic Opportunity (9).  Experiments are being planned
for school districts in Gary, Indiana and Alum Rock, California in which parents of school-age children would be
issued vouchers which are equal in value to the per-pupil
expenditures on education within the district (10).  These
vouchers could then be redeemed at any school within the
district, and the school would then receive funds from the
local school board equal to the amount of vouchers it had
collected.  In this way, parents would not be required to
enroll their children in the nearest school, and they
would be free to chose the school which they felt best for
their children's particular needs.

While the voucher system may be open to criticism from
several perspectives, it nevertheless has several potential
benefits.  For example, the transportation of children
(particularly by public transit) to other areas of their
district (or city if vouchers are instituted on a city-
wide basis) will serve to expose them to more of their
environment at an earlier age.  In addition, the closer
integration of public transit and educational facilities
can eventually lead to the types of dispersed educational
systems described previously.  For new communities, the
opportunity to realize the potential benefits of the

voucher system are perhaps greater than in an existing city because traditional school patterns will not have to be changed. By the same token, extension of the voucher idea to permit partial voucher redemption at dispersed facilities (and non-education facilities) is a strong incentive for the total integration of community service systems which may well be the most important distinction between new and existing communities.

CONCLUSIONS

There are many additional innovations in education which could have been included in this discussion. However, the purpose here was not to be exhaustive, but rather to identify some of the more critical developments in education which indicate the range of ideas of particular interest for new community planning. For identification and discussion of a wider number of educational innovations, the reader is referred to the following general reference sources:

1. Helmer, Olaf, "The Use of the Delphi Technique in Problems of Educational Innovations," The RAND Corporation, Santa Monica, California, December 1966.

2. Gordon, Theodore and Robert Ament, Forecasts of Some Technological and Scientific Developments and their Societal Consequences, Institute for the Future, Middletown, Connecticut, September 1969.

3. A comprehensive listing of numerous innovations in reports and projects sponsored by the Educational Facilities Laboratory (EFL) of the Ford Foundation can be found in:

   Educational Facilities Laboratory, Transformation of the Schoolhouse, 1969, available through EFL, 477 Madison Avenue, New York, N.Y., 10022.

REFERENCES

(1)  M. McLuhan and G. Leonard, "Learning in the Global
     Village," in Gross, Beatrice and Ronald, eds., Radi-
     cal School Reform, Simon and Schuster, New York, 1969.

(2)  "Learning on the Road," Saturday Review, May 17, 1969;
     "An Experiment: Philadelphia's School without Walls,"
     Life Magazine, May 16, 1969.

(3)  "The Parkway Program," Time Magazine, March 23, 1970.

(4)  Mario D. Fantini and Milton A. Young, Designing Educa-
     tion for Tomorrow's Cities, Holt, Rinehart and Winston,
     New York, 1970.

(5)  Edward J. Logue, Fort Lincoln New Town: Final Planning
     Report, submitted to the National Capital Planning
     Commission, Washington, D.C., April 1969.

(6)  _____, "Random Falls," The School Executive,
     March 1956.

(7)  Bernard Weinraub, "British Open a College for Drop-
     outs," The New York Times, January 12, 1971.

(8)  William Cannady, Director, Rice Design Fete IV, New
     Schools for New Towns, School of Architecture, Rice
     University, Houston, Texas, 1968.

(9)  Center for the Study of Public Policy, Education Vouchers:
     A Preliminary Report on Financing Education by Payments
     to Parents, Cambridge, Massachusetts, March 1970.

(10) William K. Stevens, "Two Cities Expected to be Named
     for School 'Voucher' System," The New York Times,
     January 23, 1971.

Recognition of opportunities for innovation in new communities must be accompanied by the institutional capability to reconcile residents, investors, jurisdictional bodies, industrial and commercial establishments and other entities whose role in the growth of the community can be identified. As distinct from a large suburban residential project in which virtually all planning is completed before development begins, a new community, if it is to be capable of accommodating change and responding to opportunity, cannot be planned in its entirety during a "pre-construction planning" stage. With this distinction in mind, this section identifies several of the institutional issues which face the new community developer.

The fundamental opportunities of new communities have been discussed previously in Part I; it is the realization of these opportunities which must serve as the basic objective of institutional control and project management in a new community development. In particular, the concern here is with opportunities for innovations in the provision of community public services so as to facilitate technological and programmatic change and accommodate continuing increases in population and demands for those services.

FUNCTIONS OF COMMUNITY INSTITUTIONS

At the very outset of the development of a city, provision must be made for essential public services, such as education, transportation, energy distribution, waste disposal and so forth. As the city grows, its population changes and so does

*This discussion is summarized from a paper entitled "Institutional Control in New Community Development," presented by William S. Saslow at The Eastern Regional Conference on Science and Technology for Public Programs at MIT on April 3, 1970.

the world around it; new needs emerge, and new technological capabilities are developed. Ideally, initial plans for provision of these services should be designed to provide sufficient flexibility to meet the needs of future residents and to accommodate anticipated, but perhaps undefined technological innovations. To illustrate several of the institutional approaches taken on contemporary new community projects, this section examines the institutional mechanisms created or proposed in three new town projects for the provision of two community public services: transportation and education. Specifically, these mechanisms are evaluated with respect to their ability to achieve a proper balance between short-term requirements of present residents and long-term interests essential to the orderly growth of the community.

In each of the new towns discussed, the requirements for provision of transportation and education are examined, as they relate to the structure of the institutions responsible for those services. Within the wide range of activities which might be regarded as public services, transportation and education were chosen as being particularly significant because of the deterministic and permanent impact of early planning decisions on the development patterns of a community. This impact is likely to assume even greater importance in the future as the planned integration of these services, i.e., educational flexibility being somewhat dependent on the means available for transporting students to dispersed facilities, becomes more critical. If one takes the approach that a transportation system is one of the "technologies" of education (in addition to buildings, equipment, etc.) then it follows that institutions responsible for these services must be congruent in their goals and geographically compatible if not highly centralized. Thus, in addition to evaluating the ability of the controlling mechanisms for transportation and education to respond to changing needs and demands, this discussion also considers the degree to which planned integration of these services is affected by the characteristics of the respective controlling institutions in each of the three cases.

MILTON KEYNES (1)

Milton Keynes is a proposed New City of 250,000 people to be located in North Buckinghamshire County, England, between London and Birmingham. The latest, and potentially, the largest, of the British New Towns, Milton Keynes contains many refinements of the policies governing the British New Towns Program and represents the most recent opportunity for British planners and policy makers to capitalize on their own extensive experience.

In a significant departure from previous new town projects, which were almost entirely developed by public Development Corporations, the British Government has set as an objective for Milton Keynes that half the investment for the city be obtained from private sources. (The present average from private sources is 10%.) In addition, half of the housing supply is to be built for owner-occupancy (as opposed to an average of about 10% for previous New Towns). The shift in the relative percentages of public and private investment will make Milton Keynes far more applicable as a model for the United States than earlier British New Towns.

Administratively, the 22,000 acre area designated by the Ministry of Housing and Local Government as the New City of Milton Keynes falls within four existing towns in Buckinghamshire County. Ultimate authority for approval of planning decisions within the County normally lies with the Buckinghamshire County Council, but responsibility for preparing and implementing the plan for the new city lies with the Milton Keynes Development Corporation, a public body created under the British New Towns Act by the Ministry of Housing and Local Government. Within this administrative framework the institutional mechanisms responsible for the provision of transportation and education are different.

Transportation

Responsibility for provision, management and operation of the public transportation system will lie with the Milton Keynes Development Corporation which, under the provision of the New Towns Acts of 1946 and 1959, will retain its development con-

217

trols until the city is essentially completed. At that time, the holdings of the Development Corporation will be transferred to the National Commission on New Towns or to local government units and the Corporation will be dissolved. During the development period, the Corporation will remain in complete control of planning decisions made with respect to the city's transportation system. As a creation of the Ministry of Housing and Local Government, the Corporation is effectively answerable only to that agency and not to the various levels of local and county government through which the future residents of Milton Keynes will express their political needs. The Corporation has only to "consult" these levels of government but is not bound by their attitudes.

As an instrument of public policy and program implementation, the Development Corporation for Milton Keynes is designed to be highly capable of reacting to new developments in transportation technologies and incorporating such developments into the public transit system with a minimum of local political interference. The advantages of this autonomy must be seen in relationship to two points. First, the history of Milton Keynes as a potential New Town began not with the interim planning proposal completed last year but with the creation of a set of objectives for the Corporation derived from close cooperation between local, county and national agencies since 1962 when the original conception for a New Town was suggested by the Buckinghamshire County Council. Thus, while the Corporation may act independently of local governments in decisions regarding transportation, the criteria by which such decisions will be made are a direct function of expressed local needs and attitudes. The cooperation between the Corporation and the region's public bodies is not likely to diminish since some other services are not under the control of the Corporation (e.g., education) and a check and balance system can be readily seen. As participants in the policy-making process of local government, the future residents of Milton Keynes will thus have an indirect, but nevertheless substantial, effect on decisions made by the Corporation.

The second point is that local participation in planning,
however well-intentioned, is likely to be oriented toward
short-term decisions and limited geographical scope.  But
investments in future transportation technologies, if and
when warranted, will be considerable and will have long-
term and geographically far-reaching implications.  It is
hard not to anticipate conflicts of judgment between local
residents whose concerns are immediate and the Development
Corporation whose horizons must be far broader.  In the
resolution of potential conflicts, therefore, the Corporation has a degree of autonomy and control which can be very
effective in protecting the broader and longer-range interests
of the total development program for Milton Keynes.

The density of residential development in Milton Keynes is
projected to reach a net average of about eight units per
acre over a thirty-year development period.  Consultants
to the Development Corporation have concluded that densities over the next decade will not support the initial provision of an economically feasible fixed right-of-way transportation system for the town.  In addition, because projected car ownership is on the order of 1.5 vehicles per
dwelling unit, it is unlikely that a fixed route service
could be offered which would be competitive with personal
vehicles.  In rejecting the short-run use of monorails, separate rights of way and other fixed route modes, the consultants have nevertheless stressed a need for reserving space
along the major road grid to allow for introduction of fixed
track systems if they should prove feasible in the future.

The public transportation system recommended for Milton Keynes,
after an evaluation of numerous alternatives, is to consist
of high quality bus service which uses the same roadways as
private vehicles.  Additionally, the eventual incorporation
of computer-controlled shared taxis of "dial-a-bus" systems
is being considered as a determinant in residential land-use
design proposals.  As an additional gesture toward accommodation of future transportation needs, the Development Corporation is preparing to reserve certain rights of way for
high-speed regional rapid transit service to augment the

existing rail link between Milton Keynes, London and other British cities.

Education

The plan for educational systems (from nursery school through higher education at a university level) for Milton Keynes is being developed by an education working party whose participants represent the Buckinghamshire County Council, the Department of Education and Science, the Development Corporation and its consultants. Determination of final educational policy, however, is the responsibility of the Education Committee of the County Council rather than that of the Development Corporation. As currently proposed, the system for schools would rely heavily on the city's transportation network to permit maximum flexibility in the use of school structures throughout the city. In addition, the shared use of scarce educational resources (e.g., staff and equipment) would be facilitated by the grouping of perhaps three secondary schools on a single campus. The relationship between educational services, communication media and cultural facilities is expected to be particularly close so as to facilitate continued opportunities for learning by residents of all ages within the new city.

The most significant innovation in educational policy currently being considered by the Education Committee and the working party is the dissolution of geographical boundaries normally defining the area served by a school facility. Reinforcing this concept, the grid layout of roads and transit should permit significant flexibility over time as the educational system evolves and as interaction among residents and facilities throughout the city increases. The fact that the "technologies" of the educational system (i.e., facilities and transit) are controlled by the Development Corporation, while education is technically the responsibility of the County Council, does not appear to constrain the comprehensive approach being pursued by the Development Corporation. Again, however, it must be recognized that the high degree of institutional cooperation in the planning for Milton Keynes

is, in part, a function of the initiating process in which
the County Council and smaller institutional units played
major parts.  Thus, a climate for effective administrative
cooperation and public service control has been nurtured for
seven or eight years and has resulted in the creation of many
opportunities for innovation in the provision of educational
services for the proposed new city.

COLUMBIA, MARYLAND (2)

Columbia is being developed by The Rouse Company with the
financial backing of the Connecticut General Life Insurance
Company and other private sources.  It has no substantial
commitment of public resources through either federal or
state development programs.  Now in its fourth year of oper-
tions, Columbia has a population of about 8000 people and
is estimated to reach a level of 80,000 people by 1980 and
an ultimate population of 120,000.

The "governing body" of Columbia is the Columbia Parks and
Recreation Association (CPRA), a nonprofit corporation, in
which all Columbia residents will have representation (through
neighborhood associations) and to which they will pay annual
dues.  The creation of CPRA was based on the developer's
desires to provide Columbia with an internal institutional
mechanism capable of supplementing services provided by its
public governing body, the Howard County Metropolitan Commission,whose jurisdiction extends beyond Columbia to include
the whole of Howard County.  In addition to this supplemental
role, the Columbia Association has been designed to serve as
the major controlling institution for development of public
facilities through the period of the New Town's development.
Its function in this role is to ensure continuity of and ad-
herence to the long-range objectives of the total development
program as well as responsiveness to the changing needs of
a growing population.  With particular emphasis on the
achievement of Columbia's long-range goals, CPRA is intended
to be primarily an instrument of the developers until the
plan for the city is substantially complete (as measured by
CPRA's ability to service adequately debt with revenues from

its assessable base). At that time, representation of the local population will be shifted to a majority share of voting control in the Association's activities.

It is this division of control, designed to serve the long-run interests of present and future Columbia residents, which has created an unanticipated problem presently faced by the developers. In its efforts to achieve a delicate balance between the short-run needs of present residents and the long-run interests of the total development plan, The Rouse Company underestimated the degree to which the early residents (now representing about 10% of the projected population for 1980) would want to assume active roles in decisions affecting the future of their community. Certainly, the structure of the Columbia Association was never intended to inhibit participation in decision-making by even the earliest residents; but the balance of power, weighted heavily toward the developer's interests (which are seen by the developers as consistent with objectives for the new community's growth), has been an irritant to much of Columbia's present population. Responding to continual demands by these residents, the Association has agreed to limited concessions designed to increase their participation in the Association's activities. However, it remains the intention of The Rouse Company and its subsidiary development corporation (Howard Research and Development) to maintain the key role played by the Association in controlling the growth of the community with a balance between long-run interests and short-term community needs. While the original community participation scheme (and timetable) may be altered, it seems unlikely that the autonomy of the Association will be reduced to the point where its effectiveness as a development control mechanism will be appreciably diminished.

Transportation

The development plan for Columbia, as for Milton Keynes, reflects a strong orientation toward an automobile-based transportation network. The road infrastructure has been designed with an eye toward future capacities which far exceed those required during the development period. At the same time, the provision of public transportation in Columbia is also being undertaken with an eye toward the future. Like one of the systems being contemplated for Milton Keynes, the present public transportation network in Columbia is a mini-bus system whose vehicles seat about 20 people.* The reservation of public transportation rights-of-way will enable Columbia to transform its system as new technologies are available (and feasible) without major disruption of other community services.

Under a grant from the Department of Transportation and Housing and Urban Development, The Rouse Company recently completed an intensive study of transportation systems and the potential for incorporating existing and projected technologies in the plan for Columbia. Whatever the modes or technical components of future public transit networks, the operation and management of the system are expected to remain under the control of the Columbia Parks and Recreation Association. The Association's political and, to some extent, financial autonomy should permit a rapid and rational response to opportunities for incorporation of technological innovations. Thus, while the routes and placement of Columbia's future public transport network have been largely predetermined, the timing of introduction of new equipment and facilities remains quite flexible. As presently structured, the Columbia Association seems capable of effectively balancing its autonomy with political determinants of decisions arising from current economic and social needs. This balance will be crucial in the Association's ability to utilize effectively the inherent flexibility of its transportation infrastructure.

Education

The plan for education in Columbia was developed from proposals made by the developer to the Howard County Board of Education which has the responsibility for building and

---

*A limited dial-a-bus system has recently replaced the minibus system in Columbia, but it utilizes the same vehicles.

operating all schools within the county. Alternative plans for differentiating Columbia's system from the county system were explored by consultants to the developer but abandoned because of political opposition (both anticipated and encountered) from county officials and citizen groups. Thus, while the school system in Columbia is operated by the County Board of Education, the educational plan was worked out through extensive negotiations which resulted in approval by the Board of most of the final proposals (e.g., school locations, size, etc.) put forth by the developer. In some cases, such as the division of levels between primary and secondary education, proposals initiated by the developer have been adopted, in whole or in part, on a county-wide basis.

The structure of the educational system for Columbia bears a direct relationship to the evolving physical form of the city. Indeed, the size and location of the city's villages and neighborhoods correspond almost directly to the size and placement of schools. The high degree to which education is integrated into the total scope of community activities can be seen by the location of school facilities within the neighborhood and village centers where most community activities are concentrated. At the same time, however, the determination of school size, neighborhood size, road and walkway patterns from an integrated planning program has resulted in a relatively static educational structure for the community, whose ability to respond to innovations in educational programs may be inhibited thereby.

A further constraint on the flexibility of Columbia's school system is, of course, the need for county-wide agreement on educational policy changes. What may look like a positive innovation for Columbia may be perceived by other county residents as detrimental to their own local interests. The issue of school size is one example in which the work group deferred to the attitudes of the County Board of Education. It was originally hoped that considerable experimentation with smaller, more dispersed schools would be possible as the new town evolved; but anticipated opposition by the Board of Education led the work group to propose a more traditional, and more rigid, educational plan.

What surfaced during the planning stage and what will probably surface in the future in Columbia and in other new towns are the critical issues of centralized vs. local control of schools and traditional vs. experimental educational policies. The necessity for incorporating Columbia's school system into the Howard County system, moreover, adds an additional layer of institutional responsibility which, by representing constituencies outside Columbia, may not be sufficiently responsive to the changing needs of the new town's growing population. In addition, unlike the Columbia Association, which is an effective protector of Columbia's long-run goals, there is little incentive for the county Board of Education, responsible exclusively to its present constituency, to adopt an equally long-range planning horizon.

MINNESOTA EXPERIMENTAL CITY (MXC) (3)

The Minnesota Experimental City, a proposed new city of 250,000 people, is projected to be built on a site (not yet finally determined) in Minnesota. Funded by both public grants and private contributions, Phase I of this comprehensive proposal was completed in 1969 at the University of Minnesota. With an emphasis on the potential for incorporating many technological innovations and experiments in all its city functions, MXC has received considerable attention for its anticipated use of highly advanced mechanical and technical systems. Among these systems being contemplated is an easily accessible subsurface tunnel complex which would house all utilities and distribution lines and, perhaps, include conveyor or trucking facilities for delivery of goods and mail. An additional innovation proposed for the city is the enclosure of a substantial area (if not the entire city) within a climate-controlled geodesic dome.

As of May 1969, which marked the completion of the first phase of study for MXC, few concrete decisions had been reached on approaches to be followed when (and if) the project reaches the development stage. However, in the course of exploring an enormous range of alternatives for eventual incorporation into a development program, many ideas have emerged from the study which are appropriate to the discussion here. Perhaps the most pertinent conclusion expressed in the Phase I Progress Report is that the three long-term functions of planning, developing and administering the city can best be accomplished by an MXC Corporation made up of individuals representing both public and private interests having a stake in the city's realization. Although the quasi-public corporation would be self-governing through the development period, it would be phased out over time in favor of a permanent governing structure.

## Transportation

If the Experimental City, in fact, reaches the development stage and maintains an emphasis on innovation and experimentation, certainly its transportation network will be a major area for such experimentation. Detailed studies are now underway exploring alternative intracity systems with particular emphasis on terminal and transfer facilities for people, goods and mail. In anticipation of integration of advanced and common technological systems, the work to date has emphasized the need for a highly centralized management and control mechanism for transportation services. The objective of the controlling mechanism would be to achieve a rational balance among expenditures for plant and vehicle as the demands on the transportation network increase with the city's growth.

Like the Milton Keynes Development Corporation and the Columbia Parks and Recreation Association, the MXC Corporation is envisioned as an entity representing the coordination and participation of varied interest groups. However, by including representatives from state and local governments and otherwise broadening its base of representation, the MXC Corporation may be much less autonomous than the Milton Keynes Corporation or CPRA. As a project specifically designed with an orientation toward social as well as techno-

226

logical experimentation, rather than as the solution to a
relatively well-defined set of practical objectives (i.e.,
land development in Columbia, population dispersion in Milton Keynes), MXC is likely to be faced with many unresolved
questions during initial development.  Much may be gained
by building a city on these premises; but there may be an
inherent danger in creating a control mechanism responsible
to many and varied interest groups and which, at the same
time, must be both quickly responsive to opportunities for
innovation and farsighted in its evaluation of long-term
benefits to be gained from short-term decisions.

Education

There exists as yet no design for an MXC educational system.
The educational workshop sessions held during Phase I of
the study have, however, begun to identify several factors
which are likely to determine the nature of the system ultimately designed.  Of particular interest is an attitude
toward the proposed new city as a "learning society" in
which the concept of student is broadened to include all
residents who wish to take part in learning activities.  In
addition, the city itself is recognized as the "raw material"
for the educational curriculum.

Anticipating the existence of institutional barriers in the
forms of tradition, legislation, sources of financing and
educational standards, the MXC proposal emphasizes the need
for close cooperation between the planners of the city and
public agencies responsible for education, particularly those
at the state level.  The proposal also anticipates that programmatic control of the educational system will, in all
likelihood, be the responsibility of state and local agencies other than the MXC Corporation.

It is interesting to note that the degree of coordination
required between planning for education and transportation
must be particularly high if the new city is to reach its
goal as a "learning society."  However, little attention has
so far been directed toward the possibilities for integration of the control mechanisms for these two services.  On

227

the contrary, in suggesting that educational control will remain in the hands of established agencies, it appears that the MXC study team has failed to recognize the increased opportunities for a better educational system which might accrue from creating a new agency -- one which is disposed toward experimentation and which is, at least, compatible with the institution (i.e., MXC Corporation) controlling other city services, particularly transportation. It remains to be seen whether continuing studies in the MXC project will focus on this issue.

CONCLUSIONS

The history of new town development, particularly in Great Britain and Europe, has been marked by the evolution, with varying degrees of success, of institutions whose function is a proper balance between short- and long-term community goals in the provision of public services. To a considerable extent, the success of these institutions is dependent on their ability to control the planned integration of service systems in a manner which permits the community to respond effectively to technological and programmatic changes as it grows and as its peoples' needs change. It is this ability which is most difficult to incorporate in institutions such as those discussed here which maintain effective control over only some of these systems (e.g., transportation but not education).

The examples discussed here have been used to illustrate a point which may be easily overlooked as we enter into an era where new community development is likely to form an integral component of federal and state growth policies. That point, breifly stated, is that there is sufficient precedent for the design of institutions capable of developing and building new towns in the United States; there is not, however, sufficient precedent to assure us that such institutions will allow us to realize fully the potential inherent in new communities for accommodating growth and change in a better way than our existing cities have done in the past. Effective institutional control of systems which are expected to change almost continuously cannot be adequately accomplished through most mechanisms presently available to our public policy makers or to private developers. Certainly the mechanisms created must be responsive and answerable to a wide range of vested interests, both public and private; but recognition that such responsibility extends to interests which cannot yet be identified, such as those of the future residents of a new community project, must act as a major consideration in finding the proper relationship between these mechanisms and the current political arena. The opinion held here is that we will achieve neither the degree of integration of services nor the degree of foresight necessary to make new communities work unless the institutions which control the provision of public services are, at least, well-coordinated or, at best, highly centralized and reasonably autonomous.

REFERENCES

(1) Proposals for Milton Keynes have been summarized from
the following publications: Llewelyn-Davies, Weeks,
Forestier-Walker & Bor, Milton Keynes: Interim Report,
London, December 1968;  Llewelyn-Davies, Richard, "New
Cities -- A British Example: Milton Keynes," Science
Technology and the Cities, U.S. House of Representa-
tives Committee on Science and Astronautics, Washington
D.C., 1969.

(2) Details on the plan for Columbia and the current status
of the city's development were summarized from recent
discussions with personnel from the staff of The Rouse
Company and from numerous articles and publications as
well as materials prepared at the Harvard Business
School.  The documents used most extensively were the
following: Mahlon Apgar IV, "Systems Management in the
New City: Columbia, Maryland," unpublished paper, Harvard Program on Technology and Society, Cambridge, 1969;
Howard Research and Development Corporation, The General
Plan and Development Program for the New Town of Columbia, Maryland, Columbia, 1965;  Christopher Jencks,
"Educational Programs for a New Community," unpublished
paper, Institute for Policy Studies, Washington, D.C.,
1964.

(3) Background information for the MXC project was taken
from the five published volumes which record the activities undertaken during the project's first phase.
The summary volume contains most of the information
cited here: University of Minnesota, Experimental City
Project, The Minnesota Experimental City Progress Report, Second Edition, May 1969.

# IV. PUBLIC POLICY, FINANCIAL, AND MARKET ANALYSES

The feasibility of applying innovations to new community development is ultimately dependent on a community's ability and willingness to meet its financial needs. The purpose of this part of the report is to lay the foundation for an analytical method which will help determine quantifiable relationships between innovations (e.g., their costs and revenue-generating potential) and the scale factors which define a new community project. An interaction among public policy, financial and market factors is essential to the determination of these relationships but is accomplished only descriptively here. Each of the factors is, however, discussed separately in the sections which follow.

From an analysis of legislative and public policy issues, an estimate of public assistance likely to be available for any proposed new community project is an essential factor in defining the community's need to support itself. The indeterminate nature of potential legislation and the lack of rigorous qualification criteria for existing legislation, however, make it difficult, if not impossible, to determine precisely (i) how much assistance a project might qualify for and (ii) how much assistance a project can actually expect to get. In view of these limitations, the public policy and legislative analysis included here is aimed at providing the basic information upon which eventual estimates of public assistance might be drawn.

The financial analysis consists of a computer model which measures the costs of the public service network associated with a new community defined by various scale factors. By calculating the revenue-generating capability of the community, the community's need for additional assistance, if any is required, can then be determined. It is at this point that an estimate of available assistance must be made.

By varying costs associated with innovative components of the public service network, relationships between scale characteristics of the community and the feasibility of public service innovations can be established. The model described below in section B is developed to an illustrative level of operation which indicates its potential usefulness as the core of an analytical method.

The market analysis, discussed in section C, describes opportunities for identifying potential new community residents and informing them of the benefits which new communities and applied innovations might provide in creating an attractive environment in which to live and work. If responses to such marketing efforts could be measured, an estimate of user willingness to support alternative mixes of public services could be translated into limits on tax rates and user charges for use in the financial model. This was well beyond the limits of this investigation but represents a useful goal in subsequent extension of the work presented here.

# A. PUBLIC POLICY AND LEGISLATIVE ANALYSIS

This section on analysis of public policy and legislation
serves a threefold function: (i) to summarize salient
features of the recently adopted Housing and Urban Development Act of 1970 and related legislation; (ii) to identify
some of the major Federal and State policy directions likely
to affect new community program implementation; and (iii)
to determine the prognosis for application of specific
assistance programs to the innovative systems in new communities treated in this study.

SOURCE MATERIAL

The Advisory Commission on Intergovernmental Relations has
acted as a primary influence on the development of a nationwide urban growth policy incorporating new communities as
one of its major thrusts. Urban and Rural America: Policies
for Future Growth, published by the Commission in 1968, is
still, three years later, the broadest, most data-filled,
definitive work on urban and rural growth. Other studies by
the ACIR examine specific subjects within the field. The
numerous volumes of Congressional Hearings before the Subcommittee on Housing and the Ad Hoc Subcommittee on Urban
Growth contain a wide range of general and specific treatment of the field. Three documents produced within the
present Administration address themselves to the overlapping
policy issues and can be regarded as indicative of future
bipartisan directions: Toward Balanced Growth: Quantity
with Quality, National Goals Research Staff, 1970; A New
Life for the Country, President's Task Force on Rural Development, 1970; and Environmental Quality, Council on Environmental Quality. Both the passed legislation and its bill
precursors, the most significant of which can be found listed
in Appendix B, deal with programs to implement these policy
directions. Therefore, rather than attempting to repeat

information amply presented in these and in several other key sources noted in Appendix B, this section limits itself to discussion of public policy and legislation.

TITLE VII OF THE HOUSING AND
URBAN DEVELOPMENT ACT OF 1970:
URBAN GROWTH AND
NEW COMMUNITY DEVELOPMENT

The recent signing into law of the Housing and Urban Development Act of 1970 brings the evolution of urban growth and new community policy over the past decade into an entirely new phase whose low key of publicity belies its major significance. From the orientation of new communities, the new law systematically overcomes the majority of barriers which have hitherto made new communities exceedingly difficult or simply unfeasible to build. Politically, a Republican administration has adopted major urbanization and economic development policies long the province of the Democrats. Merely a few months ago, the proposed Urban Growth and New Community Act of 1970 (the Ashley Bill) was regarded as most unlikely for passage; but Congress and the President have ended by signing into law an act which contains most of the essential ingredients of the original bill. In his State of the Union Message in January 1970, the President, referring to the expected population increase by the year 2000, said:

> If we were to accommodate the full 100 million persons in new communities, we would have to build a new city of 250,000 persons each month from now until the end of the century...Clearly, the problem is enormous, and we must examine alternative solutions very carefully. (1)

Samuel C. Jackson, Assistant Secretary for Metropolitan Planning and Development of DHUD, has written in 1970:

> A realistic alternative, I believe, would be to plan to accommodate 20-30 per cent of the increment of growth in new communities (1).

Developments since the recommendations on urban growth strategies by the National Goals Research Staff ("Dispersal Strategies," p.53), leading to the recent passage of the

234

Housing and Urban Development Act of 1970, have signalled
increasing momentum by numerous governmental actors in
propelling a vigorous new communities program which may
prove consonant with the emerging economic policy of expansion. The provisions of Title VII lay the groundwork
for such a program.

SUMMARY OF TITLE VII PROVISIONS

Sections 702 and 703 summarize the Findings and Declaration
of Policy concerning national urban growth (see Appendix B
for quotations from this Section), and provide for an Urban
Growth Report by the President every two years.

Section 710 describes the Findings and Purpose of development of new communities, including a comprehensive analysis
of present urban settlement deficiencies which national
urban growth and new communities might ameliorate.

Section 712, Eligible New Community Development, specifies
prerequisites for eligibility for federal support (see
Appendix B for text), many of which provide openings for
innovative applications.

Section 713, Guarantees, provides for the Secretary of HUD
(acting through the Community Development Corporation) to
guarantee the obligations of private community developers
or of state land development agencies for the purpose of
financing land acquisition and development to a limit of
$500 million of all outstanding obligations. As is seen
in the tabular comparison of the Housing and Urban Development Acts of 1968 and 1970 in Appendix B, the total outstanding guarantees permitted in the 1970 Act double those
in the 1968 Act. It is noteworthy that guarantees of mort-
gages, while greatly assisting freeing funds for new community developers, do not constitute budgetary items.

Section 714, Loans, authorizes the making of loans to private
and public developers for the purpose of assisting them to
make interest payments on indebtedness incurred by them to
finance new community development. Especially notable about

235

this new loan feature is the provision for repayment com-
mencing not later than fifteen years after the date of loan,
thereby allowing the developer to achieve sufficient land
marketing volume before he has to bear the full brunt of
heavy mortgage interest payments.  A single new community is
eligible for a loan not to exceed $20 million; and the total
loan aggregate outstanding at one time is limited to $240
million.

Section 715, Public Service Grants, permits the making of
public service grants to provide essential public services
during an initial period (not exceeding three years) before
permanent services have yet been established.

Sections 716 and 717 set Limitations on Guarantees and Loans
and establish a Revolving Fund, respectively.

Section 718, Supplementary Grants for Public Facilities,
authorizes the making of grants to any State or local public
body or agency carrying out a new community project, in no
case any grant to exceed 20% of the cost of the particular
project nor total Federal contributions to the project to
exceed 80%.  These grants, assisted by provisions of four-
teen Federal assistance programs, constitute the core of
funding sources adaptable to the financing of innovations
in new communities.  Summary descriptions of the supplemental
grants programs are to be found in Appendix B.*

Sections 719 and 720, Technical Assistance and Special Planning Assistance, provide for technical and planning aid in
such a way to induce the use of advanced technology.

---

*It should be noted that a search through The 1969 Listing of
Operating Federal Assistance Programs Compiled During the Roth
Study turned up no less than 300 programs which could be used
in varying new community situations.  They included Economic
Development Administration, HEW, Interior, Labor and a host of
other agency programs.

Section 723, New Community Demonstration Projects, addresses itself to the use of federally owned lands for model demonstrations of new communities. In view of the Public Land Law Review Commission's findings (4) of current Administration formulations of strategies for the proper disposition of Federal lands in greater metropolitan regions, and of the present control of such lands by the Office of New Communities in HUD, this provision could easily be one way of removing the land acquisition problem.

Section 728, Joint Funding, enables combination of different Federal assistance programs in joint funding of new community developments. Given the explicit recent policy of government to coordinate interdepartmental programs (e.g., transportation expenditures being coordinated with regional or new community development) in mutually reinforcing ways, this provision could aid the application of innovative technologies in new communities.

Section 729 establishes the Community Development Corporation, consisting of five members, including the Secretary of HUD, a General Manager of the Corporation appointed by the President and three persons appointed by the Secretary, not more than one to be selected from within HUD.

Section 735, the Secretary is directed to encourage State and Regional Planning.

Section 740 and 741 provide for the development of Inner City Areas, primarily by mechanisms of converting underused or inappropriately used land to beneficial uses.

Appendix B presents an outline of the financial aid provisions of the Act.

MAJOR FEDERAL AND STATE
POLICY DIRECTIONS

1. A conscious governmental policy of balanced growth involving population dispersion is now underway and can be expected to be furthered with time. While it is evident that the specific measures of a program have not yet been

resolved, the Domestic Affairs Council and other top level agencies have been working to develop a program that coordinates the efforts of various departments. The Nixon plan for executive reorganization is symptomatic of this direction and reflects in large part the recommendations of the National Goals Research Staff. Developing on themes earlier advocated by Orville Freeman and Presidents Kennedy and Johnson, President Nixon has urged that rural America be included in an overall U.S. growth policy that favors urban-rural balance.

2. New communities will undoubtedly act an important role in a balanced growth policy. Aside from the approximately 75 new communities of varying descriptions currently being built in the U.S. (see Appendix B, map), HUD has expressly stated its intention to grant support to ten new communities by June 1971. Charles Haar summarizes arguments for new communities as an integral element of the presently crystallizing growth policy:

    a. They can relieve pressures on the central city by providing open, mixed-income housing where suburban subdivisions cannot.

    b. They can improve metropolitan and urban development by offering alternatives to predominant sprawl, greater choice of housing, etc.

    c. They can help achieve national housing goals, largely through increased market aggregation capability and the application of new technology.

    d. They can help remedy inequitable and inefficient population and urban distribution, the disparities between population and employment locations and help reestablish urban-rural balance, largely through the employment of growth centers and poles.

    e. They can offer advantages to their residents, including higher quality of services, social and technological innovations and economies deriving from reduced land and services costs and greater efficiencies (5).

3.  The policy of urban-rural balance implies the general
need and applied strategies to coordinate new community
development with regional economic policy.  Whether the new
community is developed from raw farmland or around existing
growth centers (towns or cities of under 50,000 population),
they will be located and designed in order to play a func-
tional role in growth patterns.  Economic Development Areas,
Districts and Regions eligible for favored consideration can
be seen in Appendix B.

4.  The Federal government's stated intention to test innovations in new communities will be amplified by the currently
operating strategy of coordinating grant support from different departmental sources.

5.  The years since 1968 have been marked by a decline and
even turnabout of interests who formerly opposed the new
communities program, including mayors, numerous governors and
homebuilders.  According to policy statements, lobby groups
supporting the 1970 legislation included: U.S. Conference of
Mayors, the National League of Cities, the National Association of Home Builders, the National Housing Conference, the
AFL-CIO, the National Governors' Conference* and numerous
professional organizations (6,7).  Hence, without substantial
opposition, a vigorously applied new communities program
should be slowed only by friction caused by interests com-
peting for similar objectives.

6.  In the face of Federal encouragement by means of incentives, the states will develop long-term urban and regional
growth policies, programs and institutional mechanisms.  The
New York State Urban Development Corporation is the pioneering
model for statewide and community development; and there are
abundant signs that other states, including Arizona, Hawaii,
Kentucky, Massachusetts, Pennsylvania and others are pointing

---

*The first three policy positions were "Adoption of a compre-
hensive national community development policy, Adoption of a
national population growth and distribution policy and Adoption
of a new communities policy.

in similar directions.  Appendix B contains a map and chart
illustrating the incidence of enabling housing and urban
development legislation in the 50 states, as of late 1969 (8).


GRANT ASSISTANCE FOR INNOVATIONS
IN NEW COMMUNITIES

Appendix B contains an outline listing of financial aid provisions of new community supplementary grants programs.
The prospects for sufficient funding being focused on innovative services, as opposed to being retained for conventional
services, seem favorable at this time,  since innovation,
demonstration and transferability are keynotes of the new
communities policy.  Several departments of the government
have exhibited strong interest in applying technological
and programmatic innovations in new communities (e.g., the
Dashaveyor network transit system at Fort Lincoln New Town,
as well as at Dallas-Fort Worth Airport, a vacuum tube waste
disposal system at Welfare Island).


TRANSPORTATION

Funds available for urban transportation systems, particularly
demonstrative ones in new communities, will in all likelihood
increase, due not only to the rise in government expenditure
on transportation ($4.2 billion in 1960, $7.4 billion in
1970), but to the recent vulnerability of the previously
sacrosanct Highway Trust Fund and the Department of Transportation's ambition to tear loose portions of it for application to other travel modes.  The attitude is reflected
by the administrator of DOT's Urban Mass Transportation Administration, whose emphasis is on action-oriented programs
which apply advanced technology.  Thus the 2/3 and 1/2 cost
grants under the Urban Mass Transportation and Highway Planning and Construction Acts could be subject to increase and/or
diversion.  In an atmosphere of rapidly evolving air transportation technology, and with the aid of the 1/2 matching
grants of the Airport and Airway Development Act, it is
plausible to project air transport assistance as a tool to
spur economic development of lagging regions as practiced in
the Ozarks, on the one hand, and to relieve congested airways
in the urbanized corridors on the other.

## SOLID WASTE MANAGEMENT AND UTILITIES

The currently vigorous environmental campaign and increased budgetary allocations for de-pollution and solid waste programs certainly create a favorable climate for the application of innovative waste disposal systems, particularly in the experimental and demonstrative context of new communities. All three, Basic Water and Sewer Facilities Act, Water Pollution Control and Waste Treatment Works Construction Act, and Water and Waste Disposal Systems for Rural Communities Act, have traditionally been the most widely used of Federal assistance programs. The potential economies gained on the nationwide scale by successful demonstration projects in new communities lend strong incentive to their application. The use of integrated, or utility tube systems, along with their economies and environmental amenity, will be especially eligible for funding support.

## EDUCATION AND HEALTH

The current innovative changes occuring in education, described in Part III, can be expected to be well supported, perhaps more fully than conventional educational processes, given the dramatically augmenting enrollment and budget figures, weight of importance assigned education, and predominant mood of change. Responsibly and creatively innovative educational facilities in new communities would seem strong candidates for both Federal and State support, even though levels of state support of schools vary widely. For health innovations, the national scale of radical change discussed in Part III would seem to augur favorably for progressive community programs, particularly those which were able to align themselves with medical schools, general hospitals **or** other strong resources.

## REFERENCES

(1) Samuel C. Jackson, "Population Growth and New Communities: A New Venture," HUD International, May 18, 1970.

(2) National Goals Research Staff, Toward Balanced Growth: Quantity with Quality, GPO, Washington, D.C., 1970, p.54.

(3)  Ibid., p.58.

(4)  U.S. Public Land Law Review Commission, One Third of the Nation's Land, GPO, Washington, D.C., 1970.

(5)  Charles Haar, "Development of New Communities as a Method of Meeting the Challenges of Urban Growth and Population Expansion," testimony before the Ad Hoc Subcommittee of Urban Growth of the Committee on Banking and Currency in Hearings: The Quality of Urban Life, Part 2, GPO, Washington, D.C., 1970, pp.239-266.

(6)  William Lilley III, "Parties, Agencies Scrambling to Shape Future of New Communities Program," National Journal, April 4, 1970.

(7)  National Governors' Conference, Policy Positions of the National Governors' Conference 1970-1971, Washington, D.C., 1970.

(8)  Massachusetts Legislative Research Bureau:  "State Responses to Questionnaire on State Action in Urban Crisis", Boston, 1969.

## B.  FINANCIAL ANALYSIS

The financial model described below was developed as a tool
for use in evaluating the financial feasibility of public
service innovations at varying scales of new community development.  Under the basic assumption that the community
itself should ultimately support the systems which serve
it, the model calculates the amount of assistance needed
from state and federal programs to meet annual expenditure
requirements associated with a given mix of services.  Such
assistance would be the annual amount needed to meet the
difference between expenditures and the total of internally
generated revenues and the community's bonding capacity.
For a given mix of services and estimates of factors (e.g.,
tax rate) which determine total revenues, the user of the
model would then estimate the availability of state and
federal funds to meet the assistance requirement. (These
estimates would be made on the basis of the public policy
analysis described previously in this part of the report.)
If the amount of assistance required does not appear to be
obtainable, any difference would have to be borne by the
developer since, at this stage of the analysis, all other
sources of funds would be exhausted.  Unless the developer
feels that his "subsidy" could be justified by, for example,
marketing considerations, the mix of public services would
have to be changed in order to reduce costs.  By experimen-
ting with a range of different mixes of services, the mix
most appropriate for various scales of development could
be determined.

Another way of using the model is to establish minimum
standards for the level of public services associated with
the size, population level, density and staging of a community development project.  Subsequently, the incremental
costs (and revenues) generated by the inclusion of one of
the innovations outlined in Part II could be incorporated

243

in the model and evaluated with respect to the community's ability to support these incremental costs.

A third way in which the model would be used would involve the addition of incremental costs associated with various innovations at different stages in the community's growth. Thus, the timing of the community's ability to support incremental expenditures could also be evaluated.

A considerable amount of additional model development would be required to reach the level at which it would be useful in the ways described above. At the present time, the theory of the model and programming of its core routines have been refined to an operational level. The remainder of this section discusses the model at its current stage of development, illustrates its operation and identifies several steps which would be necessary to make it more accurate and more useful.

## FUNCTION OF THE FINANCIAL MODEL

One of the major differences between development of new communities and development of large-scale residential projects is that the former requires considerable investment in community public service systems while the latter can usually be incorporated into existing public service networks which serve, for example, an already highly developed metropolitan area. The function of NEWCOM is to simulate the process by which public service systems are built so as to evaluate the ability of a new community to support the public service network required to serve it. In addition, the model is intended to be used in exploring the financial feasibility of incorporating selected technological innovations into a project and to evaluate the timing of expenditures for such innovations. The structure of the model is relatively simple: a series of arithmetic functions which compare public revenues and public expenses (capital and operating) on a continuous time basis over the development period for any given project.

Several simplifying assumptions have been made which allow the model to be manageable without diluting its usefulness as a decision-making tool. Some of these assumptions follow:

1.  Although the financial responsibility for community public services may be divided among several distinct entities (municipal body, utility corporation, transportation corporation, community public service corporation, etc.), their investment criteria will be similar and their debt capacities would be calculated on a similar basis (e.g., as a capitalized function of annual revenues). Therefore, the model assumes the existence of only one public service entity for all functions defined as public services (e.g., sewage disposal, public transit, education, police, fire, energy, etc.).

2.  The development corporation may, of course, be required to act as an investor in the public service entity, but this would not increase the debt capacity of the entity. In addition, the development corporation's investment would not be in the form of equity but rather by purchase of the entity's debentures or by subsidizing the capital cost of the public service network.

3.  Although new communities may be markedly different from one another, the most important difference will occur in the values assigned to several quantitative variables, all of which will have defineable effects on the per capita revenue available to the public service entity and the costs associated with the provision of public services.

4.  Establishment of a sinking fund (which would not necessarily be required) is assumed here to approximate continuous repayment of debt.

DATA PROBLEMS

By far the most serious problem encountered in the construction and formulation of the NEWCOM model was (and is) the collection of cost information for community public service systems. There are several reasons for this difficulty:

245

1.  The governmental structure for existing cities and
    communities is characterized by an immensely com-
    plex system of overlapping agencies, authorities,
    quasi-public bodies and different levels of govern-
    ment in which responsibility for any given public
    service may be assigned to several not-so-distinct
    entities. (This, indeed, is one of the problems
    which new communities may overcome). Since expenses
    are usually allocated by agency rather than by cate-
    gories of public services, it is extremely diffi-
    cult to derive typical cost figures for the cate-
    gories in the model.

2.  There is little agreement among municipal cost ex-
    perts on the variables which have major effects on
    public service costs (for example, some experts do
    not find a close correlation between a community's
    income characteristics and its expenses for public
    services; other experts believe a high income com-
    munity will demand a higher level of public ser-
    vices with high costs).

3.  It is particularly difficult to reduce public service
    expenditures to a per capita basis since the staging
    of public service costs often must be determined
    without a clear idea of how rapidly a community
    might grow. While new communities are intended to
    "plan" growth over an extended period, experience
    in this country is not extensive enough to tell us
    whether this is really possible.

4.  A further problem is encountered in trying to esti-
    mate future costs for various types of services in
    periods of high inflation (e.g., the same problem
    one faces in trying to project construction costs).
    Since the model accommodates 10 to 25 year develop-
    ment periods, there is no way of estimating one's
    confidence in the value assigned to the parameters
    and input variables or to the results. (See the
    Validation Section.)

For purposes of getting the model running, aggregate cost estimates were derived from two sources: The Gladstone Working Papers, economic feasibility studies prepared in 1964 by Robert Gladstone and Associates for The Rouse Company, the developers of Columbia, Maryland and Earle New Town, a feasibility study prepared by the Joint Center for Urban Studies in 1969 for the State of New Jersey. In neither of these studies was the breakdown of public service costs in a form acceptable for NEWCOM. Therefore, data was transformed as accurately as possible for use here. Such transformation will undoubtedly be required even as the model is refined and additional data is found.

MODEL FORMATION

The model is a relatively simple continuous-time arithmetic cash flow device used to measure public service revenues against expenses required for the services being evaluated. The input variables, which serve as the definitional characteristics of a new community, include the following:

1. Site Area: the total size of the site.
2. Target Population: the population level for which the community is planned.
3. Development Period: the time required for the community to grow to its target population.
4. Income Characteristics: estimates of median per capita income for the community's residential population.

The status variables in the model include the following:

5. Tax Rate: the rate at which all property (assessed at 100% of market value) is taxed (this includes school taxes).
6. Annual Interest Rate: estimates of interest rates on financial obligations of the public service entity.
7. Principal Repayment Periods: also for financial obligations.
8. Commercial Rental Rate: an estimate of the median rent for commercial space used for retail and service activities.

247

9. <u>Industrial Tax Base Multiplier</u>: an estimate of the value of industrial property relative to the value of residential property.
10. <u>Capitalization Rate</u>: the rate at which commercial rentals are capitalized to determine the tax base value of commercial properties.

Values for each of the ten variables listed above are determined by the user at the start of each execution of the program. The user may also select one of three output forms available.

The operation of the model is currently dependent on an estimate of aggregate per capita costs (capital and operating) for <u>all</u> public services. Subroutines, not yet written, would be aimed at estimating costs for eight general categories of public service expenditures which include the items indicated below:

I.   ADMINISTRATION
     A.  Police
     B.  Fire
     C.  General Maintenance
     D.  Social Services
         1.  Welfare
         2.  Social Security
         3.  Unemployment
     E.  Health Services
         1.  Hospitals
         2.  Public Clinics
         3.  Ambulance Services
     F.  General Administration

II.  EDUCATION
     A.  Physical Plant
     B.  Materials
     C.  Libraries
     D.  Staffing

III. WASTE DISPOSAL

        A.  Sanitary Sewerage
        B.  Storm Sewerage
        C.  Solid Waste Management

   IV.  ENERGY
        A.  Plant and Equipment
        B.  Power Distribution Network

    V.  TRANSPORTATION
        A.  Vehicles
        B.  Collection and Distribution Network
        C.  Delivery Network
        D.  Plant and Equipment Maintenance (incl. roads)

   VI.  RECREATION
        A.  Parks and Open Space Maintenance
        B.  Cultural Facilities

  VII.  WATER  (not shown on model flow chart)
        A.  Distribution Network
        B.  Pumping Facilities
        C.  Reservoirs
        D.  Purification Facilities

 VIII.  COMMUNICATION (not shown on model flow chart)
        A.  Cable Network
        B.  Transmission and Reception Facilities

The problem of estimating costs for many of the above items
is compounded by uncertainties as to how they might be allocated among public and private entities in any specific
project.  For this reason, the subroutines in which these
costs are derived should be written to permit changing of
parameters and coefficients at the user's option.  In
addition, the model should be capable of accepting direct
annual estimates of costs and user charges when such costs
are felt to be more accurate than those calculated internally.

# NEWCOM:A PUBLIC SERVICE FINANCIAL MODEL
## FOR NEW COMMUNITY DEVELOPMENT

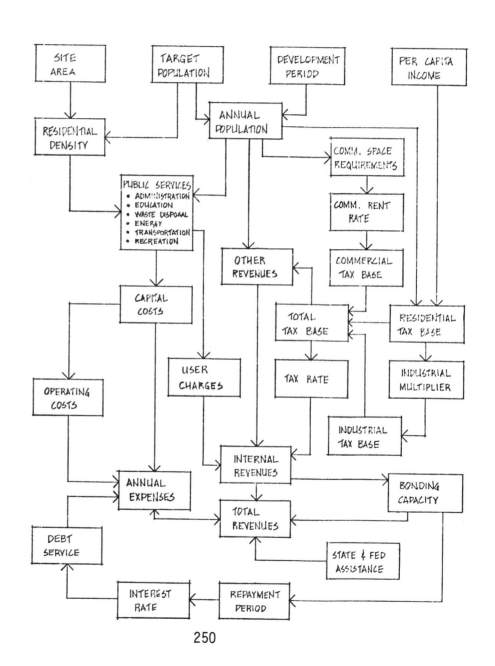

## MODEL VALIDATION

The structure of the model, as represented by the flow chart on the preceding page, was derived from an examination of several texts in municipal financial planning. With particular respect to new communities, two previous models prepared for specific new community projects were evaluated, although each differed considerably from NEWCOM in its assumptions, operation and intended use. The first was a model developed by the graduate student planning team at Harvard's GSD in its 1968 HUD-sponsored study of a new community outside Boston (New Communities: One Alternative, Harvard Graduate School of Design, 1968). Their model, written in Dynamo, never reached the operational stage largely because it attempted to reach a degree of specificity which made the model too complex to program during the eight-month duration of the project. At the expense of a similar degree of specificity, NEWCOM contains many more simplifying assumptions which may, in fact, seriously affect the model's usefulness. For example, NEWCOM does not account for differential densities within a community, a factor which would certainly change the level and costs of public services within any given new community project.

The second model used as a reference source was that developed in 1964 by Robert Gladstone and Associates for the new community of Columbia, Maryland. Columbia, started in 1965, is projected to have a population of 80,000 by 1985 and currently has a population of about 10,000. Many of the assumptions embodied in NEWCOM are similar to those used by Gladstone, particularly with respect to revenue calculations.

## PROGRAMMING

At present, the basic accounting routine of the model (written in Fortran) is accessed through a model 35 teletype connected to the BBN PDP-10 time-sharing system in Cambridge, Massachusetts. Most of the calculations currently incorporated in the core model are temporary and should be replaced by more accurate equations derived from more extensive empirical data on municipal costs and revenues. These equa-

251

tions, more specifically those which calculate costs and
user charges, can be programmed in separate subroutines
which will permit parameter changes to be made without
having to edit the core program.

A copy of the core program is included in Appendix **C**. The
variables in the model are defined below:

```
APOP  = Annual Population
TDIFF = Cumulative Surplus/Deficit
VRES  = Value of Residential Property
VCOM  = Value of Commercial Property
VIND  = Value of Industrial Property
VTAX  = Value of all Taxable Property
TREU  = Total Internal Revenues
TOTR  = Total Revenues
OPRX  = Annual Operating Expenses
CAPX  = Annual Capital Expenses
TOTX  = Total Annual Expenses
DEBX  = Annual Debt Service (interest and repayment of
          principal)

CAREQ  = State and Federal Assistance Required (cumulative)
BOND   = Available Bonding Capacity (cumulative)
UBOND  = Used Bonding Capacity (cumulative)
CAPXC  = Cumulative Capital Expenses
AREQ   = State and Federal Assistance Required (net or
          incremental)
FCOM   = Commercial Square Footage
RBOND  = Unused Bonding Square Footage
TNET   = Annual Surplus/Deficit
SREV   = Annual Revenues from Other Sources (e.g., state)
USEC   = Annual Total User Charges
TPSX   = Annual Total Public Service Expenses
ADBOND = Available Bonding Capacity (net or incremental)
ADUNBD = Unused Bonding Capacity (net)
ADUSBD = Used Bonding Capacity (net)

AREA = Site Area
TPOP = Target Population
```

```
RPOP  = Development Period
VINC  = Income per capita
RTAX  = Tax Rate
RINT  = Interest Rate on Debt
RPAY  = Principal Repayment Period
RCOM  = Commercial Rental Rate
VMIND = Industrial Tax Base Multiplier
RATE  = Capitalization Rate for Valuation of Commercial
        Property
```

MODEL OPERATION AND SENSITIVITY ANALYSIS

The printouts in this section illustrate how the model is currently used and the options given to the user in choosing output forms.

At the start of each experiment, the user is asked to input values for each of ten variables, four of which define the new community and six of which are "environmental" variables. In addition, the user chooses one of three output forms (Option 4 is reserved for a graphing routine not yet programmed). Sensitivity analysis may be performed by varying one or more of the input variables on successive experiments. This was done here varying the tax rate and holding the other variables constant; the results are compared in the summary cash flow formats (Output option 2).

In the future, it is hoped that the flexibility and usefulness of the model may be increased by two additional operations which can be performed at the user's discretion. One option will permit the user to change the parameters and coefficients which govern the model's internal calculations. The second option will permit the user to input direct estimates of costs or user charges on an annual basis and override the calculations done internally.

An additional capability being considered for the model is the inclusion of randomizing functions for use in the evaluation of specific projects in which cost estimates and parameter values have been accepted with a high degree of confidence.

253

USER SPECIFICATION OF INPUT VARIABLES:


```
 EX NEWCOM.F4
LOADING

LOADER 8K CORE
EXECUTION

INPUT AREA IN THOUSANDS OF ACRES: 10

INPUT TARGET POPULATION (IN THOUSANDS): 100

INPUT DEVELOPMENT PERIOD (10,15,20,OR 25 YEARS): 15

INPUT INCOME PER CAPITA (IN DOLLARS): 3000

INPUT TAX RATE (IN DECIMAL FRACTION): .02

INPUT ANNUAL INTEREST RATE (IN DECIMAL FRACTION): .05

INPUT DEBT REPAYMENT PERIOD (IN YEARS): 30

INPUT COMMERCIAL RENTAL RATE PER SQ. FT. (IN DOLLARS): 3

INPUT INDUSTRIAL TAX BASE MULTIPLIER: .25

INPUT CAP. RATE FOR COMMERCIAL RENT (IN DECIMAL FRACTION): .20


INPUT OUTPUT FORM DESIRED (1,2,3,OR 4)  TYPE 0 TO STOP :1
```

## 1) CASH FLOW FORMAT:

ALL AMOUNTS IN THOUSANDS OF DOLLARS

| YEAR | 1 | 2 | 3 | 4 | 5 |
|---|---|---|---|---|---|
| **EXPENSES** | | | | | |
| CAPITAL | 17730. | 17190. | 16370. | 15312. | 14059. |
| OPERATING | 555. | 1665. | 3350. | 5525. | 8101. |
| TOTAL PUB. SERV. | 18285. | 18855. | 19720. | 20837. | 22160. |
| DEBT SERVICE | 149. | 448. | 902. | 1490. | 2185. |
| TOTAL EXPENSES | 18434. | 19303. | 20622. | 22327. | 24345. |
| | | | | | |
| **REVENUES (INTERNAL)** | | | | | |
| USER CHARGES | 180. | 540. | 1087. | 1792. | 2627. |
| TAXES | 284. | 850. | 1711. | 2830. | 4149. |
| OTHER | 284. | 850. | 1711. | 2830. | 4149. |
| TOTAL INT. REV. | 747. | 2241. | 4509. | 7451. | 10926. |
| | | | | | |
| NET SURP/DEF | -17687. | -17062. | -16113. | -14876. | -13419. |
| CUM SURP/DEF | -17687. | -34750. | -50863. | -65739. | -79158. |
| | | | | | |
| **BONDING CAPACITY (NET)** | | | | | |
| AVAILIBLE | 1793. | 3586. | 5444. | 7060. | 8341. |
| UNUSED | 0. | 0. | 0. | 0. | 0. |
| USED | 1793. | 3586. | 5444. | 7060. | 8341. |
| | | | | | |
| **BONDING CAPACITY (CUM)** | | | | | |
| AVAILIBLE | 1793. | 5378. | 10822. | 17882. | 26223. |
| UNUSED | 0. | 0. | 0. | 0. | 0. |
| USED | 1793. | 5378. | 10822. | 17882. | 26223. |
| | | | | | |
| STATE AND FEDERAL | | | | | |
| ASSISTANCE (NET) | 15895. | 13477. | 10669. | 7816. | 5078. |
| STATE AND FEDERAL | | | | | |
| ASSISTANCE (CUM) | 15895. | 29371. | 40040. | 47856. | 52935. |
| | | | | | |
| POPULATION | 1500. | 4500. | 9055. | 14931. | 21896. |
| CUM. CAP. EXP. | 17730. | 34920. | 51290. | 66602. | 80661. |

255

| YEAR | 6 | 7 | 8 | 9 | 10 |
|---|---|---|---|---|---|
| **EXPENSES** | | | | | |
| CAPITAL | 12651. | 11132. | 9544. | 7927. | 6325. |
| OPERATING | 10994. | 14117. | 17383. | 20706. | 23999. |
| TOTAL PUB. SERV. | 23646. | 25249. | 26926. | 28633. | 30324. |
| DEBT SERVICE | 2966. | 3729. | 4328. | 4745. | 4963. |
| TOTAL EXPENSES | 26611. | 28978. | 31254. | 33378. | 35287. |
| | | | | | |
| **REVENUES (INTERNAL)** | | | | | |
| USER CHARGES | 3566. | 4578. | 5638. | 6715. | 7783. |
| TAXES | 5631. | 7240. | 8915. | 10619. | 12333. |
| OTHER | 5631. | 7240. | 8915. | 10619. | 12333. |
| TOTAL INT. REV. | 14828. | 19058. | 23467. | 27953. | 32449. |
| | | | | | |
| NET SURP/DEF | -11783. | -9157. | -7188. | -5008. | -2620. |
| CUM SURP/DEF | -90941. | -100098. | -107286. | -112294. | -114914. |
| | | | | | |
| **BONDING CAPACITY (NET)** | | | | | |
| AVAILIBLE | 9364. | 10152. | 10582. | 10766. | 10792. |
| UNUSED | 0. | 994. | 3393. | 5758. | 8172. |
| USED | 9364. | 9157. | 7188. | 5008. | 2620. |
| | | | | | |
| **BONDING CAPACITY (CUM)** | | | | | |
| AVAILIBLE | 35587. | 45739. | 56320. | 67086. | 77878. |
| UNUSED | 0. | 994. | 4388. | 10146. | 18319. |
| USED | 35587. | 44744. | 51932. | 56940. | 59560. |
| | | | | | |
| STATE AND FEDERAL ASSISTANCE (NET) | 2419. | 0. | 0. | 0. | 0. |
| STATE AND FEDERAL ASSISTANCE (CUM) | 55354. | 55354. | 55354. | 55354. | 55354. |
| | | | | | |
| POPULATION | 29714. | 38154. | 46981. | 55961. | 64862. |
| CUM. CAP. EXP. | 93313. | 104445. | 113989. | 121916. | 128240. |

| YEAR | 11 | 12 | 13 | 14 | 15 |
|---|---|---|---|---|---|
| **EXPENSES** | | | | | |
| CAPITAL | 4779. | 3332. | 2025. | 900. | 0. |
| OPERATING | 27176. | 30152. | 32838. | 35149. | 36999. |
| TOTAL PUB. SERV. | 31955. | 33483. | 34863. | 36050. | 37000. |
| DEBT SERVICE | 4978. | 4978. | 4785. | 4384. | 3787. |
| TOTAL EXPENSES | 36933. | 38461. | 39648. | 40434. | 40787. |
| | | | | | |
| **REVENUES (INTERNAL)** | | | | | |
| USER CHARGES | 8814. | 9779. | 10650. | 11400. | 12000. |
| TAXES | 13966. | 15495. | 16907. | 18097. | 19050. |
| OTHER | 13966. | 15495. | 16907. | 18097. | 19050. |
| TOTAL INT. REV. | 36746. | 40768. | 44465. | 47594. | 50099. |
| | | | | | |
| NET SURP/DEF | -173. | 2307. | 4816. | 7160. | 9312. |
| CUM SURP/DEF | 115087. | 112780. | 107963. | 100803. | -91491. |
| | | | | | |
| **BONDING CAPACITY (NET)** | | | | | |
| AVAILIBLE | 10311. | 9655. | 8871. | 7511. | 6012. |
| UNUSED | 10138. | 9655. | 8871. | 7511. | 6012. |
| USED | 173. | 0. | 0. | 0. | 0. |
| | | | | | |
| **BONDING CAPACITY (CUM)** | | | | | |
| AVAILIBLE | 88189. | 97844. | 106715. | 114226. | 120238. |
| UNUSED | 28456. | 40418. | 54106. | 68777. | 84101. |
| USED | 59733. | 57426. | 52609. | 45449. | 36137. |
| | | | | | |
| STATE AND FEDERAL ASSISTANCE (NET) | 0. | 0. | 0. | 0. | 0. |
| STATE AND FEDERAL ASSISTANCE (CUM) | 55354. | 55354. | 55354. | 55354. | 55354. |
| | | | | | |
| POPULATION | 73450. | 81491. | 88752. | 94999. | 99998. |
| CUM. CAP. EXP. | 133019. | 136351. | 138376. | 139276. | 139276. |

2) <u>SUMMARY CASH FLOW FORMAT</u>:

INPUT OUTPUT FORM DESIRED (1,2,3,OR 4)   TYPE 0 TO STOP :2

TAX RATE=.02:

ALL AMOUNTS IN THOUSANDS OF DOLLARS

| YEAR | 1 | 2 | 3 | 4 | 5 |
|---|---|---|---|---|---|
| TOTAL EXPENSES | 18434. | 19303. | 20622. | 22327. | 24345. |
| TOTAL INT. REV. | 747. | 2241. | 4509. | 7451. | 10926. |
| NET SURP/DEF | -17687. | -17062. | -16113. | -14876. | -13419. |

BONDING CAPACITY (CUM)

| | 1 | 2 | 3 | 4 | 5 |
|---|---|---|---|---|---|
| AVAILIBLE | 1793. | 5378. | 10822. | 17882. | 26223. |
| UNUSED | 0. | 0. | 0. | 0. | 0. |
| USED | 1793. | 5378. | 10822. | 17882. | 26223. |

| | 1 | 2 | 3 | 4 | 5 |
|---|---|---|---|---|---|
| STATE AND FEDERAL ASSISTANCE (NET) | 15895. | 13477. | 10669. | 7816. | 5078. |

INPUT OUTPUT FORM DESIRED (1,2,3,OR 4)   TYPE 0 TO STOP :2

TAX RATE=.03:

ALL AMOUNTS IN THOUSANDS OF DOLLARS

| YEAR | 1 | 2 | 3 | 4 | 5 |
|---|---|---|---|---|---|
| TOTAL EXPENSES | 18491. | 19473. | 20965. | 22893. | 24978. |
| TOTAL INT. REV. | 1031. | 3091. | 6221. | 10281. | 15076. |
| NET SURP/DEF | -17461. | -16382. | -14744. | -12612. | -9141. |

BONDING CAPACITY (CUM)

| | 1 | 2 | 3 | 4 | 5 |
|---|---|---|---|---|---|
| AVAILIBLE | 2473. | 7420. | 14930. | 24674. | 36182. |
| UNUSED | 0. | 0. | 0. | 0. | 2368. |
| USED | 2473. | 7420. | 14930. | 24674. | 33814. |

| | 1 | 2 | 3 | 4 | 5 |
|---|---|---|---|---|---|
| STATE AND FEDERAL ASSISTANCE (NET) | 14987. | 11435. | 7234. | 2369. | 0. |

TAX RATE=.02:

| YEAR | 6 | 7 | 8 | 9 | 10 |
|---|---|---|---|---|---|
| TOTAL EXPENSES | 26611. | 28978. | 31254. | 33378. | 35287. |
| TOTAL INT. REV. | 14828. | 19058. | 23467. | 27953. | 32449. |
| NET SURP/DEF | -11783. | -9157. | -7188. | -5008. | -2620. |
| BONDING CAPACITY (CUM) | | | | | |
| AVAILIBLE | 35587. | 45739. | 56320. | 67086. | 77878. |
| UNUSED | 0. | 994. | 4388. | 10146. | 18319. |
| USED | 35587. | 44744. | 51932. | 56940. | 59560. |
| STATE AND FEDERAL ASSISTANCE (NET) | 2419. | 0. | 0. | 0. | 0. |

TAX RATE=.03:

| YEAR | 6 | 7 | 8 | 9 | 10 |
|---|---|---|---|---|---|
| TOTAL EXPENSES | 26964. | 28757. | 30434. | 31978. | 33119. |
| TOTAL INT. REV. | 20459. | 26297. | 32381. | 38571. | 44782. |
| NET SURP/DEF | -6004. | -2270. | 1948. | 6594. | 11663. |
| BONDING CAPACITY (CUM) | | | | | |
| AVAILIBLE | 49102. | 63114. | 77715. | 92571. | 107477. |
| UNUSED | 9283. | 21025. | 37574. | 59024. | 85593. |
| USED | 39819. | 42088. | 40141. | 33547. | 21885. |
| STATE AND FEDERAL ASSISTANCE (NET) | 0. | 0. | 0. | 0. | 0. |

TAX RATE=.02:

| YEAR | 11 | 12 | 13 | 14 | 15 |
|------|------|------|------|------|------|
| TOTAL EXPENSES | 36933. | 38461. | 39648. | 40434. | 40787. |
| TOTAL INT. REV. | 36746. | 40768. | 44465. | 47594. | 50099. |
| NET SURP/DEF | -173. | 2307. | 4816. | 7160. | 9312. |

BONDING CAPACITY (CUM)

| | 11 | 12 | 13 | 14 | 15 |
|------|------|------|------|------|------|
| AVAILIBLE | 88189. | 97844. | 106715. | 114226. | 120238. |
| UNUSED | 28456. | 40418. | 54106. | 68777. | 84101. |
| USED | 59733. | 57426. | 52609. | 45449. | 36137. |

| STATE AND FEDERAL | | | | | |
|------|------|------|------|------|------|
| ASSISTANCE (NET) | 0. | 0. | 0. | 0. | 0. |

INPUT OUTPUT FORM DESIRED (1,2,3,OR 4)   TYPE 0 TO STOP :0


TAX RATE=.03:

| YEAR | 11 | 12 | 13 | 14 | 15 |
|------|------|------|------|------|------|
| TOTAL EXPENSES | 33779. | 33896. | 34863. | 36050. | 37000. |
| TOTAL INT. REV. | 50711. | 56263. | 61372. | 65692. | 69149. |
| NET SURP/DEF | 16932. | 22367. | 26509. | 29642. | 32149. |

BONDING CAPACITY (CUM)

| | 11 | 12 | 13 | 14 | 15 |
|------|------|------|------|------|------|
| AVAILIBLE | 121707. | 135031. | 147292. | 157660. | 165957. |
| UNUSED | 116755. | 135031. | 147292. | 157660. | 165957. |
| USED | 4952. | 0. | 0. | 0. | 0. |

| STATE AND FEDERAL | | | | | |
|------|------|------|------|------|------|
| ASSISTANCE (NET) | 0. | 0. | 0. | 0. | 0. |

INPUT OUTPUT FORM DESIRED (1,2,3,OR 4)   TYPE 0 TO STOP :0

3) <u>Supplementary</u> <u>Data</u> <u>Format</u>

| | YEAR | 1 | 2 . . . . . . . T |
|---|---|---|---|
| **EXPENSES** | | | |
| CAPITAL | | | |
| ADMINISTRATION | | — | — |
| EDUCATION | | — | — |
| WASTE DISPOSAL | | — | — |
| ENERGY | | — | — |
| TRANSPORTATION | | — | — |
| RECREATION | | — | — |
| TOTAL CAPITAL EXP. | | — | — |
| OPERATING | | | |
| ADMINISTRATION | | — | — |
| EDUCATION | | — | — |
| WASTE DISPOSAL | | — | — |
| ENERGY | | — | — |
| TRANSPORTATION | | — | — |
| RECREATION | | — | — |
| TOTAL OPER. EXP. | | — | — |
| TOTAL EXPENSES | | — | — |
| | | | |
| **USER CHARGES** | | | |
| ADMINISTRATION | | — | — |
| EDUCATION | | — | — |
| WASTE DISPOSAL | | — | — |
| ENERGY | | — | — |
| TRANSPORTATION | | — | — |
| RECREATION | | — | — |
| TOTAL USER CHARGES | | — | — |
| | | | |
| **TRANSPORTATION MILAGE** | | — | — |
| | | | |
| **COMMERCIAL SQ. FTGE** | | | |
| RETAIL | | — | — |
| SERVICE | | — | — |
| TOTAL COMM. SQ. FTGE | | — | — |
| | | | |
| **POPULATION** | | | |
| TOTAL POPULATION | | — | — |
| SCHOOL POPULATION | | — | — |
| SCHOOL SQ. FTGE | | — | — |
| | | | |
| **TAX BASE** | | | |
| RESIDENTIAL | | — | — |
| INDUSTRIAL | | — | — |
| COMMERCIAL | | — | — |
| TOTAL TAX BASE | | — | — |

261

CONCLUSIONS

As stated previously, the purpose for which NEWCOM was developed is to evaluate the ability of a proposed new community to support the public service network required to serve it. A new community, for purposes of the model, is defined by four variables: site size, target population, development period and average (mean) per capita income. While the choice of these variables was based on reasons of simplicity, it can be argued that they are insufficient to differentiate adequately between different new community projects. Although residential density is a variable calculated internally (on the basis of site size, target population and a parameter which specifies the proportion of the site used for residential development), the model would be far more representative of reality if it accommodated different densities within the same site. By the same token, the value of industrial property is calculated as a proportion of the residential tax base. Given the importance of an industrial tax base in the determination of public service revenues (and costs), the industrial component should be given far more attention than it is given in NEWCOM.

In short, the simplicity of the model casts serious doubts on its present usefulness as an analytical tool. However, two factors may be sufficient to justify the model as presently formulated:

1. The model is intended to relate the scale of development of new communities with alternative mixes of public services. It is not intended to be used for evaluation of a specific project proposal (although it is hoped that further refinement would enable the model to be used for this purpose).
2. The output of the model, while not yet systematically compared with empirical data, seems to be quite reasonable with respect to rule of thumb approximations for municipal costs and revenues.

REFERENCES

Mahlon Apgar, "Systems Management in the New City: Columbia, Maryland," discussion draft prepared for Conference on Systems Analysis in the Urban Environment, Harvard Program on Technology and Society, November 1969.

Albert Breton, "Scale Effects in Local and Metropolitan Government Expenditures," Land Economics, No. 4114, November 1965.

L. S. Burns and L. H. Klaasen, "Econometrics of Building a New Town," Review of Economics and Statistics, November 1963.

David A. Crane, Developing New Communities: Application of Technological Innovations, Department of Housing and Urban Development, Washington, D.C., 1968.

Otto Eckstein, Public Finance, Prentice-Hall, Englewood Cliffs, New Jersey, 1964.

Edward Eichler and Marshall Kaplan, The Community Builders, University of California Press, Berkeley and Los Angeles, California, 1967.

Robert M. Gladstone and Associates, "Columbia Working Papers," unpublished papers prepared for The Rouse Company, Baltimore, Maryland, 1964.

Harold Groves, Financing Government, Holt, Rinehart & Winston, New York, 1964.

James J. Grunloh, "Alternative Measures of Fiscal Capacity," Institute for Urban and Regional Studies, Washington University, St. Louis, Missouri, 1967.

Harvard Graduate School of Design, New Communities: One Alternative, Harvard University, Cambridge, Massachusetts, June 1968.

Walter Isard and Robert E. Coughlin, Municipal Costs and Revenues Resulting from Community Growth, Chandler-Davis, Wellesley, Massachusetts, 1957.

263

Joint Center for Urban Studies of MIT and Harvard, Earle
New Town, Cambridge, Massachusetts, 1969.

Nathaniel Lichfield & Paul F. Wendt, "Six English New Towns: A Financial Analysis," Town Planning Review, Vol.40, No.3, October 1964

Ruth L. Mace and Warren J. Wicker, "Do Single-Family Homes
Pay Their Own Way?," Research Monograph 15, Urban Land Institute, Washington, D.C., 1968.

David Lee Peterson, The Planned Community and the New Investors:
Economic and Political Factors in Corporate Real Estate Investment, Institute of Urban and Regional Development, University
of California, Berkeley, California, 1967.

U.S. Advisory Commission on Intergovernmental Relations,
Measures of State and Local Fiscal Capacity and Tax Efforts,
G.P.O., Washington, D.C., 1962.

Urban Systems Research and Engineering Inc., New Community
Financial Model, Cambridge, Massachusetts, 1970.

Paul F. Wendt, "Large-Scale Community Development," Journal
of Finance, Vol. 22:2, May 1967.

Paul F. Wendt and Alan R. Cerf, "Investment in Community
Development and Urban Development," Real Estate Investment,
Analysis and Taxation, McGraw-Hill, New York, 1969.

John Robert White, "Economic Assessment of Large Projects,"
The Appraisal Journal, July 1969.

W. E. Whitelaw, "Determinants of Municipal Financing,"
Harvard University Program on Urban and Regional Economics,
Paper No. 57, Cambridge, Massachusetts, November 1969.

## C.  MARKET CREATION

Technological development is not the only limiting factor
in the application of innovations to new communities.  Demand, rather than technological considerations, will determine the speed with which innovations move from the laboratory to everyday use.  Many services could be provided now
if people wanted them and were willing to pay for them.
However, diffusion time (the speed for introducing innovations into social use) has been decreasing most notably
in the last 40 years so that five and ten year diffusion
times can now be anticipated for major innovations.

The mass market is largely unprepared to create a demand,
or even exhibit an understanding of innovations of the kind
described in this report.  In the years to come, the potential market will be increasingly exposed to emerging innovations by individual sponsors operating through the mass
media (Bell will be selling picturephones, Ford may be
promoting guideways, etc.).  What there seems to be a need
for is a new community advocate body, one that could operate
at the scale of national mass media,bringing the full range
of technological and social innovations as applied in new
communities before the American public in an imaginative
way.  The purpose of this would be to better inform the
potential user and expand his awareness of alternate options for living patterns congruent with an enriched range
of options that could be provided.  In addition, feedback
mechanisms would permit an evaluation of user responsiveness to potential innovations and of user willingness to
accept incremental costs if necessary to support a desired
innovation.

The mode of informing the potential user, whether by TV or
other media, could be the use of scenarios showing detailed
glimpses into the future and how daily life transpires

amidst the new environment.  This bringing together of a
number of diverse innovations in an integrated way could
be a beginning in creating informed demand among potential
users so that when an actual innovative new community were
started, fewer people would think of themselves as experimental subjects, but rather as beneficiaries of a greatly
improved environment.

Large corporations interested in the profit potential of
new communities are especially suited as sponsors for media
representation of them.  This could be accomplished as part
of an expanded public image, or missionary, advertising
program.

A program of this nature would coincide with the current
failings of corporate dependence on exclusively market-
oriented theory, according to which progress is determined
excessively by trends and drift, insufficiently by accurate
perception of fundamental needs.  What supersedes such
dependence is a heightened general sense of expectations
of the range of the possible that the environment can provide, reinforced by a clearer popular perception of objective
performance criteria.  These altered expectations can be
formed largely by positive use of the means available to
creative manipulation -- namely the media in their numerous
forms.

Kaplan and Eichler, in their skeptical analysis of new communities, concede that "there may be untapped demand for a
type of product or products which the present firms are un-
willing or unable to offer to consumers." (1)  The view is
substantiated by Frederick Gutheim:

> The greatest obstacle to seemly cities has become
> the present low standard of demand and expectation
> of their present inhabitants, a direct expression

of their having become habituated to the present
environment and their incapacity to conceive of
any better alternative. (2)

Barbara Ward amplifies on the role of a unifying vision of
the possible city:

> There are new insights into urban planning.
> There are new technologies available to give
> the plans a solid base in fact and extrapolation.
> There are a myriad inventions -- in power, in
> traffic control, in automation -- waiting to be
> applied to urban problems.  And there are the
> resources which will in any case be spent.
> What is lacking so far is the unifying vision of
> the whole urban order as a proper field of co-
> ordinated inquiry and action. (3)

And William L. C. Wheaton, addressing himself to the role
new communities can play in remedying this failure to
reconcile vision with reality, writes:

> We particularly need planned new cities to set
> design standards for a population which has come
> to accept scattered, unorganized growth as the
> norm.  We have few distinguished examples of how
> beautiful an urban area can be.  Thus, we urgently
> need 50 to 100 standard-setting models.  With even
> a dozen demonstration new cities in the next decade
> we might logically expect the merit of those per-
> formances to attract a moderate share of all future
> building, to ease the pressure of scattered develop-
> ment, to provide substantially better environments,
> often at higher densities than can otherwise be
> provided, and to permit some real tests of the econo-
> mies of planned cities. (4)

As was emphasized in Part I, fundamental opportunities exist
in new communities to demonstrate environmental benefits
further transferable to other cities.  Peter Smithson's

267

question applies:

> What are the appropriate organization forms of
> buildings and building groups which respond to
> today's needs?  How is the response to this need
> to be communicated?  If no forms are discovered
> and no suitable language is evolved, the needs
> are not met and there remain unfulfilled, undefined
> yearnings in society as a whole. (5)

Bertrand de Jouvenel, the founder of the French Futuribles,
answers the question adeptly:

> ...Every year we are better armed to achieve what
> we want.  But what do we want?...The lack of any
> clear images of the style of life we are building
> is a cause of anxiety...a feeling that our ways of
> life are being determined entirely by technological
> advances, through no choice of ours.  Such a belief
> is widespread and fed by many incautious expressions.
>
> This belief is however quite unfounded.  It is time
> that experts represented the many different outcomes
> which can be obtained by different uses of our many
> and increasing possibilities.  This representation
> should be in pictures, according to the utopian
> tradition.  For us, television now offers a new
> technique of exposition.  A variety of modes of life
> which seem achievable can be displayed to the public
> in order to elicit its preferences; a project of
> this kind is now being undertaken by means of the
> French television. (6)

Most succinctly, de Jouvenel summarizes the problem:

> Our mind craves pictures. (7)

In the context of forecast technological and social changes
discussed in Part III, clear grounds and context exist for

the heightening of individual and social expectations of the natural, social and technological environment. The images that can gratify expectations assume magnified importance. Out of the present watershed of disillusionment and catharsis, and alongside the new "sensate" culture that is displacing traditional religious values, can rise a new image of the possible future; and it is evident that a strong continuity resides in this image from its smallest scale component of individual to its largest of world community which is particularly adaptable to the new community. Obviously, the image must be powerful; moreover, the elements that make it powerful are drama, or the ability to excite; understandability and clarity (even literalness); and plausibility.

Because of these factors, the public media constitute a logical vehicle through which to stimulate and respond to not only societal urges which the new community can satisfy, but the market and market creation needs of the private corporation toward informing the potential buyers of expanded options.

As the greatest potential unifying force in social communications, television offers the most effective tool for representing the image of a better life. It is the best means for television has the capacity for feedback participation from its audience; in this sense, Robert Theobald's idea possesses the open-ended facility for citizen response, as demonstrated in urban renewal situations in Minneapolis, Chicago, Philadelphia and Oakland:

> The catalyzing element is the use of television and radio to communicate a new vision of the city. People deeply concerned about the place where they live would communicate their concern over the "honest" medium of television, which supports sincerity and reveals falsehood. (8)

Such an application would offer special merit in a new community development situation in which a surrogate target population were involved.

To emphasize dramatic interest, film can also be used. Both film and TV can be used as a serious anticipatory representation of the future environmental choices. Additionally, newspapers, radio, magazines, exhibitions and other media can be used in ways that make the representation of the possible environment of the new community meaningful to its audience.* The media can expand the image held by the population of the range of possibility and choice of environment and make feasible the achievement of richer and fuller living in the new town or city.

In short, the image anticipates the achieved reality; its power to shape the achieved reality is enormous. The corporate developer of new communities should therefore strongly consider strategies for the use of media to represent the benfits of the communities, to obtain potential user response and, above all, at this critical moment in the history of new community development, to create a public awareness of (and a market for) technological and programmatic innovation.

REFERENCES

(1) Edward P. Eichler and Marshall Kaplan, The Community Builders, p.148.

(2) Frederick Gutheim, "Urban Space and Urban Design," in L. Wingo, ed., Cities and Space, p.117.

(3) Barbara Ward in The Economist, July 7, 1967.

(4) William L. C. Wheaton, "Form and Structure of the Metropolitan Area," in Ewald, Environment for Man, p.174.

*James Rouse's exhibition at Columbia, Maryland and subsequent media presentations mark an effort at making a popular presentation of the future environment of one new community which has met with considerable and influential success.

(5)  Peter Smithson, "The Architecture of Technology," in
     Architectural Design, July 1961.

(6)  Bertrand de Jouvenel, "Utopia for Practical Purposes,"
     in Daedalus, Spring 1965, p.444.

(7)  Bertrand de Jouvenel, Ibid., p.441.

(8)  Robert Theobald, An Alternative Future for America,
     p.140.

# V. ADVANCE DESIGN OF NEW COMMUNITY PROTOTYPES

The purpose of this part is to examine systematically the interaction between public service networks and community development patterns and to relate these networks and other design variables to the scale of development, density characteristics and staging strategies which define a community development program.

By constructing taxonomies of community forms and typologies of service area (neighborhood) forms, relationships between activities or services and community development characteristics can be established. This is useful in evaluating alternative combinations of circulation patterns and population and activity distributions which form the basis upon which the impacts of innovative systems on the community are measured. This analysis is also useful in: (i) identifying costs and benefits associated with the application of a given innovation to a community development project; and (ii) evaluating the physical and financial requirements which may be necessary to prepare (e.g., purchase rights-of-way) for the accommodation of an innovation at a later stage in the project. Once these prototypical relationships are established, the effects of particular site conditions (e.g., natural systems, topography, etc.) will operate to transform the basic community forms. When examined, the site conditions permit a more detailed evaluation of innovations being considered. In practice, the prototypical and site specific analyses would be undertaken simultaneously, rather than sequentially.

## A.  TAXONOMY OF MACROFORMS

From observation of settlement patterns -- existing, planned
and idealized (Appendix F) -- a simplified taxonomy of
macroforms (non-location-specific) can be established.*
This is useful in determining primary form attributes, independent of natural systems and adjacent urban systems, which
may predetermine or be determined by the selection of alternative internal movement, communication and utility
systems.

TAXONOMY CATEGORIES

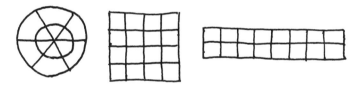

Figure 5-1

Circulation patterns

The categories are:

    1.  Three basic circulation patterns (determined by
        major movement channels) (Fig. 5-1).

        A.  Ring-radial
        B.  Grid
        C.  Linear

    2.  Relative population distributions.

        A.  Uniform distribution (Fig. 5-2).
        B.  Concentrated center, lower densities at the out-
            side and medium densities between (Fig. 5-3).

---

*Irregular patterns are not categorized nor analyzed here.
Quite often a seemingly irregular pattern when examined can
be seen to operate de facto  as one of the macroforms categorized here.  There are also hybrids which are not examined here
such as a grid system with strong diagonals generated from a
center and cutting across the grid.  This pattern takes on
characteristics of central congestion roughly similar to the
ring-radial form (1).

Figure 5-2

**Uniform population**

Figure 5-3

Concentrated center population

  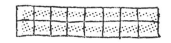

Figure 5-4

Concentrated loop population

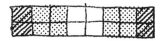 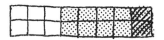

Figure 5-5          Figure 5-6

Concentrated ends    Concentrated end

Figure 5-7          Figure 5-8

Dispersed           Concentrated
activities          activities

C.  Concentrated loop, lower densities at the center
    and outside and high in between (Fig. 5-4). This
    applies to a condition where the center would ex-
    clude residential use and contain some other use
    such as recreation or commerce.
D.  Concentrated ends, lower densities in the center
    and medium in between (Fig. 5-5). This applies
    to the linear form only and would be a likely
    application for a new community that would be
    developed with an existing small town.
E.  Concentrated one end, lower densities at the
    other, and medium in between (Fig. 5-6). This
    applies to the linear form only and would likely
    be the case where the heavy end was adjacent to
    a highly attractive natural resource such as a
    lake or if it were at a relatively higher ele-
    vation, commanding impressive views.

3.  Relative activity center and service area distributions.

A.  The majority of activities (say 75%) dispersed
    into small areas evenly distributed, the remainder
    (25%) concentrated in one or several areas
    (Fig. 5-7).
B.  The majority of activities concentrated at one
    or several large areas, the remainder disaggre-
    gated into small areas, evenly distributed (Fig.
    5-8).

274

## THE BASIC CIRCULATION PATTERNS

Figure 5-9

Ring and radial systems

Figure 5-10

Transformation of ring to ring-radial

Figure 5-11

Transformation of radial to ring-radial

Figure 5-12

Second order linear

The basic circulation alternatives should not be regarded as fixed and invariant; as spatial relationships evolve through time, new demands may require new linkages and eliminate the need for others. For this reason, a comment should be made regarding the dynamics of activity locations over time which will tend to alter a ring pattern or a radial pattern toward a combination: a ring-radial. It is unrealistic, except in very special circumstances in which topographical barriers may exist, to expect that a ring system or a radial system (Fig. 5-9) will remain in its pure form for long. It is almost certain that because of its centrality, the area inside a ring will become highly attractive and demand will build up for radial links to the center (Fig. 5-10). Likewise, connectivity between the outer areas of the radial system will cause the need for circumferential links (Fig. 5-11).

In any event, both the ring form and the radial form taken separately are special variants of the linear form, the ring being a linear closed loop and the radial being several linear forms joined at their ends with the possibility of that joint becoming a common center. Other special variants of the linear form (which are branching systems) are:

1. second order linear (Fig. 5-12) and
2. second order linear composite (Fig. 5-13).

Both of these variants are especially well suited to promote the close interaction of man-made activity systems and natural systems such as waterways, parklands or farmlands.

The basic circulation pattern is, in effect, the structure of the community and the different macroforms have different characteristics of (i) accessibility, (ii) growth potential, (iii) efficiency and (iv) imageability.

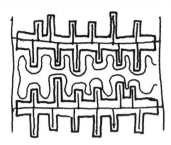

Figure 5-13

Second order linear composite

Accessibility

A carefully designed grid system can achieve a more equitable loading than a ring-radial system (1,2) and has better
attributes of accessibility.  Radial street patterns reduce
travel distances to highly attractive core centers; but
because of route convergence at the center, congestion problems can become severe, making ring-radial trips longer
in time.  The linear form is, at the smallest division, an
extended grid but has even more advantages through more efficient organization which tends to increase accessibility
to all districts.

Growth

The grid organization has the tendency to equalize growth
opportunity in all parts and can easily be expanded in
several directions, but adaptation to areas of restricted
topography can be difficult.  The ring-radial organization
has low growth potential.  Growth along closed loop circum-
ferentials is finite.  Corridor development can occur out
along the radials which, as was previously noted, gives them
linear characteristics.  The linear organization has the
highest growth potential since the growth can be simply
staged by the addition of growth modules in the direction of
the main service networks (given an unconstrained boundary
condition).*

*See Kevin Lynch, "Environmental Adaptability," Journal of
 the American Institute of Planners, Vol. 24, No. 1, 1958.

|  | GRID | RING-RADIAL | LINEAR |
|---|---|---|---|
| ACCESSIBILITY<br>Equalization of access<br>to activities in all parts | HIGH | LOW | HIGH |
| GROWTH<br>Growth potential | MEDIUM | LOW | HIGHEST |
| EFFICIENCY<br>Organization of utility services | MEDIUM | MEDIUM | HIGH |
| IMAGEABILITY<br>Image potential | MEDIUM | HIGH | HIGH |

Table 5-1

Settlement Pattern Attributes

277

Efficiency

Efficiency here refers to the organization of service nodes and networks. The patterns of service areas or activity centers are considered efficient when they are organized systematically enough to be served by regular and economical utility networks. <u>All three forms, but especially the linear, possess this potential.</u>

Imageability

Imageability is the intangible quality of stimulating in the users and observers strong and memorable feelings of environmental form. Strong perceptual anchors, such as high concentrations of structures at central areas, which can serve as orientation or reference points for all other areas, are one among several important image-producing devices.* <u>All three macroforms have potential imageability, but the ring-radial and the linear forms seem to have the highest potential for generating imageability.</u>

Table 5-1 summarizes settlement pattern attributes.

POPULATION AND ACTIVITY DISTRIBUTION

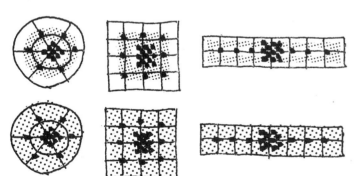

Figure 5-14

High trip time

Several recent studies have shown how trip times and costs vary for alternative combinations of population and activity center distribution (3,4).

These combinations with concentrated ring or uniform population distribution, when combined with concentrated central activities, have high trip times and costs (Fig. 5-14) (the uniform population distribution having the highest) (4).

The combination of concentrated central or concentrated ring population distributions with disaggregated and evenly

*For a full treatment of imageability, see Kevin Lynch's <u>The Image of the City</u>, MIT Press, Cambridge, Mass., 1963.

278

distributed activity centers have low trip times and costs (Fig. 5-15).

Figure 5-15

Low trip time patterns

## ALTERNATE GEOMETRICS

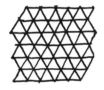

Figure 5-16

Non-orthogonal network patterns

Figure 5-17

Three-way intersection

Four-way intersection

In the previous notes on the basic circulation patterns of grid, ring-radial and linear macroforms, the main movement channels were assumed to be orthogonally related; network patterns such as hexagonal, triangular and four-directional (Fig. 5-16) would have attributes very different from rectangular patterns when applied within one of the macroforms.

The triangular and four directional patterns have serious disadvantages because of their six and eight-way intersections. For internal journeys, the hexagonal pattern would yield trip lengths equivalent to the rectangular pattern (5). The hexagonal pattern also has intersection advantages having three converging directions compared to four for the rectangular pattern. This reduces the points of potential conflict (Fig. 5-17).

These characteristics of the hexagonal pattern give it advantages if applied at a small scale such as local streets or at an intermediate scale such as collector-distributor roads.

MOBILITY IN THE COMMUNITY

The use of the word "settlement" in describing a contemporary community should be clarified. Its use is somewhat misleading in that the average American family moves once every three to five years (6). The word implies fixity and non-change. More people are leading more mobile lives, and this characteristic of transience in American life is one that could be legitimized and even celebrated in a new community. Mobility is both forced and voluntary. The forced kind is generated by (i) a forced change of employment out of the catchment area of the community and (ii) increasing space needs in the dwelling as would be required with family growth.* The voluntary kind of move is generated by expanded career opportunities in other areas, or a desire to relocate because of climate.

Mobile parks are a growing phenomenon; and while some people still consider them ugly and declassé, a growing number of people from all income levels are accepting and living in them. However, a mobile home, once situated in a park, is seldom moved. It is mobile largely in the sense of how it arrived at its final destination. With more careful attention to both the hardware design and the site design, mobile home parks could become an acceptable and vital part of a new community and could even be host to dwellings that are genuinely mobile.

---

*As defined by Peter Rossi, Why Families Move. The space needs within a dwelling are the largest single factor in motivating a move.

## B. TYPOLOGY OF SERVICE AREAS

In the same way that innovative public service systems must be evaluated in terms of their community-wide requirements and impacts, they must also be considered in relation to the service area, or local community, of which the smallest unit is the dwelling.

Service area is the expression used here to describe the minimum area of particular size, population and density needed to support a given mix of activities. Criteria for support of activities are accessibility (reasonable walking distances), financial feasibility and standards for per capita needs (e.g., for open space). In many cases the term service area can be used interchangeably with "neighborhood," "district" and even "village." However, it is not encumbered here with these traditional meanings and is more applicable to widely varying urban conditions, depending upon the mix of activities being considered. The association of activity mixes and levels with areal population and density attributes is a critical step in evaluating the impact of technological and programatic innovations on community development; by establishing the design relationships between activities and public service innovations, the scale characteristics (area, population and density) at which the innovations exert some influence on community form can be determined. This section, therefore, establishes relationships between activity levels and scale characteristics of various service areas and proceeds to examine the impact of selected innovations on those areas.

SERVICE AREA CONCEPT IN PLANNING

It is essential for planning purposes to designate and work with one or several building blocks of the community, or "community growth modules." Thus, transportation, utility, social, educational and other systems can be judged to deter-

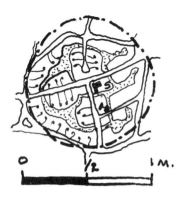

Figure 5-18

Clarence Stein neighborhood unit,
source: Gallion and Eisner,
Urban Patterns

mine how they will satisfy service area goals and needs at
the same time as they satisfy community-wide goals. The community growth module is defined as the minimum service area
which exerts a deterministic effect on dimensional or scale
characteristics of the community and which is a repeatable
unit.

In the tradition of Ebenezer Howard and Clarence Perry,
Clarence Stein's neighborhood unit of 5000 to 10,000 people,
primarily defined by its elementary school and parks within
a half-mile walk, has served as an influential model in this
country for the definition of service areas (Fig. 5-18).
The main principle of the concept is the 1/2 mile (10 minute)
maximum walk from the most remote dwelling to the central
elementary school. Abutting neighborhoods join or interlock
at secondary school and community center locations which serve
as means for fostering inter-neighborhood exchange. Three
constants are notable: (i) the neighborhoods focus inward,
toward their schools and shops at the geographic center;
(ii) the densities are only medium or medium-low; and (iii)
the arterials and other city-wide transportation channels
circumvent the neighborhoods.

COMPONENTS OF THE SERVICE AREA

The service area (or neighborhood) contains activity centers
and service networks which are supportable only at certain
levels of population and/or density.

ACTIVITY CENTERS

Activity centers,* whether single-purpose or multi-purpose,
large or small, are those magnet points of activity to which
people are attracted. Service networks are the more ubiquitous
systems of transportation utilities, water, sewerage, education
(if facilities are dispersed), recreational open space and

*As previously defined in Part II, they include employment and
 shopping opportunities, health care, education and recreation
 facilities.

282

facilities which bind the parts of the service area together, and which have cross impact with the physical form of the area.

ACTIVITY CENTERS AND POPULATION LEVELS

The tables in Appendix E present a representative inventory of activities by general category and the population levels at which their support becomes feasible in a service area. The inventory is not exhaustive, but is sufficiently comprehensive to provide the preliminary information for determining size and population parameters for community growth modules. The inventory yields several points relevant to service area design.

1. Some small-scale activities, mostly associated with children, the dwelling and short distances -- such as play spaces and convenience stores -- are constants at the smallest scales.

2. Population levels of 5000, 10,000 and particularly 20,000 and 50,000 are significant thresholds at which significant clusters of activities occur. The level of 50,000 appears to be particularly critical in the fields of education and recreation, both of which will clearly assume increased community importance in the future.

3. The population figures ascribed to the activities tend to be conservative, reflecting obsolescent, non-complementary activity patterns which in the recent past have shown indications of being organized for greater interaction. Thus, tendencies toward both centralization and decentralization are occuring simultaneously. The growth of multi-purpose activity clusters results in greater flexibility of population thresholds. Mostly, the flexibility works in favor of enabling smaller population levels to support more activity centers, particularly innovative ones such as day-care centers, dispersed employment areas

| | CELL | | SERVICE AREA (OR NEIGHBORHOOD) | | DISTRICT (OR VILLAGE) | |
|---|---|---|---|---|---|---|
| | 50 TO 500 pop. | | 4000 TO 5000 pop.** | | 10,000 TO 15,000 pop.*** | |
| | 500 MEAN* | | 5000 TO 10,000 | | 18,000 TO 45,000** | |
| POPULATION | 50 p. | 500 p. | 1500 p. | 5000 p. | 10,000 p. | 18,000 p. |
| 1.  14 PPA | 3.5 acres | 35 acres | 100 acres | 350 acres | 700 acres | 1000 acres |
| | | | | | | |
| 2.  70 PPA | | 7 a. | 20 a. | 70 a. | 140 a. | 200 a. |
| | | | | | | |
| 3. 175 PPA | | 3 a. | 8 a. | 30 a. | 60 a. | 80 a. |
| | | | | | | |
| 4. 225 PPA | | 2 a. | 6 a. | 20 a. | 40 a. | 60 a. |

Table 5-2.   COMMUNITY GROWTH MODULES OR BUILDING BLOCKS OF THE COMMUNITY (IN ACRES)

*Frank Hendricks and Christopher Alexander, "Subculture Cells," Center for Environmental Structure, Berkeley, California, 1967.

**English Mark I New Town neighborhoods 5000 to 10,000 population, noted in Andrew Derbyshire, "New Town Plans: A Critical Review," Royal Institute of Architects Journal, October 1967.

***Columbia, Maryland, as described in Morton Hoppenfeld, "A Sketch of the Columbia Planning-Building Process for Columbia, Maryland," American Institute of Planners Journal, November 1967.

and local communications and learning centers.

4. Innovative technological systems described formerly -- including network cab, transit and utilador -- serve most productively those activity centers of high density and use characteristics, particularly education, employment and recreation.

Population and densities that can be accommodated in particular area sizes are illustrated in Table 5-2. The ranges are representative of a significant density spread, for they include the relatively high density levels of English Mark I New Towns and the low and typically American new community level of Columbia, Maryland. This information is helpful in the understanding of hierarchical socio-spatial divisions that appear to operate successfully. Table 5-3 compares density levels between three U.S. and three European new communities and serves to clarify in more readily identifiable terms the meaning of the figures in Table 5-2.

| U.S. | Density ranges | | Avg. net density | |
|---|---|---|---|---|
| | dwelling units per acre | persons per acre | d.u./a | ppa |
| Reston | 3-40 | 12-43 | 6 | 22 |
| Columbia | 3.5-40 | 13-143 | 4 | 15 |
| Janss-Conejo | 3-25 | 12-89 | 3.5 | 13 |
| European | | | | |
| Harlow | 6-40 | 20-120 | 15 | 45 |
| Cumbernauld | 19-33 | 70-120 | 25 | 90 |
| Tapiola | 5-40 | 17-143 | 28 | 101 |

Table 5-3. Comparative population and dwelling unit densities in six U.S. and European new communities (7)

## DESIGN CRITERIA FOR SERVICE AREAS

Design criteria for service areas are established directly from community goals* in the early stages of design, when the basic alternatives must be evaluated. Prime criteria for early decisions are:

1. Areal size and population density.
2. Size of sub-parts or cells.
3. Degree of concentration or dispersion of activity centers within each service area (one-place synergism or multi-place, separate identity).
4. Proximity of dwellings to activity centers in time or distance for (i) walking and (ii) vehicle trips.
5. Degree of adaptability to efficient growth and change for areas, networks and user groups in terms of staging.
6. Proportion of activity centers and services to be provided within the individual service area or outside the area in community-wide activity center concentrations.
7. Impact criteria of community-wide transit on service area (for example, transit through geographic center or along periphery).
8. Degree of fit between areal design with natural systems.
9. Basic resource allocation and assignment of priorities for service area components (i.e., do transportation facilities require more expenditure than park facilities, educational or health systems?).
10. Degree of integration of public service systems of service area and community-wide levels. Another way of expressing this criterion is overlapping or congruence of service area networks. The networks can be broken down into the following general headings:

---

*See section on "New Community Capabilities for Reducing Alienation" (item no.6), for a method of aiding the establishment of community goals in the early stages prior to the formation of a user constituency.

a.  residential
b.  educational
c.  employment
d.  recreation, indoor and outdoor
e.  transportation (i) internal (pedestrian, bicycle, auto); (ii) external, community-wide (network, demand actuated); and (iii) external, inter-regional access
f.  convenience stores (and other commercial)
g.  cultural institutions
h.  natural systems and open space (i) nodes and (ii) networks
i.  utilities
j.  health and welfare
k.  communications
l.  street pattern (i) geometry, (ii) scale and spacing and (iii) access hierarchy

11.  Degree of independence as neighborhood units or the opposite, boundaryless service areas.*

---

*"Neighborhoods" or "non-neighborhoods."  Suzanne Keller examines the two extremes in The Urban Neighborhood -- "small, cohesive subunits that would help recapture the local human scale" and, on the other hand, "large anonymous urban aggregate."  She points out that Catherine Bauer summarizes the opposition to the neighborhood principle as "reactionary in effect and sentimental in concept."  C. A. Doxiadis, on the other hand, pleads for the "human dimensions" in the world's cities, of which the neighborhood provides one measure.  Columbia, Maryland embodies in rather rigidly hierarchical form the neighborhood principles described by Doxiodis, while Milton Keynes would at first seem to reflect the Bauer favor toward generalized, neutral, free-flowing patterns in which areal configurations can occur spontaneously without pre-planned structuring.  But on close examination, it becomes clear that most of the neighborhood generating elements such as schools and shops have been preestablished in a somewhat uniform distribution and exhibit a basic structure. (See Appendix D for further discussion of particular new communities.)

SERVICE AREA TYPOLOGY

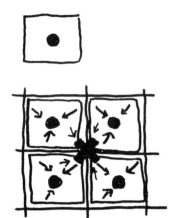

Figure 5-19

Self-contained service areas

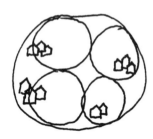

Figure 5-20

Minimum service area interchange

Whatever the size of the service areas under consideration, they can be disaggregated into three basic types, according to the pattern in which their activity centers (schools, convenience stores, social and recreational facilities, etc.) are located. We can call these models: (i) inward-oriented, (ii) interrelated and (iii) community-wide oriented.

A. Self-Contained

1. Service care activity center(s) is located internally near the geographic center of the area and strengthens a high degree of area identity. The identity can be reinforced as desired by the use of physical barriers such as arterial roads or natural landscape features which diminish interactivity between geographically adjoining areas.

   Assuming a service area 1/2 mile across, the most remote dwelling is 1/4 mile, or five minutes walk, from the activity center (at 3 mph, 20 minutes = 1 mile, 10 minutes = 1/2 mile, 5 minutes = 1/4 mile). The inward orientation of this configuration is normally modified towards an interarea oriented form by the establishment of some facility such as school or shop serving adjoining areas, as indicated by the "X" symbol in the center of Figure 5-19.

2. Household access tends to be relatively hierarchical and rigid in structure, encouraging a minimum of interchange between service areas, while not necessarily excluding it (Fig. 5-20). Columbia, Maryland is an example of this structure.

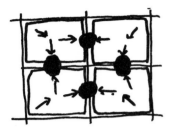

Figure 5-21

Inter-related service areas

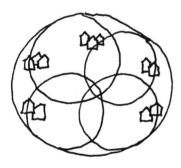

Figure 5-22

Maximum service area interchange

1. Service center(s) is located on the perimeter of the service area, where it fosters interaction between self-contained adjoining service areas. Unlike the model A, this model causes outward cross-feeding access and activity patterns (Fig. 5-21). For the 1/2 mile square area, maximum distance from dwelling to activity center remains, except for residences on the outer periphery of the total community, at the 1/4 mile, five-minute range.

2. Household access favors a more complex and expansive structure of relationships than in Model A, with greater choice and less rigid hierarchy (Fig. 5-22). More widely spaced visit locations (social, recreational, etc.) are engendered through the inter-related activity centers. As opposed to the relative autonomy and inward focus of model A, in which a large portion of needs are satisfied internally, model B implicitly encourages residents to go further afield.

Figure 5-23

Community-oriented service areas

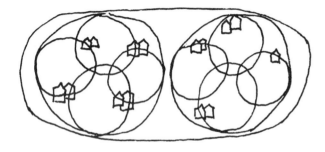

Figure 5-24

Maximum service area and community
interchange

1.   The activity center(s) is located on a main linkage
which runs along one or more perimeters of the service area and is part of the community-wide transportation system.   Thus, the activity center serves
the community-at-large as well as the particular
service area in which it is located.   In the 1/2
mile square area, distance from most remote dwelling
to activity center is 1/2 mile or a ten minute walk.
This model is oriented outwardly and interactively
with the immediately adjacent service areas, which
also use the activity centers.   It is the least
rigid and hierarchical of the three models.

2.   Of the three models discussed, this one tends toward
maximum choice and flexibility of household access
and greatest complexity of structural interrelation-
ships.   The individual service area assumes diminished significance relative to the community-wide
network; individual structure is amplified by the
availability via transit of all facilities located
along its line.

3.   Household activity pattern and range in model C are
broadest and involve the most widely spaced visit
locations of the three models.   Whereas model B
generates contacts between residents of adjacent
areas, model C provides the basis for maximum use
of community-wide facilities.

The purpose of describing the three service areas and their
structural characteristics is to identify explicitly the basic unit comprising the larger community growth module.   It
is essential to pass through these steps in order to develop
a workable approach for (i) determining fit of the physical
form to community goals at all scales, (ii) designing the
physical components and networks of the areas and the modules
and (iii) evaluating the applicability of technological and
programmatic innovations at all scales.

## Deployment of Activity Centers

The activity centers within the service areas can take either centralized or dispersed location patterns, respective to each of the three service area configurations described (Fig. 5-25).

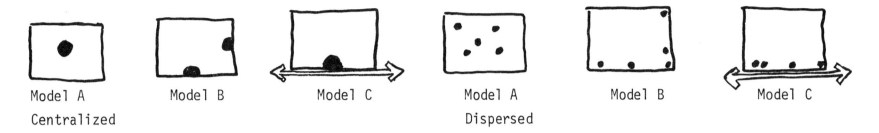

| Model A | Model B | Model C | Model A | Model B | Model C |
| Centralized | | | Dispersed | | |

Figure 5-25

Deployment of activity centers in service areas

## Transportation Linkage to Activity Centers

Similarly, the activity centers can assume either centralized or dispersed location patterns in relation to a line public transport system (Fig. 5-26).

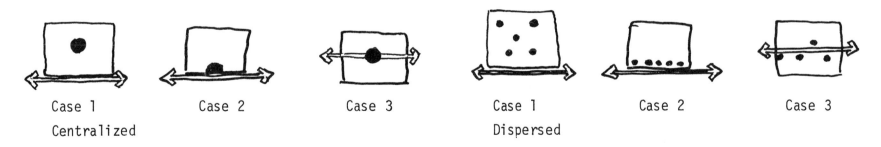

| Case 1 | Case 2 | Case 3 | Case 1 | Case 2 | Case 3 |
| Centralized | | | Dispersed | | |

Figure 5-26

Patterns of transportation linkage to activity centers

Case 1., while preserving either self-contained or inter-related relationships and identity, does not take advantage of the benefits of linking activity centers to the public transportation system. Case 2. offers the greatest potential for promoting effective use of both activity centers and the transportation systems by joining them; but this linkage occurs by sacrificing the smaller scale neighborhood identity associated with such activity center components as small convenience stores, etc. randomly located.

Case 3., if the link is a conventional street, can be inimical to the service area because of problems of disruption of area privacy, hazardous traffic, physical barrier effect and high noise levels. With a safer, quieter system such as an automated guideway this case can be considered more applicable. Combinations of the best attributes of several patterns would probably provide most effective fit with community goals.

COMPARISON OF SERVICE AREA MODELS

The two major models to which the service area must respond are (i) the discrete, autonomous sub-culture area or neighborhood (Fig. 5-27) and (ii) the interactive service area coincident with expanded access patterns (Fig. 5-27). The individual service area, whether discreet or interactive, must continue to contain or have connectivity to functions available in the older neighborhood form (elementary schools, play spaces, social meet spaces, convenience stores, job opportunities, etc.).

It must further provide convenient access to activity centers and service functions lying geographically outside of the service area on a community wide basis (Fig. 5-28).

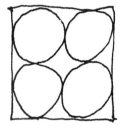

Figure 5-27

Autonomous and interactive service areas

292

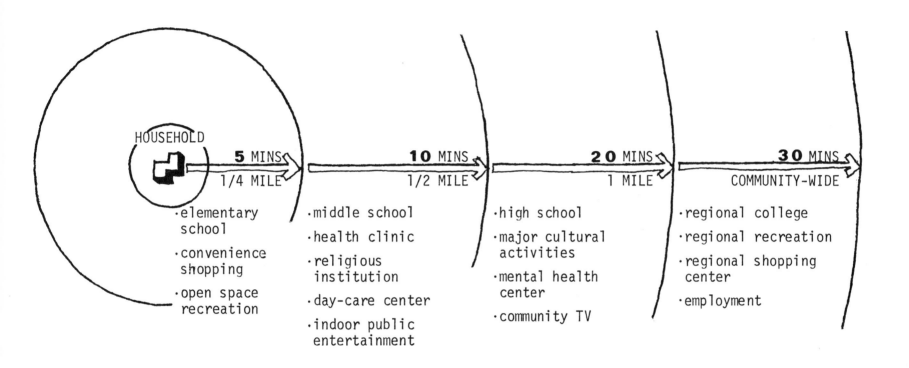

HOUSEHOLD

**5** MINS
1/4 MILE

**10** MINS
1/2 MILE

**20** MINS
1 MILE

**30** MINS
COMMUNITY-WIDE

·elementary
school

·convenience
shopping

·open space
recreation

·middle school

·health clinic

·religious
institution

·day-care center

·indoor public
entertainment

·high school

·major cultural
activities

·mental health
center

·community TV

·regional college

·regional recreation

·regional shopping
center

·employment

Improved levels of transportation tend to shorten the time/
distances cited (described in Appendix E).*  Increased access
capability will be needed to respond to trends such as (i)
shortened work week and increased leisure resulting in demand

Figure 5-28

Maximum walking distances from
household to community activities

———————————

*The access demand to services as a changing function of the
availability of improved communications technology is not
appropriate to consider here as it has been treated in Part II,
"Evolutionary Automated Movement Systems."

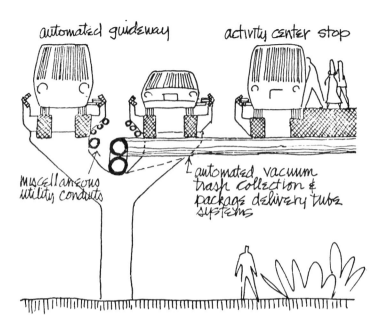

automated guideway

activity center stop

miscellaneous utility conduits

automated vacuum trash collection & package delivery tube systems

Figure 5-29

Guideway-utilador integration

for more immediately accessible recreation and cultural facilities and (ii) emerging dispersed locations for education, health care, shopping and employment (even though they will be closer to the dwelling, they will tend to be more dispersed, therefore requiring greater connectivity).

Where service networks serve highly loaded activity centers or dwelling areas, there are possibilities for integrating them. For example, where an elevated guideway is used, it can provide the structural support for an above grade utilador with new service tubes for AVAC tube trash collection and pneumatic tube delivery (Fig. 5-29).

294

Education

For all levels of schooling, the trends toward dispersed
extensions of a community-wide education system and their
integration with other community resources bear directly on
the design of pedestrian and public transportation networks,
their interfaces with public facilities, the use of advanced communications systems (e.g., community TV station,
coaxial cables, etc..) and the utilities network.  These
design considerations together with the use of non-educa-
tional facilities for educational purposes, such as described in "Education" in Part III, and the greatly increased
emphais on education in general as described in "Summary of
Social Trends" in Part I, would result in what might be
termed a "total educational environment" (Fig. 5-30).  Dispersed day-care centers would be located within a five or
ten minute walking radius of homes.  Sub-centers for human
potential expansion could also be located in a similar decentralized pattern.

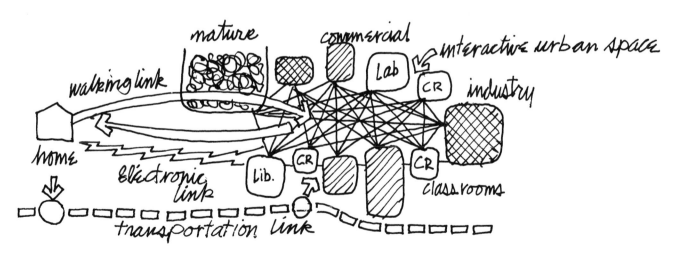

Figure 5-30

Total educational environment

## Health Facilities

Whereas much curative treatment requires the complex facilities available only in the centralized hospital, expanding paraprofessional programs and the growing emphasis on pre-paid contracts and preventive treatment will argue for the closely accessible health facilities described in "Health Services" in part III. The benefits brought about by a mother being able to bear her child in her own locale, among people she knows, extend to other facets of health care and convey to the user the security of immediate medical attention within close proximity. Location of local health centers could combine health clubs with medical care for all ages, thereby achieving the social benefits of mixing age groups achieved, for example, in the English post-World War II Peckham Experiment and British New Town health centers since.

## Transportation

Acceptable walking distances to transit stops determine sizes of service areas in much the same way that desired public transportation coverage of the community influences the urban macro-form as discussed earlier in this part and in part II. The householder within the service area needs convenient, quick linkage of all transportation systems, whether pedestrian walkway, Dial-A-Bus, line haul transit or heliport. Inter-regional, as well as inter-area, accessibility from the dwelling becomes a firm requirement, and without the time-consuming, congested access patterns typical of most cities (Fig. 5-31).

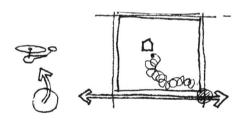

Figure 5-31

Access to full range of transportation

## Open Space and Recreation

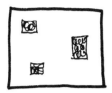

Past Pattern

Emerging Pattern

Figure 5-32

Patterns of open space linkage

New patterns of open space linkage favor inter-area and community-wide continuity which respects natural systems (Fig. 5-32) and achieves effective mesh with transportation networks, activities location and residential area configurations. This need for integration becomes a design determinant of primary force.

## Utilities

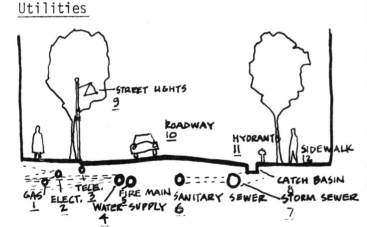

Figure 5-33

Conventional utility installations

Conventional utility installations are inefficient and costly, requiring separate digging operations (providing all are underground) for water, gas, electricity, sanitary sewer, storm sewer and telephone and inconvenient interruptions to street use for installation of laterals or repair (Fig. 5-33). The utilador concept described in part III suggests major design effects as well as service benefits, particularly for high-density areas. A modified version of the concept appears warranted in medium-density areas (Fig. 5-34). At one extreme of density -- very low -- self-contained energy production and communications systems will result in the capability for autonomy and freedom of location. At the other extreme, the physical configurations of dense activities will be influenced by the need

297

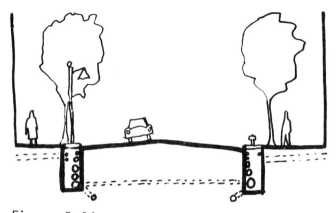

Figure 5-34

Modified utilador

Communications

for more efficiently integrated utility systems. Both
possibilities will become strong determinants of urban
form. Thus, an efficient solid-waste disposal system or
a pneumatic parcel delivery system (probably originating
with the post office network and later branching out to
accommodate department store delivery service to branch
post offices or to large residential buildings) would strongly
influence location of user activities along their length, and
of terminal facilities within the service area. Intermediate
waste treatment stations connected to the trunkline of the
waste collection system would have significant implications
for agglomerative and individual dwelling unit design as
well as for trash collecting patterns.

The advanced communications systems reviewed in part III
presage the availability of an extraordinary array of previously inaccessible or limited-access services ranging from
secretarial help or shopping at home picturevision, to instantaneous data-bank access via multi-access computer and
remote participation in local TV station broadcasting.
While it is difficult to assess the exact physical impact
on the emerging service area, it seems likely that increased
global exposure and the ability to perform remote operations
from the home will result in both (i) importance assigned to
and expectations demanded of the local service area, where
an increased amount of time is spent due to the relief provided by advanced communications from arduous errand or work-
performing trips and (ii) leisure and education travel patterns far afield stimulated by new electronic exposure with
growing economic effect on service area and residential design. The greater importance assigned to the immediate local
area raises the level of expectations of services and amenities to be provided in the service area, thereby affecting
all aspects of service area physical design.

298

## Street Patterns

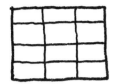

(i) Gridiron

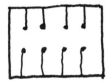

(ii) Cul-de-sac

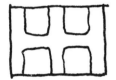

(iii) Loop

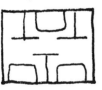

(iv) Loop and T

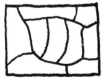

(v) Curvalinear

Despite the problems of resolving the intangibles of values and human social and ecological patterns into physical form which supports social and technological systems discussed, and of choosing among the basic street layout patterns in Figure 5-35, the rationale for decision is provided by: (i) the numerous tangible factors of density, economics of land, streets and utilities, topography and micro-climate and (ii) the initially intangible, but ultimately reducible to the tangible, measurements and reasonings associated with access to services and activities.

Each of the improved and innovative location and service factors discussed previously exert determinant influence on service area design. For example, the 1/4 mile maximum walk to the transit stop, elementary school or convenience store determines the basic area size, suggests a limited number of logical locations for the activities and favors certain street patterns over others.

A public door-to-door demand-actuated system such as Dial-A-Bus is not easily adapted to cul-de-sac or loop and T-patterns (Fig. 5-35, ii and iv); but it adapts well to patterns with through-streets (Fig. 5-35, i, v, vi, vii, viii) and at specific levels of density. Linear utility systems feasible in gridiron, hexagonal or offset grid patterns (Fig. 5-35, i, vii, viii) would likely prove impractical in cul-de-sac or loop patterns (Fig. 5-35, ii and iii).

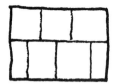

(vi) Staggered grid

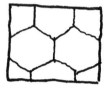

(vii) Hexagonal grid

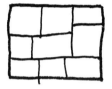

(viii) Offset grid

Figure 5-35

REFERENCES

(1) Howard T. Fisher and Nicholas A. Boukidis, "The Con-
    equences of Obliquity in Arterial Systems," Traffic
    Quarterly, January 1963.

(2) H. S. Levinson and K. R. Roberts, "System Configurations
    in Urban Transportation Planning," Highway Research Re-
    cord, No. 64, National Research Council, 1965.

(3) The Plan for Milton Keynes, Vol. 2, main consultants,
    Llewelyn-Davies Weeks Forestier-Walker and Bor, March
    1970.

(4)  George Charles Hemmens, <u>An Analysis of Urban Travel</u>
     <u>and the Spatial Structure of Urban Activities</u>, un-
     published PHD thesis, MIT Department of Urban Studies,
     January 1966.

(5)  E. M. Holroyd, <u>Theoretical Average Journey Lengths in</u>
     <u>Circular Towns with Various Routing Systems</u>, Road Re-
     search Laboratory Report No. 43, Ministry of Transport,
     U.K., 1966.

(6)  Nelson Foote and Janet Abu-Lughod, <u>Housing Choices and</u>
     <u>Housing Constraints</u>, 1960.

(7)  David A. Crane and Associates, <u>A Comparative Study of</u>
     <u>New Towns</u>, prepared for the New York State Urban Develop-
     ment Corporation, Lysander New Community, 1970.

# APPENDICES

The following appendices are included here and, referenced where appropriate in the five Parts of the report:

A. Multi-Service Cable Communication System
B. Applicable Legislation
C. Financial Model Program
D. Service Area Typology in New Community Examples
E. Activities and Population Levels
F. Macroform Prototypes and Comparative Community
   Scales

## Business:Work at Home

1. Secretarial assistance
2. Person-to-person communications
3. Computer-assisted meetings
4. Electronic mail
5. Adding machine functions
6. Access to company files
7. Message recoding

## Business:Commerce

8. Shopping transactions
9. Grocery price list (information and orders)
10. "Cashless society" transactions
11. Dedicated newspaper
12. Banking
13. Answering services
14. Real estate listings
15. Better Business Bureau
16. Special sale information
17. Budget preparation and monitoring

## Political

18. Council meetings, other local meetings
19. Voter views and participation
20. Nationwide voting surveys and voting
21. Debates on local issues
22. Free political channel for candidates
23. Access to elected officials

## Social Services - State and Federal Governments

24. Social Security
25. Immigration and naturalization
26. Taxes
27. Weather Bureau Information
28. Courts
29. Index of social services
30. General postal information
31. Welfare
32. Vocational counseling
33. Employment service
34. Disaster warnings and evacuation control
35. Marriage counseling

## Health

36. Remote diagnosis
37. Emergency medical information
38. Drugs
39. Health insurance
40. Medicare claim processing
41. Prescription communication (doctor-to-pharmacy)
42. Dietetic meal planning and scheduling
43. Ambulance/doctor/hospital coordination
44. Outpatient services
45. Medical and dental appointments and reminders
46. Advice on simple problems

## Health Cont'd

47. Doctor directory
48. Immunization information
49. Mental Health center (psychiatric consultation)
50. Suicide prevention center
51. Alcoholics Anonymous

## Household

52. Water, electric, and gas meter reading
53. Alarm systems
54. Operate household services (turn lights on, light up furnace, etc.)
55. Recipe file
56. Telegrams
57. Mail and messages
58. Daily calendar (reminders about appointments)
59. Address book
60. Equipment maintenance reminders
61. Christmas lists
62. Generate shopping lists, weekly menu
63. Cleaning information
64. Foodstorage information
65. Keeping track of food supply, household items

## Agriculture

66. Soil conditions
67. Fertilizers
68. Insecticides
69. Gardening
70. Seasonal crops

## Education

71. Correspondence schools
72. Computer tutor
73. Computer-aided instruction
74. School-related communications
75. College catalog and related information
76. Adult courses, evening courses
77. Seminars
78. Consultation with teachers, professors

## Transportation:travel

79. Department of Motor Vehicles
80. Road conditions
81. Travel advice
82. Traffic conditions
83. Vehicle maintenance reminders
84. Taxi service
85. Bus route scheduling, flight and train schedules
86. Maps
87. Travel accommodations
88. Fares and ticket reservation
89. Tour information
90. Travel and car insurance
91. Passports

## Recreation

92. Skiiing (snow conditions)
93. Camping (areas, facilities)
94. Tennis (courts, partners)
95. Golfing (courses, etc.)
96. Picnic Areas (facilities available)

## Recreation cont'd

97. Flying (lessons, airports)
98. Fishing (season, permit, etc.)
99. Hunting (season, permit, etc.)
100. Boating
101. Games (chess, bridge)

## Entertainment

103. Current cultural events
104. Local plays, movies
105. Ticket reservations
106. Restaurant reservations
107. Computer dating

## Information:General

108. Index of all services available
109. Library
110. Dictionaries
111. Encyclopedias
112. Expanded yellow page service
113. Stock market information
114. Newspapers
115. Magazines
116. Recent book publications (lists and abstracts)
117. Telephone area codes

REFERENCE: Dr. John de Mercade et al, "Multiservice Cable Telecommunication Systems: The Wired City," final report of Canada, University of Ottawa, Telecommission Study.

# APPENDIX B - APPLICABLE LEGISLATION

Extracts from the Bill "Title VII - Urban Growth and New Communities Development" (S.4368) of the Housing and Urban Development Act of 1970:

It is the policy of the Congress and the purpose of this title to provide for the development of a national urban growth policy and to encourage the rational, orderly, efficient, and economic growth, development, and redevelopment of our States, metropolitan areas, cities, countries, towns, and communities in predominantly rural areas which demonstrate a special potential for accelerated growth; to encourage the prudent use and conservation of our natural resources; and to encourage and support development which will assure our communities of adequate tax bases, community services, job opportunities, and well-balanced neighborhoods in socially, economically, and physically attractive living environments.

PART A -- DEVELOPMENT OF A NATIONAL URBAN
               GROWTH POLICY

FINDINGS AND DECLARATION OF POLICY

SEC. 702 (a)  The Congress finds that the rapid growth of urban population and uneven expansion of urban development in the United States, together with a decline in farm population, slower growth in rural areas, and migration to the cities, has created an imbalance between the Nation's needs and resources and seriously threatens our physical environment, and that the economic and social development of the Nation, the proper conservation of our

natural resources, and the achievement of satisfactory living standards depend upon the sound, orderly, and more balanced development of all areas
of the Nation.

(b)  The Congress further finds that Federal programs affect the location of population, economic
growth, and the character of urban development;
that such programs frequently conflict and result
in undesirable and costly patterns of urban development which adversely affect the environment and
wastefully use our natural resources; and that existing and future programs must be interrelated and
established priorities consistent with a national
urban growth policy.

(c)  To promote the general welfare and properly
apply the resources of the Federal Government in
strengthening the economic and social health of all
areas of the Nation and more adequately protect the
physical environment and conserve natural resources,
the Congress declares that the Federal Government,
consistent with the responsibilities of State and
local government and the private sector, must assume responsibility for the development of a national
urban growth policy which shall incorporate social,
economic, and other appropriate factors.  Such policy
shall serve as a guide in making specific decisions
at the national level which affect the pattern of
urban growth and shall provide a framework for development of interstate, State, and local growth and
stabilization policy.

(d)  The Congress further declares that the national
urban growth policy should --
    (1) favor patterns of urbanization and economic
    development and stabilization which offer a range
    of alternative locations and encourage the wise
    and balanced use of physical and human resources
    in metropolitan and urban regions as well as in
    smaller urban places which have a potential for
    accelerated growth;

    (2) foster the continued economic strength of all
    parts of the United States, including central
    cities, suburbs, smaller communities, local neigh-
    borhoods, and rural areas;

    (3) help reverse trends of migration and physi-
    cal growth which reinforce disparities among
    States, regions, and cities;

    (4) treat comprehensively the problems of poverty

and employment (including the erosion of tax bases, and the need for better community services and job opportunities) which are associated with disorderly urbanization and rural decline;

(5) develop means to encourage good housing for all Americans without regard to race or creed;

(6) define the role of the Federal Government in revitalizing existing communities and encouraging planned, large-scale urban and new community development;

(7) strengthen the capacity of general governmental institutions to contribute to balanced urban growth and stabilization; and

(8) facilitate increased coordination in the administration of Federal programs so as to encourage desirable patterns of urban growth and stabilization, the prudent use of natural resources, and the protection of the physical environment.

ELIGIBLE NEW COMMUNITY DEVELOPMENT

SEC. 712. (a) A new community development program is eligible for assistance under this part only if the Secretary determines that the program (or the new community it contemplates) --
(1) will provide an alternative to disorderly urban growth, helping preserve or enhance desirable aspects of the natural and urban environment or so improving general and economic conditions in established communities as to help reverse migration from existing cities or rural areas;

(2) will be economically feasible in terms of economic base or potential for economic growth;

(3) will contribute to the welfare of the entire area which will be substantially affected by the program and of which the land to be developed is a part;

(4) is consistent with comprehensive planning, physical and social, determined by the Secretary to provide an adequate basis for evaluating the new community development program in relation to other plans (including State, local, and private plans) and activities involving area population, housing and development trends, and transporta-

tion, water, sewerage, open space, recreation, and other relevant facilities;

(5) has received all governmental reviews and approvals required by State or local law, or by the Secretary;

(6) will contribute to good living conditions in the community, and that such community will be characterized by well balanced and diversified land use patterns and will include or be served by adequate public, community, and commerical facilities (including facilities needed for education, health and social services, recreation, and transportation) deemed satisfactory by the Secretary;

(7) makes substantial provision for housing within the means of persons of low and moderate income and that such housing will constitute an appropriate proportion of the community's housing supply; and

(8) will make significant use of advanced in design and technology with respect to land utilization, materials and methods of construction, and the provision of the community facilities and services.

(b) A new community development program approved for assistance under this part shall be undertaken by a private new community developer or State land development agency approved by the Secretary on the basis of financial, technical, and administrative ability which demonstrates capacity to carry out the program with reasonable assurance of its completion.

Outline of Financial Aid Provisions of:

HOUSING AND URBAN DEVELOPMENT ACT OF 1970

TITLE VII

| SECTION | DESCRIPTION | GRANT, ONE NEW COMMUNITY | GRANTS TOTAL |
|---|---|---|---|
| PART·B | | | |
| 1. Guarantees | Of obligations of private or public new community developers issued to finance real property acquisition and land development, in amounts up to 80% of real property value before development and 90% of estimated development cost. | maximum $50mm | $500mm |
| 2. Grants | To state land development agencies to cover difference between interest and on their taxable obligations (only type permitted) and on similar tax exempt obligations. | | |
| 3. Loans | To private and public new community developers to use in making interest payments during an initial development period (not over 15 years) on indebtedness attributable to land acquisition or land development. | $20mm | $240mm |
| 4. Supplementary Grants for Public Facilities | Authorizes $36mm for FY 1971 and $66mm each year for FY 1972 and 1973 to state or local public bodies for up to 20% of cost of 14 types of federally-aided public facility projects; provided that total federal share does not exceed 80% of project cost. | 20% cost | $36mm(FY1971) $66mm(FY1972) $66mm(FY1973) |
| 5. Technical Assistance | To developers for planning and development programs | | |
| 6. Special Planning Assistance. | To private new community developers for certain planning work which is in excess of that ordinarily needed for business purposes, up to 2/3 cost of work. | 2/3 cost | $5mm (FY1971) $10mm (FY 1972) |
| PART C | | | |
| 7. Urban Growth Patterns: Planning Grants | To governmental agencies or organizations of public officials for plans and programs for guiding and controlling urban growth. | 75%* | |
| 8. Open Space to Guide Urban Growth | For open space consolidation, grants for land interests to guide urban development. | 75%* | |

| SECTION | DESCRIPTION | GRANT, ONE NEW COMMUNITY | GRANTS TOTAL |
|---------|-------------|--------------------------|--------------|
| PART D | | | |
| 9. Inner City Developments | Urban renewal aid for revitalization of areas having obsolete commercial and other uneconomic land uses, including development of vacant and air right sites. | | |

*Directed more to existing metropolitan areas than to new communities; could apply to new community situations.

Outline of Financial Aid Provisions in Title VII of Housing and
Urban Development Act of 1970

## NEW COMMUNITY SUPPLEMENTARY GRANTS FOR PUBLIC FACILITIES

| | TITLE | DESCRIPTION | GRANT |
|---|---|---|---|
| 1. | Urban Mass Transportation | To public bodies; mass transit facilities, both public & private systems | 2/3 cost |
| 2. | Highway Planning and Construction | To state highway departments; primary and secondary roads and streets | 1/2 " |
| 3. | Airport and Airway Development | To public agencies for airport development consistent with national airport system plan. | 1/2 " |
| 4. | Health Facilities Construction | To state and local agencies and private non-profit organizations for hospitals and other health facilities (Federal share varies from state to state.) | 1/3 - 2/3 " |
| 5. | Library Construction | To states for public libraries in areas lacking them (Federal share varies from state to state.) | 1/3 - 2/3 " |
| 6. | Outdoor Recreation | To states and, through states, to political subdivisions | 1/2 " |
| 7. | Open Space Land, Urban Beautification and Improvement | To states and local public bodies for acquisition and development for park, recreation, scenic, historic uses. | 1/2 " |
| 8. | Neighborhood Facilities | To local public bodies or agencies for multi-service centers for community services. (3/4 cost in redevelopment areas) | 2/3 " (3/4) " |
| 9. | Basic Water and Sewer Facilities | To local public bodies or agencies of one or more states for construction of basic water and sewer facilities. | 1/2 " |
| 10. | Water Pollution Control, Waste Treatment Works Construction | To any state, municipalitiy or inter-municipal or interstate agency for construction of treatment works, including interceptors and outfall sewers. | |
| | | a. Normally<br>b. If state also contributes 30%<br>c. If state contributes 25% and enforceable standards exist for water into which treated waste would be discharged | 30% "<br>40% "<br>50% " |

| TITLE | DESCRIPTION | GRANT |
|---|---|---|
| 10. | d.  If in metropolitan area and conforms with a comprehensive metropolitan plan (+10% increase). | 40 - 60% " |
| 11. Water and Waste Disposal Systems for Rural Communities | To public bodies and non-profit organizations primarily serving rural communities under 5,500 in population for planning and developing water supply and waste disposal systems in rural areas. | 1/2 " |
| 12. Academic Facilities for Public Community Colleges and Technical Institutes - Two-Year Institutions | To assist public community colleges and technical institutes for construction | 1/2 " |
| 13. Academic Facilities for Colleges - Four-Year Institutions | To undergraduate institutions for construction | 1/2 " |
| 14. Public Works and Development Facilities in Economic Development areas | To states, local subdivisions, Indian tribes, and private or public non-profit organizations representing an EDA or designated growth center (80% aid in severely depressed areas) | 1/2 " (80%) " |

<u>NEW COMMUNITY SUPPLEMENTARY GRANTS FOR PUBLIC FACILITIES</u>

(Source: Department of Housing and Urban Development information and guideline summary, dated August 18, 1971)

Supplementary grants authorized by the Housing and Urban Development Act of 1970 are available for projects assisted by grants under the federal programs described below:

1. <u>Program Title</u>: Urban Mass Transportation

   (Roth, p.774*; HUD Basic Laws, 1970, p.486; major change pending)

   <u>Authorizing Legislation</u>:  Section 3 of the Urban Mass Transportation Act of 1964 (49 U.S.C. 1601 et seq.).

   <u>Administering Agency</u>:  Department of Transportation: Urban Mass Transportation Administration.

   <u>Description</u>:  Grants to assist public bodies in acquiring or improving capital equipment and facilities needed for mass transit systems, both public and private. Maximum grant is two-thirds of net project cost (that part which cannot be financed from system revenue)if the applicant meets the full planning requirements of the regular program; otherwise, the applicant may qualify under the emergency program for one-half of net project cost.

---

*Reference is made to the "1969 Listing of Operating Federal Assistance Programs Compiled During the Roth Study" (prepared by the staff of Rep. William V. Roth, Jr., House Document No. 91-177) for further information regarding the programs listed.

2. Program Title: Highway Planning and Construction

(Roth, p.752)

Popular Name: Federal-Aid Highway Program.

Authorizing Legislation: Section 120(a) of title 23, United States Code.

Administering Agency: Department of Transportation: Federal Highway Administration.

Description: Grants to State Highway Departments for building or improving primary and secondary roads and streets (Section 120(a) of title 23, United States Code, does not provide assistance for the interstate system). Grants are provided on a 50-50 matching basis (although States contribute less if they have large areas of public non-taxable lands) and may be used for planning, engineering, right-of-way acquisition, new construction, improvement, and relocation assistance.

3. Program Title: Airport and Airway Development

(P.L. 91-258)

Authorizing Legislation: Airport and Airway Development Act of 1970 (P.L. 91-258).

Administering Agency: Department of Transportation.

Description: Financial aid to public agencies for airport development consistent with the National Airport System Plan. Grants can be made for construction or improvement of airport facilities (such as runways, taxiways, and aprons); for land acquisition including advance acquisition and airspace easements; and for the acquisition of navigation aids and safety equipment.

Grants are generally limited to 50 percent.


4.  Program Title:  Health Facilities Construction

    (Roth, pp.204-07)

    Popular Name:  Hill-Burton Program.

    Authorizing Legislation:  Title VI of the Public Health
    Service Act, (42 U.S.C. 291 et seq.).

    Administering Agency:  Department of Health, Education,
    and Welfare:  Public Health Service, Health Services
    and Mental Health Administration.

    Description:  Grants to State and local agencies and
    private nonprofit organizations through State Hill-
    Burton agencies for building and equipping hospitals
    and other health facilities.  Eligible facilities include
    general hospitals, long-term care facilities, public
    health centers, rehabilitation facilities, and out-
    patient facilities.  Federal grants may be used for
    construction, modernization, and equipping of these
    facilities.  The Federal share varies from state to
    state, ranging from one-third to two-thirds of project
    cost.


4.  Program Title:  Library Construction

    (Roth, p.382; legislation pending)

    Authorizing Legislation:  Title II, Library Services and
    Construction Act (20 U.S.C.A. 355a et seq.).

    Administration Agency:  Department of Health, Education,

and Welfare: Office of Education.

Description: Grants to states for constructing public library facilities in areas lacking library facilities. The Federal share varies from state to state, ranging from one-third to two-thirds of project cost.

6. Program Title: Outdoor Recreation

(Roth, p.618)

Authorizing Legislation: Section 5 of the Land and Water Conservation Fund Act of 1965 (16 U.S.C. 460L-8).

Administering Agency: Department of Interior: Bureau of Outdoor Recreation.

Description: Grants on a 50-50 matching basis to States and, through States, to their political subdivisions for planning, acquiring, and developing public outdoor recreation areas and facilities. These include multi-purpose metropolitan parks, snow ski areas, urban playgrounds, golf courses, swimming pools, hiking and bicycling paths, nature interpretation areas, fishing piers and marinas.

7. Program Title: Open Space Land, Urban Beautification and Improvement

(Roth, pp.566 570, 572; HUD laws, p.499)

Authorizing Legislation: Title VII of the Housing Act of 1961 (42 U.S.C. 1500-1500ee).

Administering Agency: Department of Housing and Urban Development: Assistant Secretary for Metropolitan

Planning and Development.

Description: Grants to state and local public bodies for acquisition and development of land for park, recreation, conservation, scenic, and historic uses. Grants may not exceed 50 percent of the total cost of acquisition and development.

8. Program Title: Neighborhood Facilities

(Roth, p.563; HUD laws, p.433)

Authorizing Legislation: Section 703 of the Housing and Urban Development Act of 1965 (42 U.S.C. 3103).

Administering Agency: Department of Housing and Urban Development: Assistant Secretary for Metropolitan Planning and Development.

Description: Grants to local public bodies or agencies to aid in construction or rehabilitation of multi-service neighborhood centers which offer programs of health, recreation, social, and similar community services. Grants may cover two-thirds of the development cost, or three-fourths in areas designated for redevelopment under section 401, Public Works and Economic Development Act of 1965.

9. Program Title: Basic Water and Sewer Facilities

(Roth, p.569; HUD laws, p.432)

Authorizing Legislation: Section 702 of the Housing and Urban Development Act of 1965 (42 U.S.C. 3101).

Administering Agency: Housing and Urban Development:
Assistant Secretary for Metropolitan Planning and
Development.

Description: Grants to local public bodies or agencies
of one or more States for the construction of basic
community water and sewer facilities needed to promote
efficient and orderly growth and development. Grants
cover up to 50 percent of land and construction costs.

10. Program Title: Water Pollution Control, Waste Treatment
Works Construction

(Roth, p.633)

Authorizing Legislation: Section 8 of the Federal
Water Pollution Control Act (33 U.S.C. 466).

Administering Agency: Department of Interior: Federal
Water Pollution Control Administration.

Description: Under this program, grants can be made
to any State, municipality, or intermunicipal or interstate agency for the construction of waste treatment
works, including interceptors and outfall sewers. A
grant may not exceed 30 percent of the estimated reasonable cost of construction, except that the grant may
be increased to 40 percent of project cost if the State
contributes 25 percent and there are enforceable water
quality standards for the water into which the treated
waste would be discharged. The amount of the grant may
be increased by 10 percent, in metropolitan areas, if
the project conforms with a comprehensive metropolitan
plan.

11. Program Title: Water and Waste Disposal Systems for
Rural Communities

(Roth, pp.43, 46)

Authorizing Legislation: Section 306 (a) (2) of the Consolidated Farmers Home Administration Act (7 U.S.C. 1926).

Administering Agency: Department of Agriculture: Farmers Home Administration.

Description: This program provides grants to public bodies and nonprofit organizations primarily serving rural communities under 5,500 in population for planning and developing water supply and waste disposal systems in rural areas. When needed to reduce user charges to reasonable levels, applicants may obtain grants of up to 50 percent of development cost.

12. Program Title: Academic Facilities for Public Community Colleges and Technical Institutes -- Two Year Institutions

(Roth, p.363; major legislation pending)

Authorizing Legislation: Section 103 of the Higher Education Facilities Act of 1963 (20 U.S.C.A. 713).

Administering Agency: Department of Health, Education, and Welfare: Office of Education.

Description: Grants to assist public community colleges and public technical institutes in building, rehabilitating or improving academic and related facilities. Grants may be made for up to 50 percent of the construction cost.

13. Program Title: Academic Facilities for Colleges -- Four Year Institutions

(Roth, p.363; major legislation pending)

Authorizing Legislation:  Section 104 of the Higher Education Facilities Act of 1963 (20 U.S.C.A. 714).

Administering Agency:  Department of Health, Education, and Welfare:  Office of Education.

Description:  Grants to assist four year undergraduate institutions in building, rehabilitating or improving needed academic and related facilities.  Grants may be made for up to 50 percent of the construction cost.


14. Program Title:  Public Works and Development Facilities in Economic Development Areas

(Roth, p.97; HUD laws: p.435)

Authorizing Legislation:  Section 101 (a) (1) of the Public Works and Economic Development Act of 1965 (42 U.S.C. 3121).

Administering Agency:  Department of Commerce:  Economic Development Administration.

Description:  Grants to States, local subdivisions, Indian tribes, and private or public nonprofit organizations or associations representing an economic redevelopment area or designated growth center.  The grants may not exceed 50 percent of the development costs for such public facilities as water and sewer facilities, access roads to industrial parks or area harbor facilities, railroad sidings, public tourism facilities, vocational schools, flood control projects, and site improvements for industrial parks.  Severely depressed areas that cannot match public funds may receive grants to bring the Federal contributions up to 80 percent of the project cost.

Outline of Financial Aid Provisions of:

<u>HOUSING AND URBAN DEVELOPMENT ACT OF 1968 (P.L. 90-448)</u>

<u>TITLE IV</u>

| SECTION | DESCRIPTION | GRANT, ONE NEW COMMUNITY | GRANTS TOTAL |
|---------|-------------|-------------------------|--------------|
| 1. Guarantees | Of obligations of private (only) new community developers issued to finance real property acquisition and land development, in amounts of the less of 80% of value of property after development, or the sum of 75% of land value before development plus 90% of actual cost of land development. | maximum $50mm | $250mm |
| 2. Supplementary Grants for Public Facilities | To states and local public bodies to assist new community development projects. Total federal contribution to project limited to 80%. | 20% of cost | maximum $5mm (FY1969) $25mm (FY 1970) |

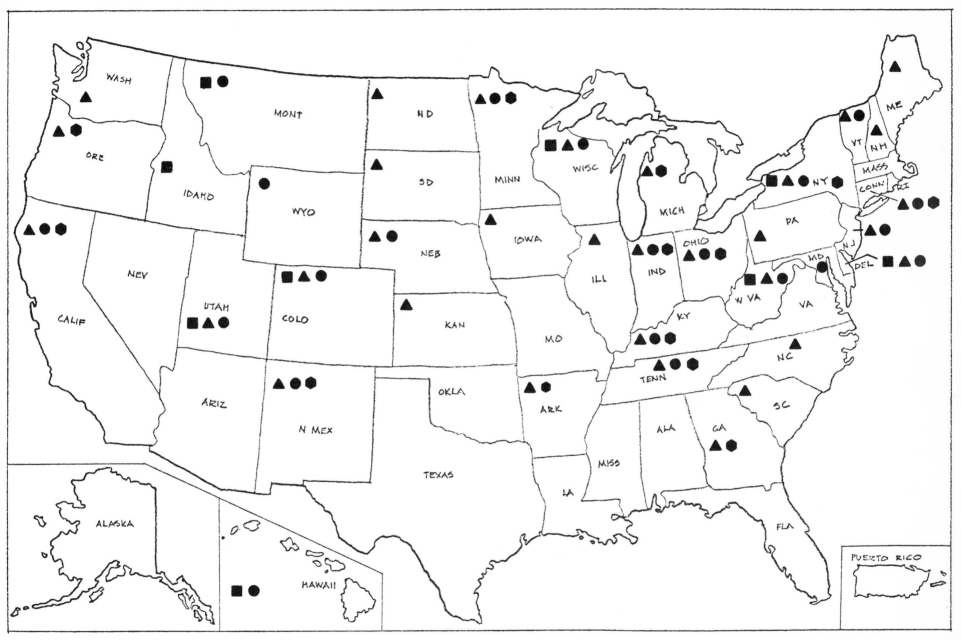

SURVEY OF STATE LEGISLATION FOR
URBAN AND RURAL DEVELOPMENT ACTIVITIES

SOURCE: See Appendix D

KEY:
■ State Land Development Agency
▲ Areawide Regional Planning District
⬟ Comprehensive State Plan
⬡ Regionalization of Urban Functions

B-18

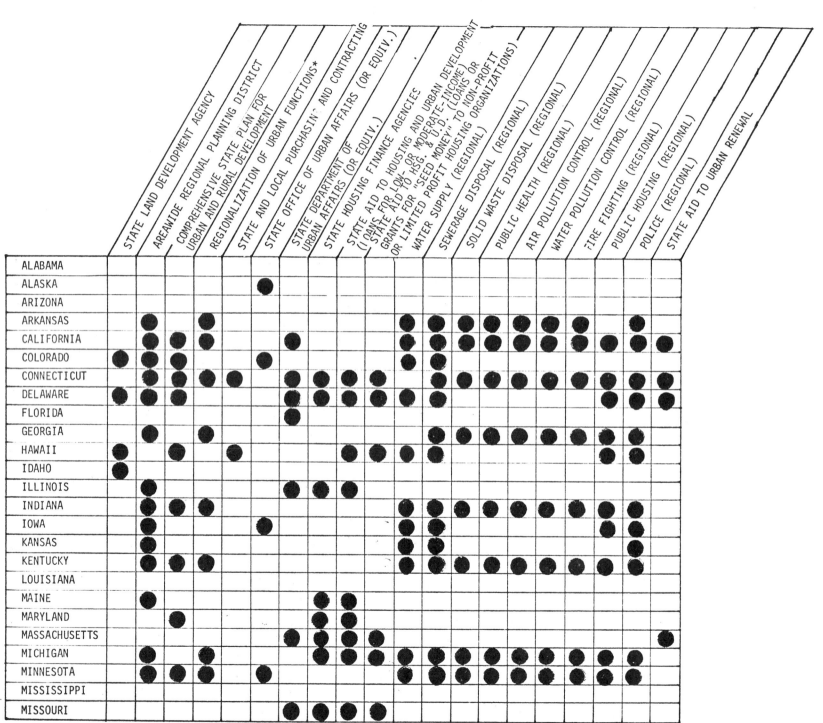

| State | State Land Development Agency | Areawide Regional Planning District | Comprehensive State Plan for Urban and Rural Development | Regionalization of Urban Functions* | State and Local Purchasing and Contracting | State Office of Urban Affairs (or Equiv.) | State Department of Urban Affairs (or Equiv.) | State Housing Finance Agencies | State Aid to Housing and Urban Development (Loans for Low- or Moderate-Income) | State Aid to Hsg. & U.D. (Loans or Grants for "Seed Money" to Non-Profit or Limited Profit Housing Organizations) | Water Supply (Regional) | Sewerage Disposal (Regional) | Solid Waste Disposal (Regional) | Public Health (Regional) | Air Pollution Control (Regional) | Water Pollution Control (Regional) | Fire Fighting (Regional) | Public Housing (Regional) | Police (Regional) | State Aid to Urban Renewal |
|---|---|---|---|---|---|---|---|---|---|---|---|---|---|---|---|---|---|---|---|---|
| MONTANA | ● | | ● | | ● | | | | | | | | | | | | | | | |
| NEBRASKA | | ● | ● | | | | | | ● | ● | | | | | | | | ● | | |
| NEVADA | | | | | | | | | | | | | | | | | | | | |
| NEW HAMPSHIRE | | ● | | | | | | | | | | | | | | | | | | |
| NEW JERSEY | | ● | ● | | | ● | ● | ● | ● | ● | | | | | | | | ● | ● | ● |
| NEW MEXICO | | ● | ● | ● | | | | | ● | ● | ● | ● | ● | ● | ● | ● | | ● | ● | |
| NEW YORK | ● | ● | ● | ● | | ● | | ● | ● | ● | ● | ● | ● | ● | ● | ● | ● | ● | ● | ● |
| NORTH CAROLINA | | ● | | | | ● | | ● | ● | | | | | | | | ● | ● | | |
| NORTH DAKOTA | | ● | | | | | | | | | | | | | | | | | | |
| OHIO | | ● | ● | ● | | ● | | | | ● | ● | ● | | ● | ● | ● | ● | ● | | |
| OKLAHOMA | | | | | | | | | | | | | | | | | | | | |
| OREGON | | ● | | ● | | ● | | | | ● | ● | ● | ● | ● | ● | ● | | ● | ● | |
| PENNSYLVANIA | | ● | | | | | ● | | | ● | ● | | | | | | | ● | | ● |
| RHODE ISLAND | | | | | | | ● | | ● | | | | | | | | | | | |
| SOUTH CAROLINA | | ● | | | | ● | | | | | | | | | | | ● | | | |
| SOUTH DAKOTA | | ● | | | | | | | | | | | | | | | | | | |
| TENNESSEE | | ● | | ● | ● | | ● | | | ● | ● | ● | ● | ● | ● | ● | ● | ● | ● | |
| TEXAS | | ● | | | | ● | | | | | | | | | | | | | | |
| UTAH | ● | ● | | ● | | | | | | ● | ● | | | | | | | | | |
| VERMONT | | ● | ● | | | ● | | ● | ● | ● | ● | ● | ● | ● | ● | ● | | | | |
| VIRGINIA | | ● | | | | ● | | | | | | | | | | | | | | |
| WASHINGTON | | ● | | | | ● | | | | ● | ● | | | | | | | | | |
| WEST VIRGINIA | ● | ● | ● | | | | ● | ● | ● | ● | ● | | | | | | | | | |
| WISCONSIN | ● | ● | ● | | | ● | | | | | | | | | | | | | | |
| WYOMING | | | ● | | | | | | | | | | | | | | | | | |

*Public housing, urban renewal, Model Cities, code enforcement, zoning legislation, building regulation, water supply, sewerage disposal, solid waste disposal, public transit, public health, air pollution control, water pollution control, police, fire fighting, valuation of property for tax purposes.

B-20

REFERENCES

STATES LEGISLATION RESEARCH

(1) Advisory Commission on Intergovernmental Relations, 1970 Cumulative ACIR State Legislative Program, 1970.

_____, Urban America and the Federal System, 1969.

_____, State Aid to Local Government,1969.
(all available through GPO, Washington, D.C.).

(2) American Bar Association: 1969 Committee Reports, New York, 1969
_____, 1970 Committee Reports, New York, 1970.

(3) Massachusetts Legislative Research Bureau: "State Responses to Questionnaire on State Action in Urban Crisis", Boston, September 1969.

(4) Massachusetts Legislative Research Bureau, Report Relative to New Towns, Boston, 1970.

(5) Metropolitan Area Planning Council, Commonwealth of Massachusetts, Federal and State Assisted Housing Programs (3 Vols.), Boston, October 1968.

(6) New York State Legislature, New York State Urban Development Corporation Acts.(1968),New York, 1968.

(7) Policy Institute of the Syracuse University Research Corporation, The Lysander New Community, (Vols. I and II), New York, 1967.

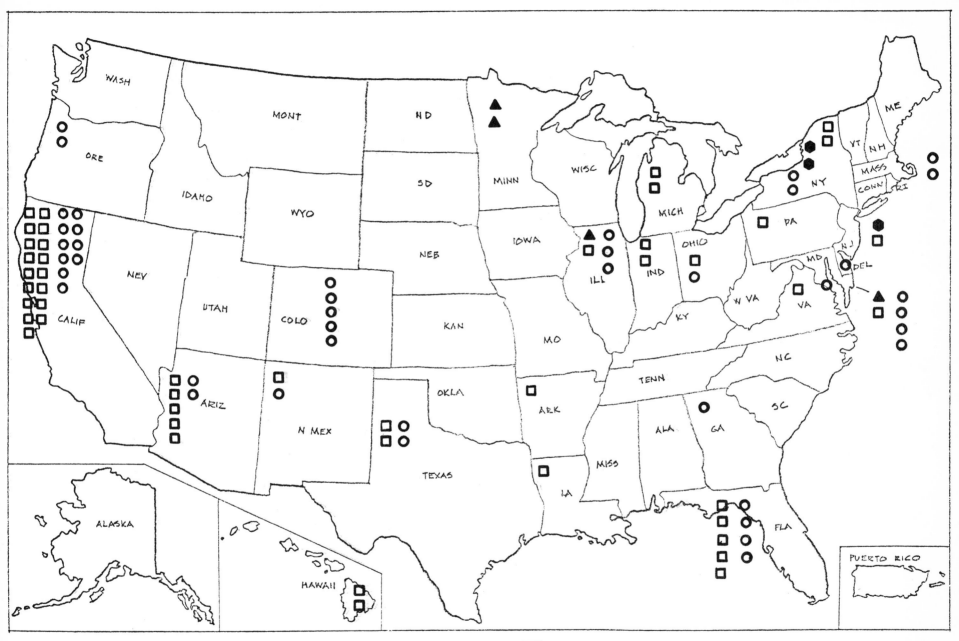

SURVEY OF NEW COMMUNITY AND LARGE-SCALE
DEVELOPMENT ACTIVITY IN THE U.S. COMPLETED
OR UNDER CONSTRUCTION SINCE 1947 *

* n.b. sources and definitions overleaf

KEY:
▲ Federally supported new community
⬟ State-supported new community
☐ Privately financed new community
◯ Privately financed large development, pop. 10-50,000

B-22

REFERENCES FOR SURVEY OF NEW COMMUNITIES:

1.  DHUD (New Communities Division): "Survey and Analysis of Large Developments and New Communities Completed or Under Construction in the U.S. Since 1947" (February 1969)

2.  Regional Economic Development Institute (for DHUD): Transportation Requirements and Effects of New Communities (May 1968)

3.  House & Home: "New Towns for America", February, 1964

4.  Advisory Commission on Intergovernmental Relations: Urban and Rural America: Policies for Future Growth (1968)

5.  Edward Eichler and Marshall Kaplan: The Community Builders, University of California Press, 1967

6.  Thomas A. Dames and William L. Grecco: "A Survey of New Town Planning Considerations" in Traffic Quarterly, Winter 1966

7.  Urban Land Institute: The Community Builder's Handbook, Urban Land Institute, Washington, D.C., 1964

DEFINITIONS:

DHUD's basic definition of new community is accepted here (eg. overall plan; economic base and regional impact; social and geographic identity; self-government; sufficient size to provide social diversity and all urban functions necessary to its residents; source of primary employment and community revenues), except that large developments with population in excess of 50,000 are included under the "new community" category in recognition that their achievement of critical mass enables them to fulfill the majority of urban functions, and dims the tenuous distinction between the larger "large developments" and "new communities."

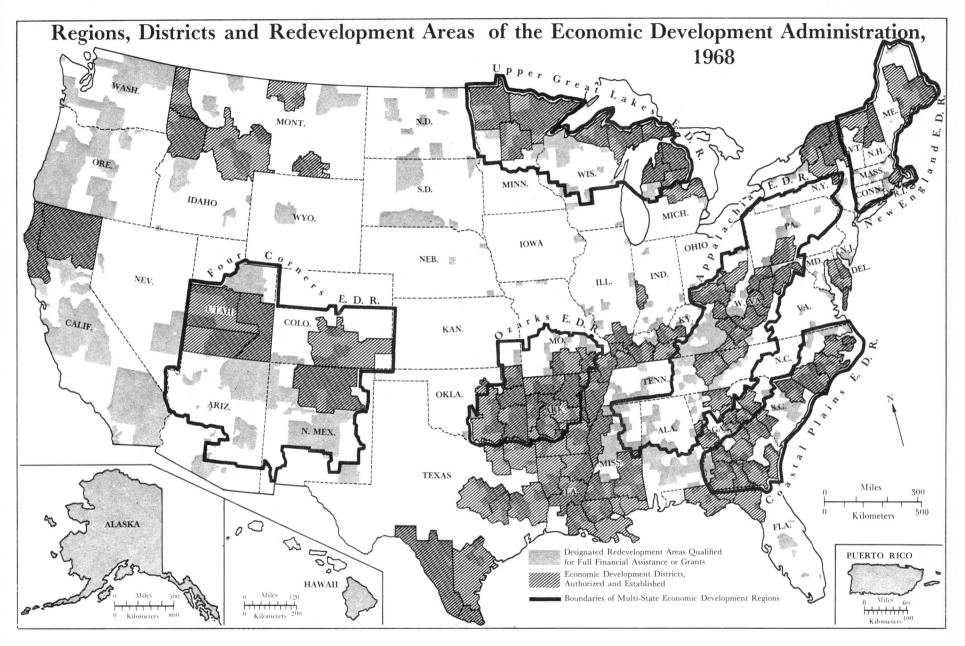

# Regions, Districts and Redevelopment Areas of the Economic Development Administration, 1968

Designated Redevelopment Areas Qualified for Full Financial Assistance or Grants

Economic Development Districts, Authorized and Established

Boundaries of Multi-State Economic Development Regions

SOURCE: Lloyd Rodwin: *Nations and Cities: A Comparison of Strategies for Urban Growth*, Boston, 1970.
Permission by the author and Houghton Mifflin Company to reproduce this map is appreciately acknowledged. .

REFERENCES

URBAN GROWTH AND
NEW COMMUNITIES POLICY

(1) Advisory Commission on Intergovernmental Relations, Urban and Rural America: Policies for Future Growth, 1968.

(2) Council on Environmental Quality, Environmental Quality, First Annual Report, GPO, Washington, D.C., 1970.

(3) Anthony Downs, "Alternative Forms of Future Urban Growth in the U.S.", American Institute of Planners Journal, January 1970.

(4) Victor Gruen Associates, New Cities USA, commissioned by DHUD, Washington, D.C., 1966.

(5) Albert Mayer, "Urban Modes and the Continuum", in Architectural Record, October 1969 - January 1970.

(6) National Committee on Urban Growth Policy (ed. Donald Canty), The New City, Urban America, Washington, D.C., 1969,

(7) National Governors' Conference, Policy Positions of the National Governors' Conference 1970 - 71, Washington, D.C., August 1970.

(8) National Goals Committee, Goals for Americans, Washington, D.C., 1960.

(9) National Goals Research Staff, Toward Balanced Growth: Quantity with Quality, GPO, Washington, D.C., 1970.

(10) Jerome Pickard, Dimensions of Metropolitanism, Urban Land Institute, Washington, D.C., 1967.

(11) President's Task Force on Rural Development, A New Life for the Country, GPO, Washington, D.C., 1970.

(12) Lloyd Rodwin, Nations and Cities: A Comparison of Strategies for Urban Growth, Houghton Mifflin, New York, 1970.

(13) Charles L. Schultz, <u>Setting National Priorities</u>:
     <u>The 1971 Budget</u>, Brookings Institution, Washington,
     D.C., 1970.

(14) James Sundquist, "Where Shall They Live?", <u>Public</u>
     <u>Interest</u>, Winter 1970.

(15) U.S. Congress, <u>Hearings Before the Committee on Banking</u>
     <u>and Currency</u>, Housing Subcommittee
     Part I - June 2-5, 1970, on housing, urban development
     Part II - June 8-11, 1970, on housing, urban development

     <u>National Housing Goals</u>, May, June, 1969

     <u>Hearings Before the Ad Hoc Subcommittee on Urban Growth</u>
     Part I <u>Population Trends</u>, 1970.
     Part II <u>The Quality of Urban Life</u>, 1970
     (all available through GPO, Washington, D.C., 1969).

(16) U.S. Department of Agriculture, <u>Providing Quality En-</u>
     <u>vironment in Our Communities</u>, Graduate School of the
     Department of Agriculture, Washington, D.C., 1968.

(17) U.S. Department of Health, Education and Welfare,
     <u>Toward a Social Report</u>, GPO, Washington, D.C., 1969.

(18) William L.C. Wheaton, "Form and Structure of the
     Metropolitan Area" in William Ewald (ed.), <u>Environ-</u>
     <u>ment for Man</u>, Indiana University Press, 1970.

REFERENCES

FEDERAL LEGISLATION

(1)  Norman Beckman, "Legislative Review - 1968 - 1969: Planning and Urban Development", American Institute of Planners Journal, September 1970.

(2)  Commonwealth of Massachussetts, Legislative Research Council of, Report Relative to New Towns, Boston, July 1970.

(3)  Department of Housing and Urban Development, "New Community Supplementary Grants for Public Facilities", mimeo. information sheet, August 1970.

(4)  MIT/Harvard Joint Center for Urban Studies, Earle New Town, Cambridge, 1969.

(5)  Eugene J. Morris and Henry S. Halprin, Urban Renewal and Housing, "Summary and Analysis of Housing and Urban Development Act of 1968:, Practicing Law Institute, New York, 1969.

(6)  Office of Economic Opportunity (Prepared for Executive Office of the President), Catalog of Federal Domestic Assistance, GPO, Washington, D.C., 1969.

(7)  U.S. Congress, Housing and Urban Development Act of 1968, P.L. 90-448.

(8)  U.S. House of Representatives, 1969 Listing of Operating Federal Assistance Programs Compiled During the Roth Study, GPO, Washington, D.C. (House Document No. 91-177), 1969.

REFERENCES

RECENT FEDERAL LEGISLATION ON
URBAN GROWTH AND NEW COMMUNITIES
IN PROCESS

H.R. 13217, July 30, 1969, "Balanced Urbanization
Policy and Planning Act" (Rep. Dwyer).

S. 3228, December 9, 1969, "Balanced Urbanization Policy and Planning Act" (Sen. Muskie).

H.R. 16643, March 24, 1970, "Housing and Urban Development Act of 1970" (Rep. Widnall).

H.R. 16647, March 25, 1970, "Urban Growth and New Community Act of 1970" (Rep. Ashley).

S. 3460, March 25, 1970, "Urban Growth and New Community
Development Act of 1970" (Sens. Muskie, Sparkman).

H.R. 19250, September 16, 1970, "Urban Growth and New
Community Development Act of 1970" (Rep. Widnall).

"Report of the Committee on Banking and Currency, U.S.
Senate to Accompany S. 4368, September 21, 1970.

H.R. 19436, September 23, 1970, "Housing and Urban Development Act of 1970" (Rep. Patman, also Ashley, etc.).

"Conference Report for Housing and Urban Development Act
of 1970" (to accompany H.R. 19436), December 17, 1970,
(since passed and signed into law, The Housing and Urban
Development Act of 1970).

# APPENDIX C--FINANCIAL MODEL PROGRAM

```
        DIMENSION APOP(40),TDIFF(40),VRES(40),VCOM(40),
      1 VTAX(40),VIND(40),TREV(40),TOTR(40),OPRX(40),
      2 CAPX(40),TOTX(40),DEBX(40),BOND(40),UBOND(40),CAPXC(40),
      3 AREQ(40),FCOM(40),TDEBT(40),RBOND(40),TNET(40),SREV(40)
        DIMENSION CAPXA(40),CAPXH(40),CAPXW(40),CAPXE(40)
      1 ,CPAXR(40),OPRXA(40),OPRXH(40),OPRXW(40),CAREQ(40),
      2 OPRXE(40),OPRXT(40),OPRXR(40),CAPXT(40)
        DIMENSION USEC(40),TPSX(40),ADBOND(40),ADUNBD(40),ADUSBD(40)
C ZERO ALL ARRAYS
        DO 10 K=1,40
        APOP(K)=0
        CAPXC(K)=0
        USEC(K)=0
        TDIFF(K)=0

        VRES(K)=0
        SREV(K)=0
        VCOM(K)=0
        VIND(K)=0
        VTAX(K)=0
        TREV(K)=0
        TOTR(K)=0
        OPRX(K)=0
        CAPX(K)=0
        TOTX(K)=0
        TNET(K)=0
        TDEBT(K)=0
        RBOND(K)=0
        DEBX(K)=0
        BOND(K)=0
        AREQ(K)=0
        FCOM(K)=0
10      CONTINUE
C   INITIALIZE YEAR COUNTER (I) TO ZERO
        I=0
        DIFF=0
C   INPUT EXOGENEOUS AND INPUT VARIABLES
        TYPE 920
        ACCEPT 999,AREA
        TYPE 921
        ACCEPT 999,TPOP
        TYPE 922
        ACCEPT 999,RPOP
        TYPE 923
        ACCEPT 999,VINPC
        TYPE 925
        ACCEPT 999,RTAX
        TYPE 926
        ACCEPT 999,RINT
        TYPE 927
        ACCEPT 999, RPAY
        TYPE 928
        ACCEPT 999,RCOM
        TYPE 929
        ACCEPT 999,VMIND
        TYPE 930
```

```
            ACCEPT 999,RATE
720         TYPE 980
980         FORMAT(1H ,//,' INPUT OUTPUT FORM DESIRED (1,2,3,OR 4)
   1        TYPE 0 TO STOP :',$)
            ACCEPT 999,OUTPUT
            IF(OUTPUT.EQ.0)CALL EXIT                          Page 2
C START OF CALCULATIONS
100         J=I
            I=I+1
            IF(J.EQ.0)GO TO 11
            CAREQ(I)=CAREQ(J)
            IF(J.NE.0)TDIFF(J)=TDIFF(J)+TNET(J)
            IF(J.NE.0)TDIFF(I)=TDIFF(J)
            IF (J.NE.0)CAPXC(J)=CAPXC(J)+CAPX(J)
            IF(J.NE.0)CAPXC(I)=CAPXC(J)
            IF(J.NE.0)TDIFF(I)=TDIFF(J)
            IF(J.NE.0)UBOND(J)=BOND(J)-RBOND(J)
            IF(J.NE.0) TDEBT(I)=TDEBT(J)
11          IF (I.EQ.41) GO TO 901
C CHECK TO SEE IF COMMUNITY HAS REACHED END OF DEVELOPMENT
C         PERIOD.
            IF (I.EQ. (RPOP+1)) GO TO 600
C TRANSFER TO POPULATION CALCULATION SECTION
            GO TO 111
C POPULATION DENSITY CALCULATION
101         DPOP=TPOP/(0.5*AREA)
C TRANSFER TO PUBLIC SERVICE CALCULATION SECTION.
            GO TO 500
50          CONTINUE
C VALUE CALCULATIONS - RESIDENTIAL
            VRES(I)=APOP(I)*VINPC*2.5
C INDUSTRIAL
            VIND(I)= VMIND*VRES(I)
C TRANSFER TO COMMERCIAL SQ.FOOTAGE CALCULATION SECTION.
            GO TO 310
102         CONTINUE
            VCOM(I)= RCOM*FCOM(I)/RATE
C TAX BASE AND REVENUE CALCULATIONS
            VTAX(I)=VRES(I) + VCOM(I) + VIND(I)
            TREV(I)= RTAX * VTAX(I)
            SREV(I)=TREV(I)
C USER CHARGES CALCULATION
            USEC(I)=120*APOP(I)
C         THE ABOVE CALCULATION IS TEMPORARY
C TOTAL REVENUE CALCULATION
            TOTR(I)= TREV(I) +USEC(I) + SREV(I)
C BONDING CAPACITY CALCULATION
            BOND(I)= 0.2 * TOTR(I)/ (RINT+ (1/RPAY))
            IF(J.NE.0)ADBOND(I)= BOND(I) - BOND(J)
            IF(J.EQ.0)ADBOND(I)=BOND(I)
C EXPENSE CALCULATIONS (INCLUDING DEBT SERVICE)
C ON TOTAL DEBT TO DATE)
            DEBX(I)=0.2*TOTR(I) * TDEBT(I)/BOND(I)
            TOTX(I)= OPRX(I) + CAPX(I) + DEBX(I)
C FIND DIFFERENCE BETWEEN INCOME AND EXPENSES
            DIFF= TOTR(I) - TOTX(I)
C CHECK FOR SURPLUS OR DEFICIT
            IF (DIFF.GE.0) GO TO 150
C    DEFICIT EXISTS. CHECK AVAILIBLE BONDING FOR EXHAUSTION
            IF ( (BOND(I)-TDEBT(I)) .LE. 0) GO TO 140
C    DEFICIT EXISTS, SOME BONDING CAPACITY REMAINS.
C    CALCULATE REMAINING CAPACITY
            RBOND(I)=BOND(I)-TDEBT(I)
C CALCULATE ADDITIONAL DEBT SERVICE REQUIRED TO COVER
C     ENTIRE DEFICIT
            ADEBX= 0.2*TOTR(I) * DIFF/BOND(I)
```

```
C  CHECK REMAINING BONDING AGAINST DEFICIT AND ADDITIONAL
C       DEBT SERVICE
          IF( (RBOND(I)+DIFF+ADEBTX) .LT. 0) GO TO 160
C REMAINING BONDING CAPACITY SUFFICIENT TO COVER DEFICIT    Page 3
C  CALCULATE ADDITIONAL (NET) UNUSED AND USED BONDING CAPACITY
190       TNET(I)=DIFF+ADEBTX
          ADUSBD(I)=-TNET(I)
          ADUNBD(I)=ADBOND(I)-ADUSBD(I)
          TDEBT(I)=TDEBT(I)-TNET(I)
          DEBX(I)= 0.2*TOTR(I) * TDEBT(I)/BOND(I)
          TOTX(I)= OPRX(I)+CAPX(I)+DEBX(I)
          RBOND(I)=BOND(I)-TDEBT(I)
C RETURN TO START
          GO TO 100
C REMAINING BONDING CAPACITY NOT SUFFICIENT
C   TO COVER DEFICIT
160       CONTINUE
          ADUNBD(I)=0
          ADUSBD(I)=RBOND(I)
          TDEBT(I)=BOND(I)
          DEBX(I)= 0.2 * TOTR(I)
          TOTX(I)=OPRX(I)+CAPX(I)+DEBX(I)
          AREQ(I)=-TOTR(I)-RBOND(I)+TOTX(I)
          CAREQ(I)=CAREQ(I)+AREQ(I)
          TNET(I)=TOTR(I)-TOTX(I)
          RBOND(I)=0
C RETURN TO START
          GO TO 100
C  SURPLUS EXISTS. SUBTRACT SURPLUS FROM ACCLUMULATED DEBT
150       IF(TDEBT(I).GE.DIFF) GO TO 151
          ADUNBD(I)=ADBOND(I)
          ADUSBD(I)=0
          TDEBT(I)=0
          TNET(I)=DIFF
          RBOND(I)=BOND(I)
          GO TO 100
151       ADUNBD(I)=ADBOND(I)
          ADUSBD(I)=0
          TDEBT(I)=TDEBT(I)-DIFF
          RBOND(I)=BOND(I)-TDEBT(I)
          TNET(I)=DIFF
C RETURN TO START
          GO TO 100
C AVAILIBLE BONDING EXHAUSTED. GOVERNMENT ASSISTANCE
C  REQUIRED.
140       AREQ(I)= -DIFF -BOND(I) +TDEBT(I)
          CAREQ(I)=CAREQ(I)+AREQ(I)
          ADUNBD(I)=0
          ADUSBD(I)=0
          RBOND(I)=0
          TNET(I)=DIFF
C RETURN TO START
          GO TO 100
C CALCULATION FOR COMMERCIAL SPACE REQUIREMANTS.
C DETERMINE MULTIPLIER ADJUSTMENT
310       IF(I.LE.(RPOP/5))GO TO 311
          IF (I.LE.(2*RPOP/5))GO TO 312
          IF(I.LE.(3*RPOP/5))GO TO 313
          IF (I.LE.(4*RPOP/5)) GO TO 314
C IN THE FIFTH PERIOD
          FCOM(I)=10*APOP(I)
          GO TO 102
C YEAR IS IN THE FIRST PERIOD
311       FCOM(I)=0.5*10*APOP(I)
          GO TO 102
C IN THE SECOND PERIOD
312       FCOM(I)=0.67*10*APOP(I)
```

```
        GO TO 102
C IN THE THIRD PERIOD
313     FCOM(I)=0.75*10*APOP(I)
        GO TO 102
C IN THE FOURTH PERIOD
314     FCOM(I)=0.88*10*APOP(I)
        GO TO 102
C CALCULATION OF POPULATION
C DETERMINE TIME PERIOD OF MODEL
111     IF(RPOP.EQ.10)GO TO 210
        IF(RPOP.EQ.15)GO TO 215
        IF(RPOP.EQ.20)GO TO 220
        IF(RPOP.NE.25)GO TO 800
C DEVELOPMENT PERIOD IS 25 YEARS
        APOP(I)=(-1383.40+2824.28*I+59.54*I**2-0.41*I**3)*TPOP/100
        APOP(I)=APOP(I)/1000
        GO TO 101
C DEVELOPMENT PERIOD IS 10 YEARS
210     APOP(I)=(5446.43-7915.67*I+4217.26*I**2-248.02*I**3)*TPOP/100
        APOP(I)=APOP(I)/1000
        GO TO 101
C DEVELOPMENT PERIOD IS 15 YEARS
215     APOP(I)=(288.46+239.47*I+1010.99*I**2-38.92*I**3)*TPOP/100
        APOP(I)=APOP(I)/1000
        GO TO 101
C DEVELOPMENT PERIOD IS 20 YEARS
220     APOP(I)=(-947.71+2156.09*I+299.36*I**2-7.74*I**3)*TPOP/100
        APOP(I)=APOP(I)/1000
        GO TO 101
C THIS IS THE OUTPUT SECTION
600     IF(OUTPUT.EQ.0)GO TO 700
        IF(OUTPUT.EQ.1)GO TO 610
        IF(OUTPUT.EQ.2)GO TO 620
        IF(OUTPUT.EQ.3)GO TO 630
        IF(OUTPUT.EQ.4)GO TO 640
        GO TO 710
610     TYPE 650
        M=1
        N=5
C THIS IS THE LONG FORM OF OUTPUT (#1)
650     FORMAT(1H-T20,'ALL AMOUNTS IN THOUSANDS OF DOLLARS')
651     FORMAT(1H-T10,'YEAR'T24,5(I2,'          ')//)
652     FORMAT(1H 'EXPENSES'/'   CAPITAL'T21,5(F7.0,'  '))
653     FORMAT('     OPERATING'T21,5(F7.0,'  '))
654     FORMAT('  TOTAL PUB. SERV.'T21,5(F7.0,'  '))
655     FORMAT('    DEBT SERVICE'T21,5(F7.0,'  '))
656     FORMAT('  TOTAL EXPENSES'T21,5(F7.0,'  '))
657     FORMAT('-REVENUES (INTERNAL)'/'    USER CHARGES'
     1 T21,5(F7.0,'  '))
658     FORMAT('     TAXES'T21,5(F7.0,'  '))
665     FORMAT('     OTHER'T21,5(F7.0,'  '))
659     FORMAT('  TOTAL INT. REV.'T21,5(F7.0,'  '))
660     FORMAT('-NET SURP/DEF'T21,5(F7.0,'  '))
666     FORMAT(' CUM SURP/DEF'T21,5(F7.0,'  '))
1000    FORMAT('-BONDING CAPACITY (NET)'/'    AVAILIBLE'
     1 T21,5(F7.0,'  '))
1001    FORMAT('     UNUSED',T21,5(F7.0,'  '))
1002    FORMAT('     USED',T21,5(F7.0,'  '))
661     FORMAT('-BONDING CAPACITY (CUM)'/'    AVAILIBLE'T21,5(F7.0,'  '))
662     FORMAT('     UNUSED'T21,5(F7.0,'  '))
667     FORMAT('     USED'T21,5(F7.0,'  '))
663     FORMAT('-STATE AND FEDERAL'/'   ASSISTANCE (NET)'
     1 T21,5(F7.0,'  '))
1003    FORMAT(' STATE AND FEDERAL'/'   ASSISTANCE (CUM)'
     1 T21,5(F7.0,'  '))
664     FORMAT('-POPULATION'T21,5(F7.0,'  '))
```

```
668     FORMAT(' CUM. CAP. EXP.'T21,5(F7.0,' '))
999     FORMAT(F)
731     TYPE 651 ,(L,L=M,N)

        TYPE 652,(CAPX(L),L=M,N)                                    Page 5
        DO 21 I=M,N
21      APOP(I)=APOP(I)*1000
        TYPE 653,( OPRX(L), L=M,N)
        TYPE 654,( TPSX(L),L=M,N)
        TYPE 655, ( DEBX(L),L=M,N)
        TYPE 656,(TOTX(L),L=M,N)
        TYPE 657,(USEC(L),L=M,N)
        TYPE 658,(TREV(L),L=M,N)
        TYPE 665,(SREV(L),L=M,N)
        TYPE 659,(TOTR(L),L=M,N)
        TYPE 660,(TNET(L),L=M,N)
        TYPE 666,(TDIFF(L),L=M,N)
        TYPE 1000,(ADBOND(L),L=M,N)
        TYPE 1001,(ADUNBD(L),L=M,N)
        TYPE 1002,(ADUSBD(L),L=M,N)
        TYPE 661,(BOND(L),L=M,N)
        TYPE 662,(RBOND(L),L=M,N)
        TYPE 667,(UBOND(L),L=M,N)
        TYPE 663,(AREQ(L),L=M,N)
        TYPE 1003,(CAREQ(L),L=M,N)
        TYPE 664,(APOP(L),L=M,N)
        TYPE 668,(CAPXC(L),L=M,N)
730     M=M+5
        N=N+5
        IF(N.EQ.(RPOP+5))  GO TO 720
        GO TO 731
C THIS IS THE SUMMARY FORM OF OUTPUT (#2)
620     M=1
        N=5
        TYPE 650
631     TYPE 651,(L,L=M,N)
        TYPE 656,(TOTX(L),L=M,N)
        TYPE 659,(TOTR(L),L=M,N)
        TYPE 660,(TNET(L),L=M,N)
        TYPE 661,(BOND(L),L=M,N)
        TYPE 662,(RBOND(L),L=M,N)
        TYPE 667,(UBOND(L),L=M,N)
        TYPE 663,(AREQ(L),L=M,N)
        M=M+5
        N=N+5
        IF(N.EQ.(RPOP+5) )GO TO 720
        GO TO 631
C CALCULATION OF PUBLIC SERVICE COSTS
500     OPRX(I)= 370 * APOP(I)
        CAPX(I)= 180 * (TPOP-APOP(I))
        TPSX(I)=OPRX(I)+CAPX(I)
        GO TO 50
920     FORMAT(' INPUT AREA IN THOUSANDS OF ACRES: ',S)
921     FORMAT(' INPUT TARGET POPULATION (IN THOUSANDS): ',S)
922     FORMAT(' INPUT DEVELOPMENT PERIOD (10,15,20,OR 25 YEARS): ',S)
923     FORMAT(' INPUT INCOME PER CAPITA (IN DOLLARS): ',S)
925     FORMAT(' INPUT TAX RATE (IN DECIMAL FRACTION): ',S)
926     FORMAT(' INPUT ANNUAL INTEREST RATE (IN
      1 DECIMAL FRACTION): ',S)
927     FORMAT(' INPUT DEBT REPAYMENT PERIOD (IN YEARS): ',S)
928     FORMAT(' INPUT COMMERCIAL RENTAL RATE PER SQ. FT.
      1 (IN DOLLARS): ',S)
929     FORMAT(' INPUT INDUSTRIAL TAX BASE MULTIPLIER: ',S)
930     FORMAT(' INPUT CAP. RATE FOR COMMERCIAL RENT (IN DECIMAL
      1 FRACTION): ',S)                630     CONTINUE      800     CONTINUE
710             CONTINUE               700     CONTINUE      901     CONTINUE
640     CONTINUE
```

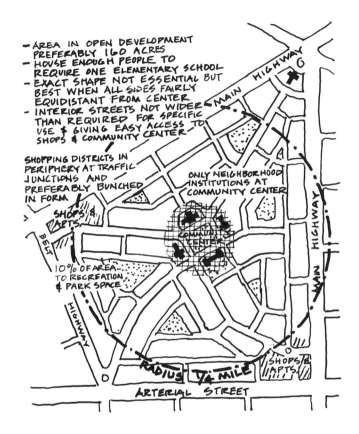

- AREA IN OPEN DEVELOPMENT PREFERABLY 160 ACRES
- HOUSE ENOUGH PEOPLE TO REQUIRE ONE ELEMENTARY SCHOOL
- EXACT SHAPE NOT ESSENTIAL BUT BEST WHEN ALL SIDES FAIRLY EQUIDISTANT FROM CENTER
- INTERIOR STREETS NOT WIDER THAN REQUIRED FOR SPECIFIC USE & GIVING EASY ACCESS TO SHOPS & COMMUNITY CENTER

SHOPPING DISTRICTS IN PERIPHERY AT TRAFFIC JUNCTIONS AND PREFERABLY BUNCHED IN FORM

SHOPS & APTS.

10% OF AREA TO RECREATION & PARK SPACE

ONLY NEIGHBORHOOD INSTITUTIONS AT COMMUNITY CENTER

COMMUNITY CENTER

RADIUS 1/4 MILE

SHOPS & APTS

ARTERIAL STREET

Figure D-1

Clarence Perry neighborhood unit
(Source: Gallion and Eisner: Urban Patterns)

This appendix reviews several of the more significant examples of new communities in which service area concepts have been applied and will serve the purposes of (i) illustrating graphically the physical consequences of the three basic conceptual models of service areas*; (ii) demonstrating the evolution of the concepts in significant new communities over the last forty years and the direction of future changes; and (iii) laying the basis for evaluating the impact at service area level of, and access to, improved and innovative community services.

## Model A: Self-Contained Service Area

1.  Clarence Perry's scheme for the neighborhood unit (Fig. D-1) advocated in the 1929 New York Region Survey, set the leading precedent for neighborhood design for the next thirty years.  It was based on extensive studies of the number of families required to support facilities, principally the elementary school, and on the basic walking radius of 1/4 mile from outlying homes to the elementary school and associated community center.  The underlying principle was that an urban neighborhood should be regarded both as a unit of a larger whole and as a distinct entity in itself.  The scheme contained provision for size, boundaries, open spaces, institution sites, local commerce and internal street

---

*The three basic models are self-contained, inter-related and community oriented, as discussed in part IV.

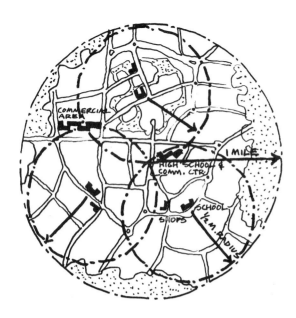

Figure D-2

Clarence Stein: three inter-
locking neighborhood units

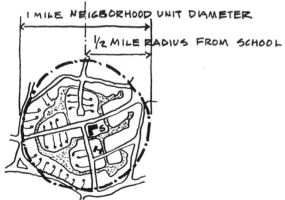

Figure D-3

Clarence Stein: one neighborhood unit
(source: Gallion and Eisner, Op. Cit.)

system. It was most closely worked out for a population of approximately 6000 with a school enrollment
of 1000.

2.  Clarence Stein's neighborhood scheme, best known in
    Radburn, followed along much the same lines. Radius
    from elementary school to outer boundary became 1/2
    mile, and a more highly developed system of pedes-
    trian and vehicle ways was introduced (Figs. D-2,3).

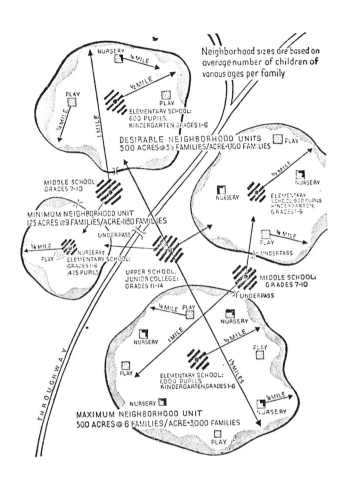

3. The directions established by Perry and Stein are seen in later illustrative diagrams by N. L. Englehardt, the school planning expert of the '40's and '50's (Fig. D-4). The primacy of the school in neighborhood planning remains constant for neighborhoods ranging from 1200 to 3000 families. The radius of 1/2 mile maximum walking distance to elementary school is maintained, but 1/4 mile is the proposed distance to playgrounds and nursery schools.

Figure D-4

N. L. Englehardt: neighborhood sizes based on number of children in families
        (Source: Gallion and Eisner, Op. Cit.)

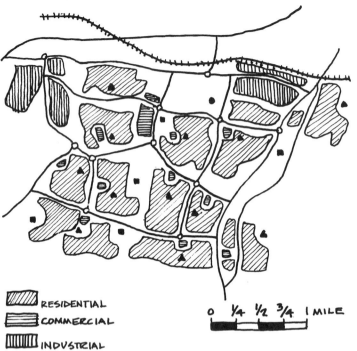

4. Discrete, boundary-defined neighborhoods similar in contents and configuration to those of Perry and Stein are employed in Harlow, one of the first generation and most influential of English new towns (Fig. D-5). Whereas the sizes of neighborhoods vary from 1/4 mile to 3/4 mile radius, walking distance to elementary school stays at 1/4 mile. As in the Stein schemes, secondary schools are used to link adjoining neighborhoods; an extensive parkways network weaves among the neighborhoods, and through-streets do not intrude into residential areas.

RESIDENTIAL
COMMERCIAL
INDUSTRIAL
▲ PRIMARY SCHOOL
■ SECONDARY SCHOOL
● COLLEGE

0  1/4  1/2  3/4  1 MILE

Figure D-5

Harlow, England (Mark I New Town)

(Source: Lloyd Rodwin : The British New Towns Policy)

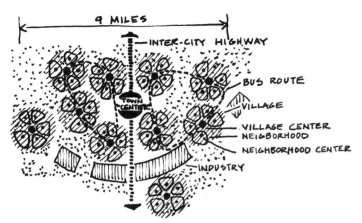

Figure D-6

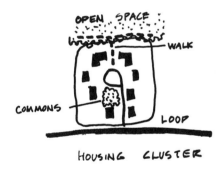

Figure D-7

## 5. COLUMBIA, MARYLAND

Columbia develops further the neighborhood principles of Perry, Stein and the new town of Harlow within the overall planning context of the entire new community. An orderly but also firm hierarchy of housing cluster (Fig. D-7), neighborhood (Fig. D-8), village (Fig. D-10) and town (Fig. D-6) is established. Whereas the planners of Columbia emphasize the system of overlapping communities, chiefly by means of village centers serving several adjacent neighborhoods and of a planned loop bus route,* structure is hierarchical and rather rigid. The stated ambition of the planners is to establish patterns "as complex and overlapping as in every living city"* by encouraging activity patterns which cut across service areas, but the forces of density and housing types and of self-contained sufficiency and physically hierarchical layout are structured so as to inhibit such complex and unpredictable overlapping.

*Morton Hoppenfeld, "A Sketch of the Planning Building Process for Columbia, Maryland," American Institute of Planners Journal, November 1967.

5. Columbia, Maryland (Cont'd)

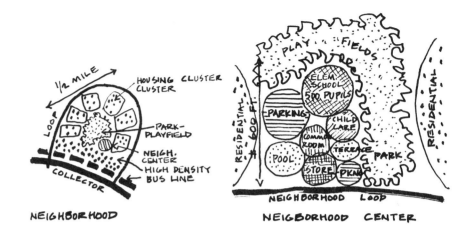

Figure D-8                    Figure D-9

(Source: Morton Hoppenfeld, Op. Cit.)

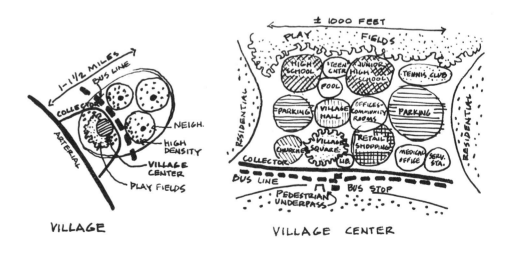

Figure D-10                   Figure D-11

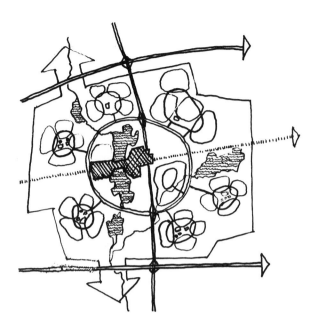

Figure D-12

Jonathan New Town

(Source: Jonathan Development Corporation, Jonathan: Design and
Development (Jonathan, Minn, 1970)

## 6. JONATHAN, MINNESOTA

Jonathan's villages contain approximately 7000 persons,
each with its internal road system, elementary schools,
municipal facilities and convenience village center
(Fig. D-12). On the basis of preliminary information,
both the village and overall community structure appear
similar to that of Columbia. The use of pedestrian
walkways and varying institutional and village center
identities are cited by the developer as means of
considerable interchange between villages, but Figure
D-12 does not strongly substantiate the concepts. It
should be noted that the Jonathan land use maps for
actual road and village situations suggest more inter-
communication between all villages by means of inter-
connecting roads. But at this point, Jonathan service
areas appear to belong to model (A) type, an updating
of the Perry and Stein schemes.

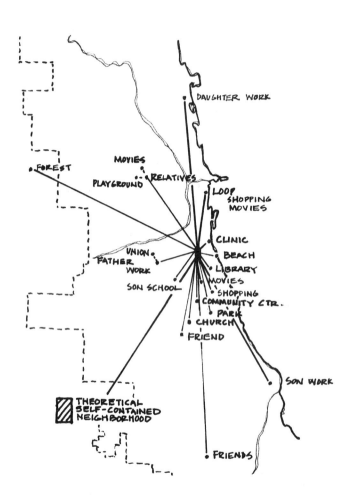

## Model B: Inter-Related Service Areas

Figures D-13 and D-14 illustrate graphically the activity patterns which tend to push the service center toward greater outward orientation. The diagram in Figure D-13 is at once an argument for the arrangement of service area facilities within convenient distance from the home and for efficient transportation networks to reduce the time, cost and strain of travel in the community.

Figure D-13

Household daily activities in Chicago household (Source: Gallion & Eisner, Urban Patterns)

Figure D-14 demonstrates empirically the real patterns
which constitute -- at least in part -- the basis for
the inter-area related configurations of model (B).

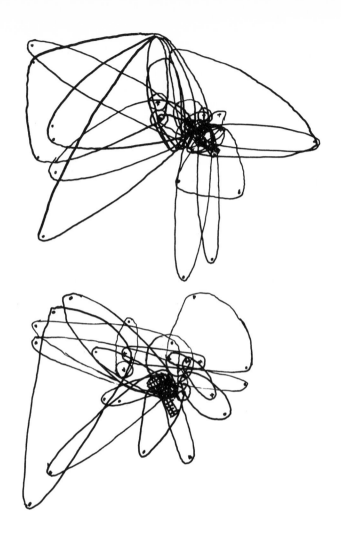

Figure D-14

Illustrative household activity patterns
from pilot study: top figure shows recreation pattern, lower figure shows
visiting patterns (Source: F. Stuart
Chapin, Urban Land Use Planning, New
York, 1957)

| A | County Seat Administration | M | Industry |
|---|---|---|---|
| B | Airport | N | Merchandising |
| C | Sports | P | Railroad |
| D | Professional Offices | R | Orchards |
| E | Stadium | S | Homes and Apartments |
| F | Hotel | T | Temple and Cemetery |
| G | Sanitarium | U | Research |
| H | Small Industry | V | Zoo |
| J | Small Farms | W | Schools |
| K | Park | | |
| L | Motor Inn | | |

Area of Plan is
Two Square Miles

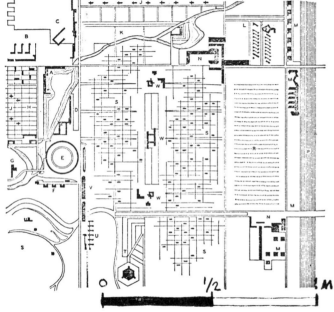

O          1/2          1 M.

Figure D-15

Broadacre City
(Source:  Frank Lloyd Wright, The Living City,
New York, 1961)

## 1.  BROADACRE  CITY

Broadacre  City by Frank Lloyd Wright (Fig. D-15) was
an important attempt at not only overcoming some of the
adverse effects of the self-contained, inward-focusing
neighborhood, but of enabling each neighborhood to use
more fully the attributes of the total community by
locating them within reasonable distances (less than
1 mile) from the residential areas.  Given the low density (minimum of one **acre** per dwelling unit), this plan
achieved remarkable compactness of a wide range of
community activities.  In a sense, each Broadacres City
became an unusually diversified superblock, with many
city activities as well as the rural benefits of the
countryside accessible within a half to one mile walk.
The individual service area or neighborhood effectively
disappeared in the total, but near community.

## 2. WARRINGTON NEW TOWN, ENGLAND

Warrington (Fig. D-16) adopts a system of district distributor street spacing of 3/4 mile, with local distributor spacing of 440 yards. The public transit network is thereby able to achieve optimum spacing of 1/4 mile for bus stops. The grid system de-emphasizes the neighborhood unit in favor of an open-ended activity location pattern closely related to the pedestrian and vehicular lattice network and favoring inter-area communication.

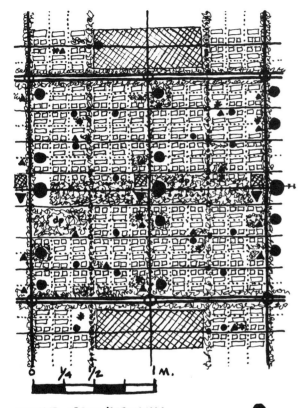

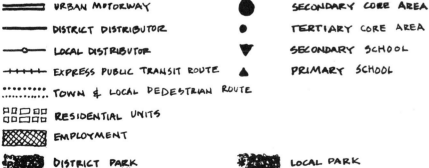

Figure D-16
WARRINGTON, ENGLAND: Urban Structure
(Source: Austin-Smith Lord Partnership:
Warrington New Town, Warrington, England, 1969)

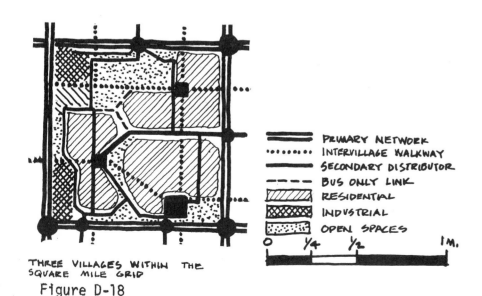

## 3. WASHINGTON NEW TOWN, ENGLAND

Washington (Figs. D-17, 18) employs a basic square mile grid within which villages, each with its own center, share a local center and open space, schools and community facilities. Activity center nodes are located at the interstices between adjoining villages and square mile grids in order to impel interaction between adjoining service areas, as illustrated in Figure D-19. At the same time as walking distance to village centers and elementary schools remains at 1/4 to 1/2 mile, accessibility to inter-village, inter-area centers is no more than 1/2 mile, fostering greater and more complex exchange than was typical of the self-contained villages of model (A) towns.

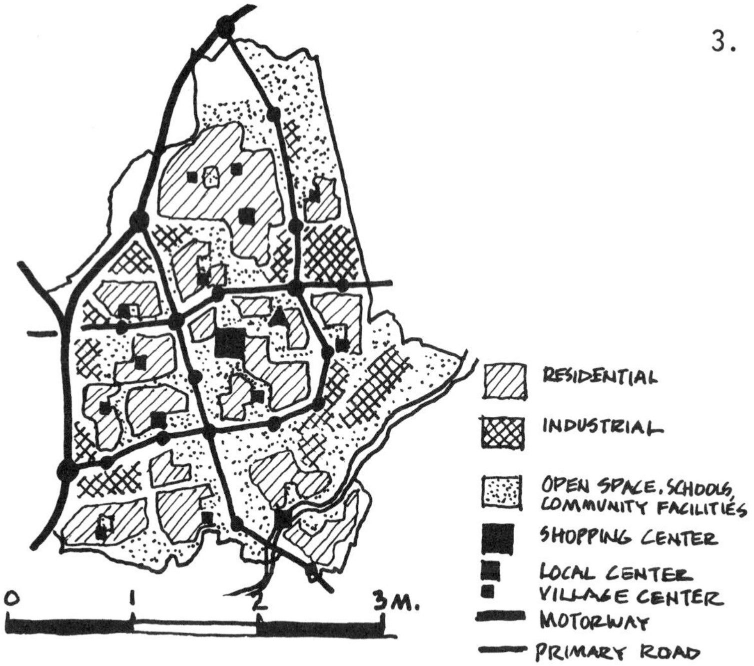

RESIDENTIAL

INDUSTRIAL

OPEN SPACE, SCHOOLS, COMMUNITY FACILITIES

SHOPPING CENTER

LOCAL CENTER
VILLAGE CENTER

MOTORWAY

PRIMARY ROAD

0   1   2   3 M.

WASHINGTON: VILLAGES AND CENTERS

Figure D-17

PRIMARY NETWORK

INTERVILLAGE WALKWAY

SECONDARY DISTRIBUTOR

BUS ONLY LINK

RESIDENTIAL

INDUSTRIAL

OPEN SPACES

0   1/4   1/2   1 M.

THREE VILLAGES WITHIN THE SQUARE MILE GRID

Figure D-18

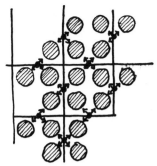

ACCESSIBILITY BETWEEN VILLAGES:
WITHIN ONE MILE OF NODES, ADJOINING A
VILLAGE, 6 TO 10 VILLAGES CAN
GENERALLY BE REACHED

Figure D-19
(Source: Llewelyn-Davies Weeks and
Partners: Washington New Town Master
Plan and Report, Baynard Press,
London, 1966)

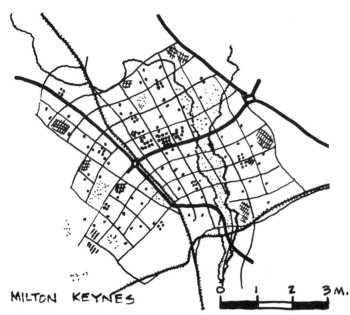

MILTON KEYNES

0  1  2  3 M.

Figure D-20

## 4. MILTON KEYNES, ENGLAND

Milton Keynes (Fig. D-20) carries further the community and service area concepts applied at Washington. The service area center becomes a non-center, located at the edges of the mile-square service area close to the pedestrian underpasses connecting areas under the through streets of the community grid (Fig. D-21) and encouraging interactivity between adjacent areas.

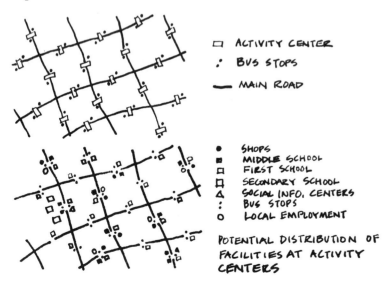

□ ACTIVITY CENTER
∴ BUS STOPS
— MAIN ROAD

● SHOPS
▣ MIDDLE SCHOOL
□ FIRST SCHOOL
⌂ SECONDARY SCHOOL
△ SOCIAL INFO. CENTERS
∴ BUS STOPS
○ LOCAL EMPLOYMENT

POTENTIAL DISTRIBUTION OF
FACILITIES AT ACTIVITY
CENTERS

Figure D-21
(Source: Llewelyn Davies Weeks Forestier-Walker and Bor: The Plan for Milton Keynes, HMSO, London, 1970)

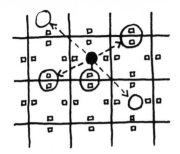

Figure D-22

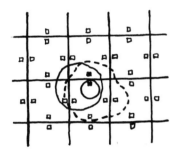

Figure D-23
(Source: Architecture D'Aujourdui,
October - November, 1969)

In similar vein, the notion of neighborhood is deliberately rejected in order to encourage maximum interaction between adjoining areas. Figure D-22 shows the locations of activities frequented by a given family. Figure D-23 expresses the zones of influence possible for a grouping of schools, stores or other activities. Different categories of activity benefit by their location near one another; and individuals and families meet people from many neighboring service areas at the activity nodes they frequent -- whether school, employment, store or club.

## Model C: Community-Wide Oriented Service Areas

The third service area model is premised on proximity to a
central, community-wide activity center, usually linear
but also possibly radial or loop in form.  In order to
maintain the short walking distances required for a concentrated activity spine to serve effectively the impinging
service areas, higher densities are usually developed in
these areas.  The areas retain their typical features, such
as schools, parks and convenience stores.  However, they
have the additional accessibility to the wide range of
services and contacts belonging to the community-wide
activity spine.  In order to optimize facile access to all
facilities along the length of the activity spine, a
public transportation system with frequent stops is implied.

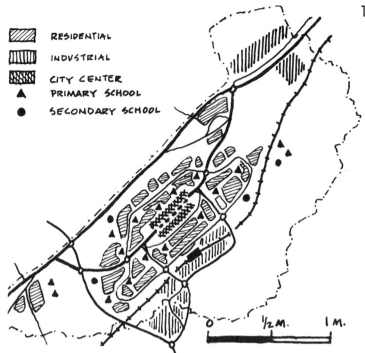

RESIDENTIAL
INDUSTRIAL
CITY CENTER
▲ PRIMARY SCHOOL
● SECONDARY SCHOOL

0    ½ M.    1 M.

Figure D-24

Cumbernauld new town

1. CUMBERNAULD NEW TOWN, SCOTLAND

Cumbernauld (Figs. D-24, 25) is probably the most familiar example of the new community of service areas with orientation that is primarily community-wide. The majority of the service areas, while possessing their own elementary schools and local centers, lie within convenient walking distance of the high-density town center.

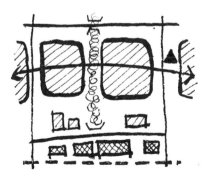

Figure D-25

Cumbernauld neighborhood

## 2. NUNS' ISLAND, MONTREAL

Nuns' Island (Fig. D-26) applies an organizing concept strikingly similar to that of Cumbernauld, with a central activity spine fed into by impinging service areas which are delineated by the road pattern. Distances are also comparable.

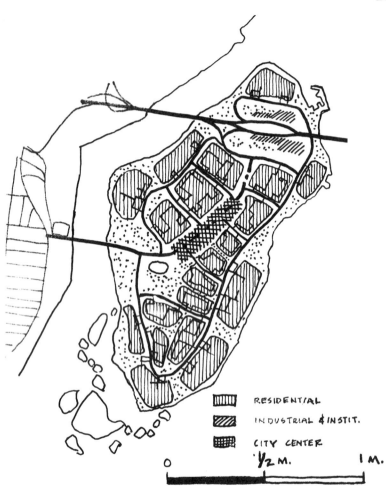

RESIDENTIAL

INDUSTRIAL & INSTIT.

CITY CENTER

0          ½ M.          1 M.

Figure D-26

Nuns' Island or Ile-St-Paul, Montreal

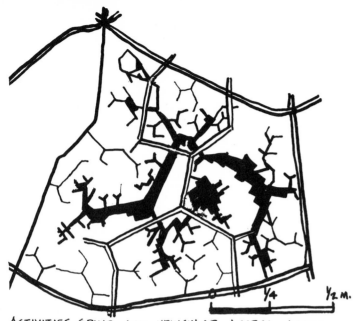

ACTIVITIES SPINE AND VEHICULAR ACCESS WAYS

Figure D-27

### 3. TOULOUSE-LE-MIRAIL, FRANCE

Toulouse-le-Mirail (Figs. D-27, 28) emphasizes a continuous spine zone of concentrated activity and density in the collective community life of the street. Its hexagonal patterns reduce conflict at intersections and provide branching access. The pedestrian spine, which weaves irregularly among the service areas brings its continuous and varied activity centers within easy walking distance of all homes. Vehicular traffic is barred from the central areas. A greenways network ties one area to another and to the activity spine. Service areas assume diminished significance relative to the primacy of the community activity concourse.

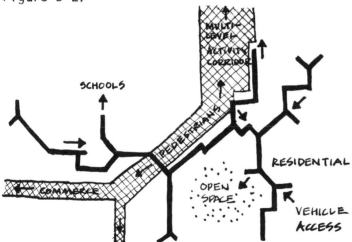

ACTIVITIES/ACCESS HIERARCHY

Figure D-28

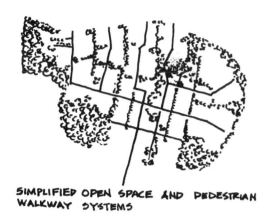

SIMPLIFIED OPEN SPACE AND PEDESTRIAN WALKWAY SYSTEMS

Figure D-29

SIMPLIFIED AUTO AND PUBLIC TRANSIT MOVEMENT SYSTEMS

Figure D-30
(Source: Harvard University Graduate School of Design: New Communities: One Alternative, Cambridge, 1968)

## 4. HARVARD NEW COMMUNITIES STUDY: ONE ALTERNATIVE

Based on a high-density settlement pattern strongly related to a central activity corridor by means of pedestrian, vehicle and public transit systems, the Harvard scheme placed primary emphasis on the mixing of service area populations through the community networks (Figs. D-29/32).

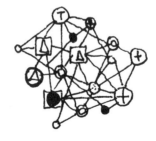

Figure D-31

The compact new community provides diversity and choice of activity within easy reach of the home

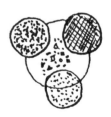

Figure D-32

Overlap of activity patterns encourages mixing of distinct social, ethnic and economic groups

REFERENCES

Charles Abrams, "Blueprints for American Cities," The City is the Frontier, Columbia University Press, 1965.

Christopher Alexander, "The Pattern of Streets," Architectural Forum, April, 1965.

Christopher Alexander, "The City is Not a Tree," Architectural Forum, April-May, 1965.

American Public Health Association, Committee on the Hygiene of Housing, Planning the Neighborhood, Public Administration Service, Chicago, 1960.

"Le Villes Nouvelles," Architecture D'Aujourd'hui, Vol. 146, October-November, 1969.

Austin-Smith Lord Partnership, Warrington New Town: Consultant's Proposals for the Draft Master Plan, Warrington, England, 1969.

Harland Bartholomew, Land Uses in American Cities, Harvard University, Cambridge, 1965.

Warren G. Bennis and Philip E. Slater, The Temporary Society, New York, 1964.

A. Baburov, A. Gutnov, G. Djumenton, S. Kharitonova, I. Lezava, S. Sadovskij, The Ideal Communist City, New York, Brazilier, 1968.

Stuart Chapin, Urban Land Use Planning, Harper and Row, New York, 1957.

Serge Chermayeff and Alexander Tzonis, Advanced Studies in Urban Environments, Yale University, New Haven, 1967.

David A. Crane and Associates, Fort Lincoln New Town: Final Planning Report, Philadelphia, 1969.

David A. Crane and Associates, A Comparative Study of New Towns, prepared for the New York State Urban Development Corporation, Philadelphia, 1969.

James Dahir, The Neighborhood Unit Plan, Its Spread and Acceptance, Russell Sage Foundation, New York, 1947.

James Dahir, Communities for Better Living, Harper, New York, 1950.

Joseph de Chiara and Lee Koppelman, Planning Design Criteria, Van Nostrand, New York, 1969.

Karl Deutsch, "On Social Communication and the Metropolis," in Lloyd Rodwin, ed., The Future Metropolis, Brazilier, New York, 1961.

Lillian M. Dobriner, The Suburban Community, Putnam, New York, 1958.

Edward P. Eichler and Marshall Kaplan, The Community Builders, University of California Press, Berkeley, 1967.

Arthur B. Gallion and Simon Eisner, The Urban Pattern, Van Nostrand, New York, 1963.

Herbert Gans, The Levittowners, Pantheon, New York, 1967.

Herbert Gans, People and Plans, Basic Books, New York, 1968.

Paul and Percival Goodman, Communitas, Random House, New York, 1947.

Great Britain Ministry of Housing and Local Government, The Needs of New Communities, London, Her Majesty's Stationery Office, 1967.

Harvard University Graduate School of Design, New Communities: One Alternative, Cambridge, 1968.

Harvard University Graduate School of Design, Criteria for a New Center of Urban Development, Cambridge, 1967.

Harvard University Graduate School of Design, Comparative Housing Study, Cambridge, 1958.

Lawrence Hayworth, The Good City.

Ludwig Hilberseimer, The New City, Theobald, Chicago, 1944.

O. T. Hoffmann and Christoph Repenthin, Neue Urbane Wohnformer, Verlag Ullstein, Berlin, 1956.

Morton Hoppenfeld, "A Sketch of the Planning-Building Process for Columbia, Maryland, American Institute of Planners Journal, November 1967.

Ebenezer Howard, Garden Cities of Tomorrow, Faber and Faber, London, 1945.

Reginald Isaacs, "Are Urban Neighborhoods Possible?", Journal of Housing, July-August, 1948.

Reginald Isaacs, "The Neighborhood Theory,"American Institute of Planners Journal, Spring, 1948.

Suzanne Keller, The Urban Neighborhood: A Sociological Perspective, Random House, New York, 1963.

Jane Jacobs, The Death and Life of Great American Cities, Random House, New York, 1961.

Jonathan Development Corporation, Jonathan: Design and Development, Jonathan, Minnesota, 1970.

Le Corbusier, La Ville Radieuse, Orion, New York, 1967.

Llewelyn-Davies Weeks and Partners, Washington New Town Master Plan and Report, London, Baynard Press, 1966.

Llewelyn-Davies Weeks Forestier-Walker and Bor, The Plan for Milton Keynes, HMSO, London, 1970.

Albert Mayer, The Urgent Future, McGraw-Hill, New York, 1967.

Martin Meyerson, "What Specific Implication Does Expanding Technology Have Upon the Problem of Metropolitan Areas?", in Seminar E, Conference on Space, Science and Urban Life, Washington, D.C., NASA, 1963.

G. Duncan Mitchell, Neighborhood and Community, Liverpool Estate, London, 1954.

Lewis Mumford, "The Neighborhood and the Neighborhood Unit," Town Planning Review, Vol. 24, No. 4, January 1954, pp.256-70.

Frederick J. Osborn and Arnold Whittick, The New Towns: The Answer to Megalopolis, MIT Press, Cambridge, revised 1969.

Innes H. Pearse, M.D. and Lucy H. Crocker, The Peckham Experiment: A Study in the Living Structure of Society, Allen and Unwin, London, 1943.

Clarence Perry, "The Neighborhood Unit," Regional Survey of New York and Its Environs, Vol. 7, Committee on the Regional Plan and Its Environs, New York, 1929.

Pras, Schoenauer, Seeman, Ile St. Paul or Nuns' Island: A Report on the Preliminary Studies for the Development of, prepared for Quebec Home and Mortgage Corporation, Montreal, 1963.

Thomas A. Reiner, The Place of the Ideal Community: Urban Planning, University of Pennsylvania Press, Philadelphia, 1963.

The Rouse Company, Columbia, A New City, Columbia, Maryland, 1966.

Paul Ritter, Planning for Man and Motor, Macmillan, New York, 1964.

Lloyd Rodwin, The British New Towns Policy, Harvard University Press, Cambridge, 1956.

Clarence Stein, Toward New Towns for America, MIT Press, Cambridge, 1967.

United Nations, Department of Economic and Social Affairs, Planning of Metropolitan Areas and New Towns, United Nations, New York, 1967.

Roland L. Warren, The Community in America, Rand McNally, Chicago, 1963.

Melvin Webber, "Order in Diversity: Community without Pro-pinquity," in Cities and Space: The Future Use of Urban Land, London Wingo, ed., Johns Hopkins Press, Baltimore, 1963.

Whittlesey and Conklin, Reston Master Plan, New York, 1962.

Carol Withers, Plainville, USA, New York, 1945.

Frank Lloyd Wright, The Living City, Brazilier, New York, 1961.

Peter Willmott, "Social Research and New Communities," in American Institute of Planners Journal, November 1967.

René Bussière, Les Modeles de Villes: Recherche Préliminaire, Centre de Recherche d'Urbanisme, Paris, 1967.

PREAMBLE:  ECONOMIES OF SCALE

In the planning of a community, many externalities act to
affect the feasibility of specific components at given
scales of development.  A device for graphically presenting
the feasibility of particular innovative developments, together with standard urban components at various scales of
development, is shown in the Table    .  This table summarizes
much of the information  presented in Table E-2.

It is not intended to indicate the ultimate feasibility of
any entry at the scale indicated, but rather to be a first
cut measure of feasibility based on past experience and
present judgment.

Population figures in the chart over 280,000 are not included
since in a recent government study of public expenditures
and employment in three representative states for communities
of 25,000 to 250,000, it was indicated that at least up to
the 250,000 level, cities do not, in general, demonstrate
any tendency toward either major economies or diseconomies
of scale.  For the larger cities (over 250,000) in these
states, however, there was some tendency for population size
to associate with higher per capita public spending and employment .*    This can be taken to indicate the benefit of
assigning an upper limit of 250,000 for the population size
of a new community.  The "economies of scale" under that
limit, then, are those scales of development at which specific innovations or clusters of service components become
feasible: this is sometimes referred to, in a term borrowed
from nuclear physics, as "critical mass."

In the table, 50% of the total land devoted to the residential area approximates that used by several communities
(e.g., Reston and Columbia).  For six communities presently

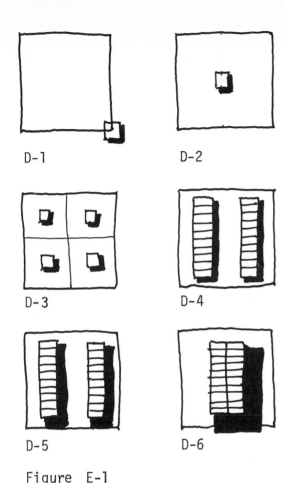

D-1

D-2

D-3

D-4

D-5

D-6

Figure E-1

in progress, the proportion of residential land is as follows: Cumbernauld, 21%; Tapiola, 24%; Jonathan, 30%; Columbia, 54%; Reston, 56%; and Janss-Conejo, 70%.

For purposes of comparison, several gross residential densities ranging from 5 to 25 dwelling units per acre are listed. These gross densities are arrived at by using combinations of six basic net densities (fig. E-1 ).

D-1. Four-acre lots (one **person** per acre -- representative of "estate" or "ranch" densities)
D-2. One-acre lots (3-5 ppa -- representative of "estate" densities)
D-3. Quarter-acre lots (14 ppa -- representative of suburban densities)
D-4. Twenty DU's per acre (70 ppa -- town house or garden apartment)
D-5. Fifty DU's per acre (170 ppa -- 3-story walkup)
D-6. Seventy DU's per acre (245 ppa -- 6-story midrise)

These basic net densities are distributed with the total residential land in various proportions (Fig. E-2 ), which are roughly comparable to a range of densities representing recreational or second home developments at the low end of the scale to para-urban developments at the high end.

*Advisory Commission on Intergovernmental Relations, Urban and Rural America: Policies for Future Growth, GPO, Washington D.c., 1968.

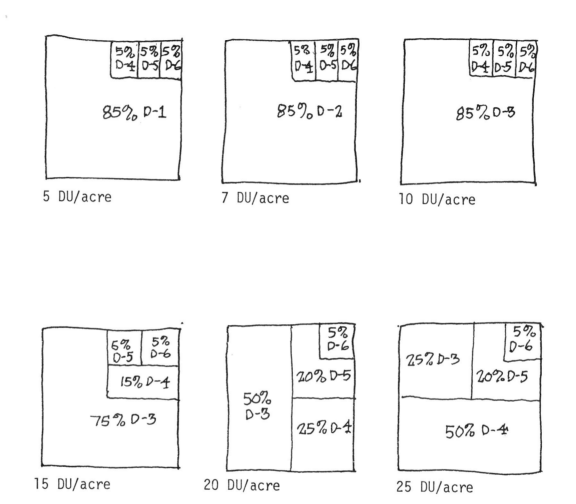

| | | |
|---|---|---|
| 5% D-4 | 5% D-5 | 5% D-6 |
| | 85% D-1 | |

5 DU/acre

| | | |
|---|---|---|
| 5% D-4 | 5% D-5 | 5% D-6 |
| | 85% D-2 | |

7 DU/acre

| | | |
|---|---|---|
| 5% D-4 | 5% D-5 | 5% D-6 |
| | 85% D-3 | |

10 DU/acre

| | |
|---|---|
| 5% D-5 | 5% D-6 |
| | 15% D-4 |
| | 75% D-3 |

15 DU/acre

| | |
|---|---|
| | 5% D-6 |
| 50% D-3 | 20% D-5 |
| | 25% D-4 |

20 DU/acre

| | |
|---|---|
| 25% D-3 | 5% D-6 |
| | 20% D-5 |
| | 50% D-4 |

25 DU/acre

Figure  E-2

Alternate diagrammatic dispersal of residential types, gross residential areas

These diagrams, illustrating the densities in Table E-1 (top row), are one set among many possible sets of population distribution.

## CLUSTERS OF SERVICE COMPONENTS BY POPULATION*

**A.**  4000-5000 population
Education: day care centers, creche[+], primary school
Recreation: play areas, restaurant, bar or saloon, outdoor pools
Commercial: automobile service station, convenience stores
(grocery, delicatessen, drugs), bank branch office
Health: doctors' surgery
Institutional: public meeting room

**B.**  7000-10,000 population
Education: middle school, educational resources center or library
Recreation: arts center, gallery, small boat rental
Employment: offices, multi-service centers, light industry
Commercial: supermarket
Transportation: public parking areas
Health: medical arts diagnosis and treatment center
Institutional: fire station, police station, waste treat-
ment plant, assembly hall

**C.**  14,000-20,000 population
Education: high school
Recreation: indoor swimming pool, ice rink, health club,
cinema, play fields
Commercial: department store, local shopping center
Transportation: bus and taxi service, interurban bus station
Health: 100 bed hospital

**D.**  50,000-70,000 population
Education: vocational college, community junior college,
community TV station
Recreation: gold course, tennis club, marina, drive-in
cinema, bowling alley, night club
Employment: heavy industry
Commercial: hotel-motel
Transportation: interurban VTOL metroport
Health: 225 bed hospital, mental health clinic
Institutional: main city hall

---

*For a complete table of service components and their scale
attributes, refer to the tables beginning E-6.
+Live-in child care center.

Matrix cell figures
are in 1000's

Top figure represents
total dwelling units

Bottom figure represents
total population at
3.5 persons per unit

| CLUSTER GROUP | DWELLING UNITS PER GROSS RESIDENTIAL ACRE | | | | | | COMMUNITY TOTAL ACRES | GROSS RESIDENTIAL ACRES @ 50% |
|---|---|---|---|---|---|---|---|---|
| | 5 | 7 | 10 | 15 | 20 | 25 | | |
| A ▶ | 1 / 4 | 2 / 7 | 3 / 9 | 4 / 14 | 5 / 17 | 6 / 20 | 500 | 250 |
| B ▶ | 3 / 10 | 4 / 14 | 5 / 17 | 8 / 28 | 10 / 35 | 13 / 45 | 1000 | 500 |
| C ▶ | 4 / 14 | 5 / 17 | 7 / 26 | 11 / 39 | 15 / 52 | 19 / 66 | 1500 | 750 |
| | 5 / 17 | 7 / 24 | 10 / 35 | 15 / 52 | 20 / 70 | 25 / 87 | 2000 | 1000 |
| | 10 / 35 | 14 / 50 | 20 / 70 | 30 / 105 | 40 / 140 | 50 / 175 | 4000 | 2000 |
| D ▶ | 15 / 52 | 21 / 73 | 30 / 105 | 45 / 155 | 60 / 210 | 75 / 260 | 6000 | 3000 |
| | 20 / 70 | 28 / 98 | 40 / 140 | 60 / 210 | 80 / 280 | | 8000 | 4000 |
| | 25 / 87 | 35 / 120 | 50 / 175 | 75 / 260 | | | 10,000 | 5000 |
| | 30 / 105 | 42 / 145 | 60 / 210 | | | | 12,000 | 6000 |
| | 35 / 120 | 49 / 170 | 70 / 245 | | | | 14,000 | 7000 |
| | 40 / 140 | 56 / 195 | 80 / 280 | | | | 16,000 | 8000 |

INDUSTRIALIZED SYSTEMS HOUSING*

NETWORK CAB TRANSIT    DIAL-A-BUS

CATV

Table E-1   Economies of Scale: Scale of development required for levels of aggregated service components within the community

*Assuming 100% industrialized housing in community.

E-5

1

## EDUCATION

Column headers:
- POPULATION
- 500 - 1000
- 1000 - 5000
- 5000 - 8000
- 8000 - 12,000
- 12,000 - 20,000
- 20,000 - 30,000
- 30,000 - 40,000
- 40,000 - 50,000
- 50,000 - 100,000
- 100,000 - 250,000
- 250,000 - 1,000,000
- 1,000,000 -
- SCALE FLEXIBILITY (▼ AND/OR ▶)
- FREQUENCY OF USE (SCALE ▮ — ▮▮▮▮)
- MAXIMUM WALKING DISTANCE (mins.)
- USERS: CHILDREN / ADOLESCENTS / YOUNG COUPLES / YOUNG SINGLES / MIDDLE-AGED / ELDERLY
- DEGREE OF PRODUCTIVE FIT WITH INNOVATIVE SYSTEM:
- DIAL-A-BUS / LINE-HAUL TRANSIT / UTILIDOR / ADVANCED COMMUNICATIONS

| Activity | Population | Scale Flexibility | Max Walking Distance |
|---|---|---|---|
| DAY CARE CENTER | 500 | ▼▶ | 10 |
| CHILDREN'S PLAY SPACE | 300-700 | ▼ |  |
| ELEMENTARY SCHOOL | 1800 | ▶ | 10 |
| MIDDLE SCHOOL | 5000 | ▼▶ | 15 |
| LIBRARY, EDUC RESOURCES CENTER |  | ▶ | 15 |
| HIGH SCHOOL | 9000 | ◀ | 20 |
| DISPERSED DAY CARE CENTERS | 20,000 | ◀ | 10 |
| DISPERSED SCHOOL AND COLLEGE FACILITIES | 50,000 | ▶ | 15 |
| CENTRALIZED EDUCATIONAL COMPLEXES |  | ▶ | 20 |
| COMMUNITY TV STATION |  | ▶▶ | 20 |
| VOCATIONAL COLLEGE |  | ▶▶▶ | 20 |
| COMMUNITY COLLEGE |  | ▶▶ | 30 |
| JUNIOR COLLEGE |  | ▶ | 30 |
| COLLEGE | 100,000 | ◀ |  |
| UNIVERSITY | 500,000 | ▶ |  |
| GRADUATE UNIVERSITY | 1,000,000 | ◀▶ |  |
| FREE UNIVERSITY | 3,000,000 | ◀ |  |

Population; Scale Flexibility; Frequency of Use; Maximum Walking Distance; Degree of Productive Fit with Innovative Systems

**2**

**RECREATION**

| Facility | Population | Scale Flexibility | Maximum Walking Distance (mins.) |
|---|---|---|---|
| COMMUNAL GARDEN | 100 | ◄ ► | 5 |
| INFANTS' PLAY SPACE | | ◄ ► | 1 |
| CHILDREN'S PLAY SPACE | 300-700 | ◄ ► | 3 |
| RESTAURANT | 2000 | ► | 10 |
| LOCAL PARK | 2000-4000 | ◄ ► | 10 |
| PLAYGROUND | 5000 | ◄ ► | 10 |
| BAR, SALOON | | ◄ ► | 15 |
| GYMNASIUM, MEETING ROOMS, ARTS AND CRAFTS | 10,000 | ◄ | 15 |
| LOCAL MUSEUM | | ◄ ► | 30 |
| ART GALLERY | | ◄ ► | 30 |
| SMALL CRAFT AND BOATING RENTAL | | ◄ | 30 |
| COMMUNITY THEATER, AUDITORIUM | 20,000 | ◄ ► | 20 |
| SPECIAL RESTAURANT | | ◄ ► | 30 |
| COFFEE HOUSE, NIGHT CLUB, ETC | | ◄ ► | 20 |
| PLAYFIELD | | ◄ ► | 15 |
| INDOOR SWIMMING POOL | | ◄ ► | 15 |
| MOVIE THEATER | | ◄ ► | 15 |
| HEALTH CLUB | | ◄ ► | 15 |
| ICE RINK | | ◄ ► | 20 |
| COMMUNITY TV STATION | | ► | 20 |

Population column ranges (headers): POPULATION; 500 – 1000; 1000 – 5000; 5000 – 8000; 8000 – 12,000; 12,000 – 20,000; 20,000 – 30,000; 30,000 – 40,000; 40,000 – 50,000; 50,000 – 100,000; 100,000 – 250,000; 250,000 – 1,000,000; 1,000,000

Additional columns: SCALE FLEXIBILITY (◄ AND/OR ►); FREQUENCY OF USE (SCALE # – ▥); MAXIMUM WALKING DISTANCE (mins.); USERS: CHILDREN, ADOLESCENTS, YOUNG COUPLES, YOUNG SINGLES, MIDDLE-AGED, ELDERLY; DEGREE OF PRODUCTIVE FIT WITH INNOVATIVE SYSTEM: DIAL-A-BUS, LINE-HAUL TRANSIT, UTILADOR, ADVANCED COMMUNICATIONS

Population; Scale Flexibility; Frequency of Use; Maximum Walking Distance; Degree of Productive Fit with Innovative Systems

## 2 RECREATION (CONT'D)

| | POPULATION | SCALE FLEXIBILITY | FREQUENCY OF USE | MAXIMUM WALKING DISTANCE (mins.) |
|---|---|---|---|---|
| DRIVE-IN THEATER | 50,000 | | | 20 |
| GOLF COURSE | | | | 20 |
| GOLF DRIVING RANGE | | | | 30 |
| TENNIS CLUB | | | | 20 |
| SWIMMING BEACH | | | | 30 |
| MARINA | | | | 30 |
| CONVENTION HALL | 100,000 | | | 30 |
| FOOTBALL/BASEBALL STADIUM | | | | 30 |
| OLYMPIC SWIMMING POOL | | | | 20 |
| LOCAL TV STATION | 250,000 | | | 20 |
| REGIONAL PARK | 500,000 | | | 30 |
| AMUSEMENT PARK | | | | 30 |
| SYMPHONY ORCHESTRA | 1,000,000 | | | 30 |
| ZOO | | | | 30 |

Population; Scale Flexibility; Frequency of Use; Maximum Walking Distance; Degree of Productive Fit with Innovative Systems

| 3<br><br>HEALTH | POPULATION 500 – 1000 | 1000 – 5000 | 5000 – 8000 | 8000 – 12,000 | 12,000 – 20,000 | 20,000 – 30,000 | 30,000 – 40,000 | 40,000 – 50,000 | 50,000 – 100,000 | 100,000 – 250,000 | 250,000 – 1,000,000 | 1,000,000 – | SCALE FLEXIBILITY (▼ AND/OR ▲) | FREQUENCY OF USE (SCALE 1 – ) | MAXIMUM WALKING DISTANCE (mins.) | USERS: CHILDREN | ADOLESCENTS | YOUNG COUPLES | YOUNG SINGLES | MIDDLE-AGED | ELDERLY | DEGREE OF PRODUCTIVE FIT WITH INNOVATIVE SYSTEM: | DIAL-A-BUS | LINE-HAUL TRANSIT | UTILADOR | ADVANCED COMMUNICATIONS |
|---|---|---|---|---|---|---|---|---|---|---|---|---|---|---|---|---|---|---|---|---|---|---|---|---|---|---|
| 2 CHRONIC DISEASE BEDS | | 1000 | | | | | | | | | | | | | | | | | | | | | | | | |
| 4 NURSING HOME BEDS | | | | | | | | | | | | | | | | | | | | | | | | | | |
| 5 MENTAL HOSPITAL BEDS | | | | | | | | | | | | | | | | | | | | | | | | | | |
| DIAGNOSIS AND TREATMENT CENTER | | | | 10,000 | | | | | | | | | ◄ ► | | 10 | | | | | | | | | | | |
| WELFARE AGENCY | | | | | | 25,000 | | | | | | | ◄ ► | | 20 | | | | | | | | | | | |
| 100-BED HOSPITAL | | | | | | | | | | | | | | | 20 | | | | | | | | | | | |
| PUBLIC HEALTH CENTER | | | | | | | 35,000 | | | | | | ► | | 20 | | | | | | | | | | | |
| 225 BED HOSPITAL | | | | | | | | 50,000 | | | | | | | 20 | | | | | | | | | | | |
| MENTAL HEALTH CLINIC | | | | | | | | | | | | | ◄ ► | | 20 | | | | | | | | | | | |
| REHAB. CENTER | | | | | | | | 75,000 | | | | | ◄ | | 20 | | | | | | | | | | | |
| 340 BED HOSPITAL | | | | | | | | | | | | | | | 60 | | | | | | | | | | | |
| 450 BED HOSPITAL | | | | | 100,000 | | | | | | | | | | 60 | | | | | | | | | | | |

Population; Scale Flexibility. Frequency of Use; Maximum Walking Distance; Degree of Productive
Fit with Innovative Systems

| | POPULATION | 500 - 1000 | 1000 - 5000 | 5000 - 8000 | 8000 - 12,000 | 12,000 - 20,000 | 20,000 - 30,000 | 30,000 - 40,000 | 40,000 - 50,000 | 50,000 - 100,000 | 100,000 - 250,000 | 250,000 - 1,000,000 | 1,000,000 - | SCALE FLEXIBILITY (▲ AND/OR ▼) | FREQUENCY OF USE (SCALE ▓ - ▓) | MAXIMUM WALKING DISTANCE (mins.) | USERS: | CHILDREN | ADOLESCENTS | YOUNG COUPLES | YOUNG SINGLES | MIDDLE-AGED | ELDERLY | DEGREE OF PRODUCTIVE | FIT WITH INNOVATIVE SYSTEM: | DIAL-A-BUS | LINE-HAUL TRANSIT | UTILADOR | ADVANCED COMMUNICATIONS |
|---|---|---|---|---|---|---|---|---|---|---|---|---|---|---|---|---|---|---|---|---|---|---|---|---|---|---|---|---|---|
| **EMPLOYMENT:** | | | | | | | | | | | | | | | | | | | | | | | | | | | | | |
| OFFICE COMPLEX | | | | | ▓ 10,000 | | | | | | | | | ◀▶◀▶ | | 30 | | ▓ | ▓ | ▓ | ▓ | ▓ | ▓ | | | ▓ | ▓ | ▓ | ▓ |
| SERVICES COMPLES | | | | | ▓ | | | | | | | | | ◀▶◀▶ | | 30 | | | | | | | | | | | | | |
| LIGHT INDUSTRY | | | | | ▓ | | | | | | | | | ◀▶◀▶ | ▓ | 30 | | | | | | | | | | | | | |
| LOCAL "NEIGHBORHOOD" INDUS-TRIAL AND COMMERCIAL COOPORATIVES | | | | | ▓ | | | | | | | | | ◀▶◀▶ | | 15 | | | | | | | | | | | | | |
| HEAVY INDUSTRY | | | | | | | | | ▓ 50,000 | | | | | ◀▶◀▶ | ▓ | 30 | | ▓ | ▓ | ▓ | | | | | | | | | |
| INDUSTRIAL PARK | | | | | | | | 100,000 | | ▓ | | | | ◀▶◀▶ | ▓ | 30 | | | | | | | | | | ▓ | ▓ | ▓ | ▓ |
| DISPERSED EMPLOYMENT FACILITIES | | | | | | | | | ▓ | | | | | | ▓ | 20 | | | | | | | | | | | | | |

Population; Scale Flexibility; Frequency of Use; Maximum Walking Distance; Degree of Productive Fit with Innovative System

5

## TRANSPORTATION

| | POPULATION | SCALE FLEXIBILITY (▼ AND/OR ▲) | FREQUENCY OF USE (SCALE ⫼ - ⫼) | MAXIMUM WALKING DISTANCE (mins.) | USERS: CHILDREN / ADOLESCENTS / YOUNG COUPLES / YOUNG SINGLES / MIDDLE-AGED / ELDERLY | DEGREE OF PRODUCTIVE FIT WITH INNOVATIVE SYSTEM: DIAL-A-BUS / LINE-HAUL TRANSIT / UTILADOR / ADVANCED COMMUNICATIONS |
|---|---|---|---|---|---|---|
| PRIVATE PARKING | 100 (500–1000) | | | 100' | | |
| AUTO SERVICE STATION | 2000 (1000–5000) | | | | | |
| PUBLIC PARKING | (8000–12,000) | ▲ | | 3 | | |
| PUBLIC BUS TRANSPORT | 20,000 (12,000–20,000) | ▲ ▽ | | 5 | | |
| TAXI SERVICE | | ▲ ▽ | | 100' | | |
| BUS STATION | | ▲ ▽ | | 30 | | |
| V/STOL STOP | | ▲ ▽ | | 20 | | |
| TRAIN STATION | 50,000 (50,000–100,000) | ▲ ▽ | | 30 | | |
| SMALL GEN'L AVIATION AIRPORT | | ▲ | | 30 | | |
| INTER-CITY AIRPORT | | ▲ ▽ | | | | |

Column headings — POPULATION sub-ranges:
500 – 1000; 1000 – 5000; 5000 – 8000; 8000 – 12,000; 12,000 – 20,000; 20,000 – 30,000; 30,000 – 40,000; 40,000 – 50,000; 50,000 – 100,000; 100,000 – 250,000; 250,000 – 1,000,000; 1,000,000 –

Population: Scale Flexibility; Frequency of Use; Maximum Walking Distance; Degree of Productive Fit with Innovative Systems

6

INSTITUTIONAL:

| | POPULATION | SCALE FLEXIBILITY (▲ AND/OR ▼) | FREQUENCY OF USE (SCALE ▮ – ▥) | MAXIMUM WALKING DISTANCE (mins.) | USERS | DEGREE OF PRODUCTIVE FIT WITH INNOVATIVE SYSTEM |
|---|---|---|---|---|---|---|
| POST OFFICE | 100 | | | 10 | | |
| LIBRARY | 500 | | | 15 | | |
| CHURCH | | | | 10 | | |
| TOWN HALL | 5000 | | | | | |
| FIRE STATION | 10,000 | | | | | |
| POLICE STATION | | | | | | |
| WASTE DISPOSAL PLANT (ADVANCED TECHNOLOGY) | | | | | | |
| DISPERSED COMMUNITY CLINICS | 15,000 | | | | | |
| MULTI-PURPOSE CENTERS | 30,000 | | | | | |
| UTILITIES OFFICE | 50,000 | | | | | |
| AIRPORT | | | | | | |
| RAILWAY STATION | | | | | | |
| CITY HALL | | | | | | |
| WASTE DISPOSAL PLANT (CONVENTIONAL) | | | | | | |

Population column scale: 500 – 1000; 1000 – 5000; 5000 – 8000; 8000 – 12,000; 12,000 – 20,000; 20,000 – 30,000; 30,000 – 40,000; 40,000 – 50,000; 50,000 – 100,000; 100,000 – 250,000; 250,000 – 1,000,000; 1,000,000 –

Users: CHILDREN; ADOLESCENTS; YOUNG COUPLES; YOUNG SINGLES; MIDDLE-AGED; ELDERLY

Degree of Productive Fit with Innovative System: DIAL-A-BUS; LINE-HAUL TRANSIT; UTILADOR; ADVANCED COMMUNICATIONS

Population: Scale Flexibility; Frequency of Use; Maximum Walking Distance; Degree of Productive
Fit with Innovative System

# 7

## COMMERCIAL

| COMMERCIAL | POPULATION | SCALE FLEXIBILITY (▼ AND/OR ▶) | FREQUENCY OF USE (SCALE ▮ – ▥) | MAXIMUM WALKING DISTANCE (mins.) | USERS | DEGREE OF PRODUCTIVE FIT WITH INNOVATIVE SYSTEM |
|---|---|---|---|---|---|---|
| CORNER STORE | 500 | ▶ | | 10 | | |
| CONVENIENCE GROCERY STORE | 2000 | ▶ | | 10 | | |
| DELICATESSEN AND BAKERY | 3000 | ▶ | | 10 | | |
| DRUG STORE | | ▶ | | 10 | | |
| SNACK BAR | | ▶ | | 10 | | |
| LIQUOR | | ▶ | | 15 | | |
| BEAUTY PARLOR | | ▶ | | 15 | | |
| SERVICE STATION | 5000 | ▶ | | 15 | | |
| BANK OFFICE | | ▶ | | 15 | | |
| HARDWARE | | ▶ | | 15 | | |
| BARBER SHOP | | ▶ | | 15 | | |
| SINGLE-PURPOSE STORE | 10,000 | ▶ | | 20 | | |
| SUPERMARKET | | ▶ | | 15 | | |
| NEWS AND PERIODICALS/ STATIONERY | | ▶ | | 10 | | |
| DEPARTMENT STORE | 20,000 | ▶ | | | | |
| LOCAL SHOPPING CENTER | | ▶ | | 15 | | |
| HOTEL/MOTEL | | ◀ ▶ | | 20 | | |
| REGIONAL SHOPPING CENTER | 150,000 | ▶ | | 30 | | |

Users columns: CHILDREN, ADOLESCENTS, YOUNG COUPLES, YOUNG SINGLES, MIDDLE-AGED, ELDERLY

Degree of Productive Fit columns: DIAL-A-BUS, LINE-HAUL TRANSIT, UTILADOR, ADVANCED COMMUNICATIONS

Population; Scale Flexibility; Frequency of Use; Maximum Walking Distance; Degree of Productive Fit with Innovative System

REFERENCES

American Public Health Association, Planning the Neighborhood, Public Administration Service, Chicago, 1960.

F. Stuart Chapin, Jr., Urban Land Use Planning, University of Illinois Press, Urbana, 1965.

Joseph de Chiara and Lee Koppelman, Planning Design Criteria, Van Nostrand, New York, 1969.

Arthur B. Gallion and Simon Eisner, The Urban Pattern, Van Nostrand, New York, 1963.

Great Britain, Ministry of Housing and Local Government, The Needs of New Communities, HMSO, London, 1967.

Harvard Graduate School of Design, Criteria for a Center of Urban Development, unpublished, 1967.

Clarence A. Perry, "The Neighborhood Unit" in Neighborhood and Community Planning, Vol. VII of New York State Regional Survey, New York, 1929.

Urban Land Institute, Council of Community Builders, The Community Builders' Handbook, Urban Land Institute, Washington, D.C., 1964.

It should be noted that there is considerable divergence among these sources on the population figures cited as required to support various activities. Therefore, some interpolation and reasoned estimating has been used.

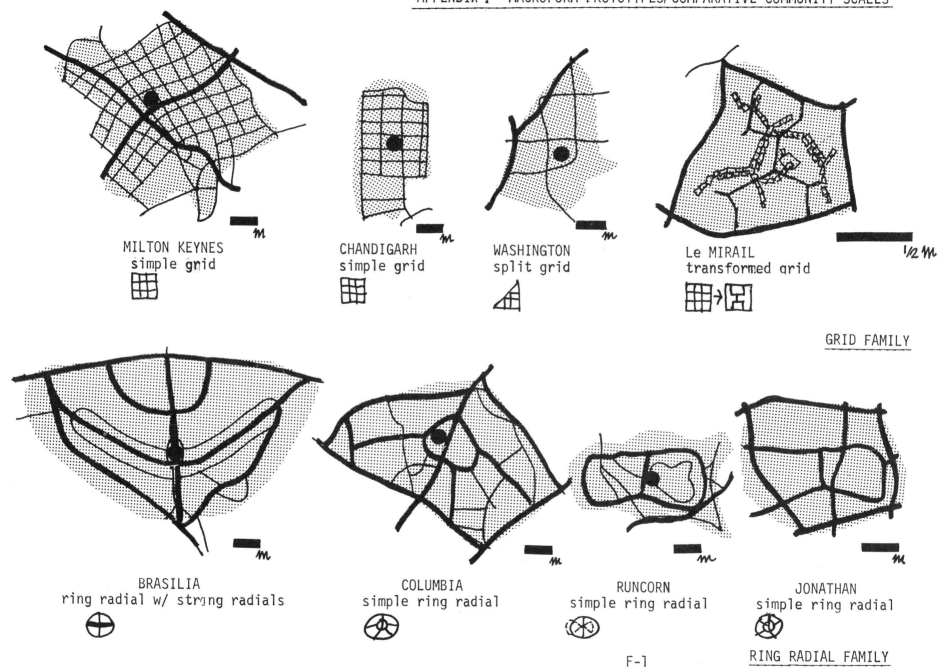

MILTON KEYNES
simple grid

CHANDIGARH
simple grid

WASHINGTON
split grid

Le MIRAIL
transformed grid

½ m

GRID FAMILY

BRASILIA
ring radial w/ strong radials

COLUMBIA
simple ring radial

RUNCORN
simple ring radial

JONATHAN
simple ring radial

F-1

RING RADIAL FAMILY

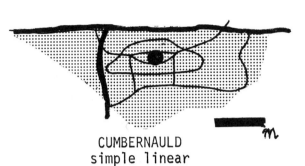

CUMBERNAULD
simple linear

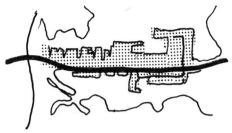

PAMPUS, AMSTERDAM NEW TOWN
second order linear

EPCOT (WALT DISNEY WORLD)
linear ring-radial composite

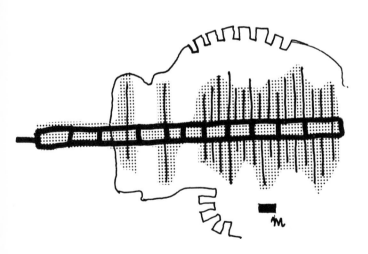

PLAN FOR TOKYO BAY
second order linear

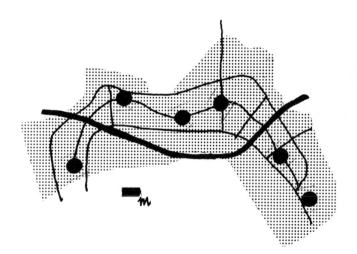

PLAN OF CENTRAL LANCASHIRE
linear sequential-multiple centers

LINEAR FAMILY

F-2

# COMPARATIVE COMMUNITY SCALES

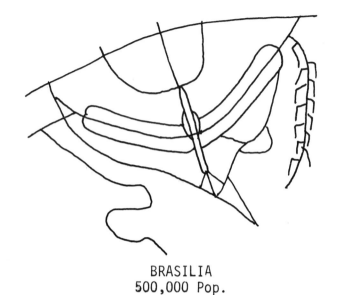

BRASILIA
500,000 Pop.

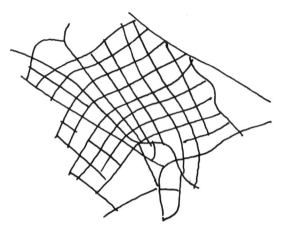

MILTON KEYNES
250,000 Pop.
17,300 acres

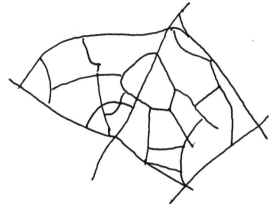

COLUMBIA
110,000 Pop.
14,100 acres

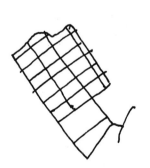

CHANDIGARH
500,000 Pop.

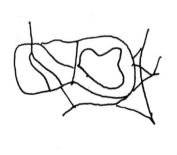

RUNCORN
100,000 Pop.
7,250 acres

RESTON
75,000 Pop.
6,750 acres

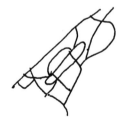

CUMBERNAULD
70,000 Pop.
4,150 acres

VALLINGBY
10,000 Pop.

TAPIOLA
17,000 Pop.

5 M

F-3